CHRIST AND THE OTHER

How should we relate to 'others' – those within a particular tradition, those of different traditions, and those who are oppressed? In the light of these anxieties, and building on the work of Andrew Shanks, this book offers a vision of Christ as 'the Shaken One', rooted in community with others. Shaped through dialogue with the theologies of John Hick and Lesslie Newbigin, Adams urges Christian communities to attend more deeply to the demands of ecumenical, dialogical and political theologies, to embody an ever greater 'solidarity of others' – a quality of community better demonstrating Christlike 'other-regard'.

To Sheryl

EL Oct
2010

Christ and the Other

In Dialogue with Hick and Newbigin

GRAHAM ADAMS

Congregational Federation and Luther King House,
Manchester, UK

ASHGATE

Published by
Ashgate Publishing Limited
Wey Court East
Union Road
Farnham
Surrey, GU9 7PT
England

Ashgate Publishing Company
Suite 420
101 Cherry Street
Burlington
VT 05401-4405
USA

www.ashgate.com

British Library Cataloguing in Publication Data
Adams, Graham.
   Christ and the other:in dialogue with Hick and Newbigin.
   1. Jesus Christ–Person and offices. 2. Christianity and other religions. 3. Religious pluralism–Christianity.
   I. Title II. Hick, John, 1922– III. Newbigin, Lesslie.
   232-dc22

Library of Congress Cataloging-in-Publication Data
Adams, Graham, 1975–
   Christ and the other: in dialogue with Hick and Newbigin / Graham Adams.
     p cm.
   Includes bibliographical references and index.
   ISBN 978-1-4094-0028-8 (hardcover : alk. paper) 1. Christianity—Philosophy. 2. Jesus Christ—Person and offices. 3. Christianity and other religions. 4. Communities—Religious aspects—Christianity. 5. Hick, John, 1922–6. Newbigin, Lesslie. I. Title.
   BR100.A33 2010
   232'.8—dc22

                                                                                2010014646

ISBN 9781409400288 (hbk)
ISBN 9780754698784 (ebk)

Mixed Sources
Product group from well-managed forests and other controlled sources
www.fsc.org Cert no. SA-COC-1565
© 1996 Forest Stewardship Council

Printed and bound in Great Britain by
MPG Books Group, UK

Contents

Preface   *vii*

Introduction   1

1   Why Christ and the Other?   5

2   The Christology of John Hick: Partially Shaken   27

3   The Christology of Newbigin: Partially Shaken   49

4   An Alternative Vision: Biblically Shaken   73

5   The Shaken One and the Other Within   95

6   The Shaken One and the Other Beyond   119

7   The Shaken One and the Invisible Other   145

8   Conclusions and Recommendations   167

Bibliography   *183*
Index   *199*

Preface

The substance of this book is concerned with the relationality or sociality of being human: we are fully human only in and through relationship with each other. It is right, then, that in the construction of this book I should aim to acknowledge the communities of people, past and present, on whom my particular argument depends. So I want to express my thanks not only to the following known people but for so many 'others' who have influenced and helped to shape this work, though I cannot name their contribution directly. I begin by apologizing to any such others who feel I ought to be more aware of and explicit about their role, and want to thank you all – including those in the wider culture who inform my worldview, whether in politics, commerce, the media or voluntary organizations, or acquaintances I have made briefly through work or socially; those particular colleagues in ministry, or students, with whom I have agreed or disagreed or who simply hold a vision of the Christian tradition which differs from mine; and those activists or opinion-shapers whom I have encountered only through traces of their efforts or hearsay but who have underpinned so much of my outlook and practice.

While it is one thing to write this, but it would be another to act on it, I also specifically want to acknowledge those whose struggles and experiences are exposed to us only briefly, through the media, in statistics or in our neighbourhoods, who have helped to conscientize me to the inequalities and injustices in our social structures. This includes, whether far away or close to home, those living in debt or poverty; those who are currently surviving violence; those who are witnessing to their belittlement at the hands of authority-figures or living out their learned lack of self-esteem or self-belief; and those who demonstrate glimpses of the people they still might become, if we can commit socially to identifying and resourcing the potential of each other.

I am thankful, too, for those whom I can name who have been alongside me: my parents, for their encouragement; my friends at Lees Street Congregational Church, Manchester, for their love and patience, and the wider family of church, including the Council for World Mission for its diverse partnership and its granting of an academic scholarship; my teachers, tutors and colleagues, in school and various theological academies, especially Northern College, which granted me the Mona Powell Fellowship to help with my doctoral studies (2002–2008), the community of Luther King House Educational Trust in Manchester, the Department of Theology and Religious Studies at the University of Leeds, especially Dr Jacqui Stewart and Dr Alistair McFadyen; the Congregational Federation Training Board, particularly Revd Dr Janet Wootton, Revd Dr Richard Cleaves and Revd Dr Alan Argent for their encouragement over several years; and to Canon Andrew Shanks, Prof John Hick and Prof Gavin D'Costa for their conversations and advice.

I express my sincere thanks to Revd Kate Gray for her helpful observations, and Dr Jacqui Stewart, again, whose incisive insights and support have been invaluable throughout this process; and to Sarah Lloyd at Ashgate.

And to Sheryl, patiently encouraging me all the way; for each evening I had to go to the computer again, each amusing addition to my draft text, and each loving assurance that I should do this. Thank you.

Graham Adams
March 2010

Introduction

We live in a world of anxieties. In our current age, for a variety of reasons, people are anxious about identity, whether as individuals in a consumerized world or as communities struggling to make sense of 'who we are' in the light of 'others' who are different from but related in complex ways to 'us'. Nevertheless, we also live in a world in which there are movements towards solidarities with one another, attempts to express connection and to find common cause. Religious traditions are informed by this context no less than they aim to affect it themselves.

I write this book from within the Christian tradition, believing that Jesus Christ offers particular resources to enable us to navigate these anxieties and generate a distinctive quality and potency of 'solidarity' – not solidarity merely amongst those who present like-mindedness or commonality, but solidarity amongst those more conscious of differences. Even so, the christological tradition is also shaped by these anxieties, so it is important for us to be self-critical, to strive to identify those forces or ideologies which distort the relationships integral to the particularity of Christ and his corporate Body. In other words, I argue that Jesus, being human and thus partly constituted by social relations, is necessarily subject to the cultural and religious forces of his particular history and his meaning is shaped by ongoing reflections through the generations. Nevertheless, by way of the constructive christology[1] offered here, I assert that the christological tradition gives hope for our engagement with each other and our capacity to transform human relationships.

In particular, I am concerned with the ways in which human beings objectify each other. We tend either to demonize or to idealize others, to reduce them to partial versions of themselves; that is, we dehumanize each other. We do this also in relation to Jesus and the tradition surrounding him. I identify specifically three kinds of otherness which need our attention. Firstly, there are those others within our own tradition or group whom we objectify and suppress, so as to streamline our self-understanding, ignoring various dissonances and debates within our history or community. Secondly, there are those others beyond our tradition, those of the other traditions, about whose identity we generalize, so we can more conveniently fix their meaning in our worldview, whether uncritically or only critically. Thirdly, there are those others who are barely visible to the traditions, those who are marginalized in sociopolitical terms, who suffer most in an unjust world. Each kind of 'other' is significant in our understanding of the person and tradition of Jesus, whilst I argue

---

[1]   I write 'christology' with a small 'c' to emphasize that it is a constructive *discipline*. A capital 'C', instead, gives the impression that we are simply identifying and understanding a named individual, but we are doing more than that.

also that Jesus in community with others enables us to engage with the humanity of each other and become more fully human through such engagement.

In Chapter 1 I explain further the contexts and concepts of the argument. I introduce the constructive notion of Jesus 'the Shaken One', one who is shaken by the otherness of each other while also enabling our mutual shakenness, such that we can become more fully human with each other. I root this in my personal and church experiences and build on it through engagement with Andrew Shanks, Peter C. Hodgson, Slavoj Žižek and Walter Wink. I also explain the relevance of the theologies of John Hick and Lesslie Newbigin, by virtue of their attempts to consider the nature of the Christian tradition in light of religious otherness and their contrasting ways of expressing solidarity between those of different experiences and perspectives. This book is partly a dialogue between them, meaning to take them seriously in their contexts, though it brings to bear questions and issues which are not explicitly theirs in order to construct an alternative vision of Jesus as 'the Shaken One'.

Chapters 2 and 3 are then studies of the christologies of Hick and Newbigin, respectively. I outline their own contexts and perspectives before analysing them with regards to their sensitivity to the three kinds of otherness. Though Hick is relatively attentive to religious otherness and Newbigin is more attentive to the otherness of his own tradition, I argue that both are only 'partially shaken'; that is, they continue to objectify the others, those within their tradition, those of other traditions and those relatively invisible to the traditions.

In Chapter 4, I consider some biblical resources for my christological vision of Jesus as 'the Shaken One', identifying the complex relationship between Jesus' historicization of a distinct myth and the mythicization of his history. I refer particularly to Wink's understanding of 'the myth of the Human Being' and offer traces of Jesus' embodiment of such a myth, in and through relationship with each kind of 'other'.

Chapters 5, 6 and 7 then explore each dimension of otherness in turn. In Chapter 5, I consider how the Shaken One prompts the re-shaping of our particular tradition – its history, its claims to know, and its power relations, with reference also to the relationality intrinsic to trinitarian theology. In Chapter 6, the question is how the Shaken One redefines our engagement with other religious traditions. The answer is deeply pluralistic, as constituted in part through conversation with John B. Cobb Jr. Chapter 7 explores the Shaken One's implications for liberative praxis: in what ways is the question of solidarity with and liberation of those who are relatively oppressed conditioned by Western constructs? How can we express and enact our common humanity, a supposedly universal vision, without reverting to imperialism?

Chapter 8 brings the threads together with some recommendations for the thinking and praxis of churches. What does it mean for us to be attentive or open to the otherness of each kind of other and thus to become more fully human in and through such engagement? I argue that this constructive christology is consciously a reinterpretation of the tradition; that it affirms the distinctiveness of the Christian tradition, including its vision of universal scope which I express in terms of our 'mutual humanization'; but such distinctiveness is dependent upon and demands persistent engagement with the other – within the tradition, beyond it, and relatively invisible to it. Without such engagement we are only partially shaken by Jesus the Shaken One.

Chapter 1
Why Christ and the Other?

This book is about three significant issues in human social relationships – *identity*, *difference* and *solidarity*. I argue that an alternative vision of Jesus Christ, understood in community with 'others', is needed to help us address them constructively. They are significant, for churches and the world, because of anxieties about who 'we' are, as constituents of a particular social group or tradition, in relation to 'the others', and the related ethical question: with whom should we be in solidarity? In fact, as I hope to demonstrate throughout, we are really all 'other' to one another, including Jesus; thus we ought to aim to be a 'solidarity *of* others',[1] yet we tend instead to think in terms of being in solidarity *with* others, implying a 'privileged vantage point from which I or we look at others as other'.[2] Whilst we find ourselves seeing, and objectifying, 'them' as 'the other', the challenge is for us to recognize ourselves also as 'other' and that we are actively part of the othering processes. Jesus, his community and our vision of him are also subject to these processes, yet I argue that the Christian tradition can enable us to see these realities in such a way that we might reshape the world in terms of God's *basileia*.[3]

This demands a constructive christology, which I see in terms of Jesus 'the Shaken One'. This notion is a development of Shanks's concept of 'shakenness': to use Žižek's term, it consists of a 'traumatic encounter' with an other, which, as Shanks suggests, confronts us with the partialities of our worldview and experience, so opens us up towards transcendence.[4] I argue that Jesus embodies such a reality in his relationships, being deeply attentive to others' otherness, and that he effects others' shakenness. While Shanks understands it primarily as something that happens to us, I suggest we should actively foster shakenness with each other.

---

[1]   Anselm Min, *The Solidarity of Others in a Divided World: A Postmodern Theology after Postmodernism* (New York and London, 2004), pp. 1, 82.

[2]   Ibid., p. 82.

[3]   I use the feminine Greek term, *basileia*, meaning 'empire', rather than the English 'kingdom', to problematize assumptions about God's kingly power, and to contrast God's realm politically with the Roman Empire. See Elisabeth Schüssler Fiorenza, *Jesus – Miriam's Child, Sophia's Prophet: Critical Issues in Feminist Christology* (London, 1995), pp. 14–18, 92, and Fiorenza, *Jesus and the Politics of Interpretation* (London, 2000), pp. 28, 166–70.

[4]   Slavoj Žižek, *Did Somebody Say Totalitarianism? Five Interventions in the (Mis)Use of a Notion* (London, 2001), p. 58; Andrew Shanks, *God and Modernity: A New and Better Way to Do Theology* (London, 2000), p. 5.

'Other' Experiences

Identity, Difference and Solidarity

What are the personal contexts and observations which inform this quest for a constructive christology? Regarding the question of 'identity', I have experienced it as compound for as long as I can remember. My mother is Welsh and my father is English, so I am both Welsh and English. Since marrying Sheryl, whose mother is Singaporean Chinese and whose father is white English, my appreciation of the multi-faceted nature of identity has grown further. For most official documents require Sheryl to define herself as 'Other', which feels somewhat dismissive with regards to the richness of ethnic heritage. For we are all 'other' to one another. It is, for Min, about difference being significant, but not absolute,[5] such that we should be free and able to affirm both difference and commonality; after all, identity can consist of a solidarity of the different. This is my experience.

As for my Christian identity, the same is true: identity, difference and solidarity are interrelated. I was brought up in a Congregational church and am now a minister of a church which also belongs to the Congregational Federation, a small but mainstream denomination in the UK. This gives me a particular notion of 'church', in which all members are understood to be equal and able to participate in church meetings where we aim to discern God's way forward for the church in our locality. This suggests the importance of Christian attentiveness to the particularity of time and place; for what God asks of us in this local church might be quite unlike what God is asking of 'others' in a different local church, though we can still aim to be in solidarity with each other. I increasingly want to emphasize that this implies a distinctive theology of revelation. For the idea is that, through our corporate engagement with scripture and in prayer, we discern and discover together the Word which God is speaking – not by way of a monologue, but rooted in our dialogue with each 'other'. (The nuances of this may not be typical of all Congregationalists, since many would still anticipate that God speaks more through the preacher than the conversation of the gathered Body, but it is of the very nature of my Congregationalism that I am wary of the presumption that a single individual – person or church – might 'represent' a whole tradition. It is due to a lack of attentiveness to differences within a group or tradition that we expect one to represent the whole, but still one's relation to the whole must be affirmed.)

Congregational identity is not, however, the whole story. Firstly, an international youth workcamp in Penrhys, a housing estate in South Wales, with members of thirty Protestant denominations, opened me to all kinds of global connections, contradictions and inequalities. Identity was further developed, secondly, through the ecumenical nature of my Contextual Theology course and placements in Manchester; and thirdly, in encounters with people of other religious traditions, notably on a study tour of Israel/Palestine in 1999. Studying theology as the only

---

[5]   Min, p. 2.

Congregationalist gave rise to contrasting reactions: some included me as one of 'the others' (for there were a handful of individuals from small denominations), or forgot that I was not identified by use only of the dominant categories; but others made concerted efforts to see that I was remembered (some being bewildered by a 'continuing' Congregationalist, but genuinely supportive, and some presuming that I must represent all Congregationalists – generalizing on the basis of minimal experience[6]). The challenge was to aim for a 'solidarity *of* others'. My religious identity is thus also compound: I am a committed Congregationalist, but not necessarily a typical one; I see myself as an 'ecumenical' Christian, a progressive, a constructive theologian, and, like Peter C. Hodgson, 'committed to the agenda of liberal theology as modified in the direction of liberation theology and pluralistic inquiry'.[7] Thus I might have more in common with some who are not religious than with many who are; I sometimes relish being nonconformist, an individualist, but it means a great deal to identify loyally with my tribe.

As part of these developments, especially through studying Contextual Theology, I encountered the work of both John Hick and Lesslie Newbigin. They are located ecclesiologically not too far from my Congregational part of the Reformation, being Presbyterians, and their theologies speak to these concerns about our identity, our relatedness to the religious other, and the question of our solidarity – that is, they discuss the nature of Christian faith in the modern world, and the possibilities for how we might relate to others. Their different visions of Jesus epitomize the contrasting ways in which they handle such concerns.

With regards to my understanding of solidarity – with whom am I called to be in solidarity? – my childhood and Christian nurture were largely coloured by a compassionate Christian conservatism. This taught me that we should show concern for those who are less fortunate; but I was not inclined to push against the *status quo*. First, the youth workcamp in an estate shaped by multiple deprivations; secondly, discussions at university about politics; and thirdly, my experiences in Manchester, including ministry in an inner-city ward, have conscientized me to the prophetic nature of faith. Who am I, in relation to those children who walk the streets without an adult knowing or apparently caring where they are? Who am I, and who is the Church, in relation to those whose low self-esteem is deeply ingrained? Who am I, in relation to those who have sought asylum in this country, but now suffer the indignity of legal limbo and social prejudice? I am an educated, middle-class, white man. In that light, I increasingly see my politics as social democratic – disturbed by inequality and social exclusion, committed to public space and the power of education, and concerned for democracy, human rights, non-violence, internationalist mutuality over narrowly national self-interest, and

---

[6] See below, pp. 11-12, with regards to Benhabib's distinction between 'generalized' and 'concrete' others.

[7] Peter C. Hodgson, *Winds of the Spirit: A Constructive Christian Theology* (London, 1994), p. 17.

sustainable forms of development[8] – though I am far better at the theory than the practice. Attention to the sociopolitical 'others', those relatively marginalized and oppressed, has raised questions for me about global capitalism, which Min, for example, sees today as '*the* context of contexts'.[9] Globalization will reappear through this work, including in relation to the theologies of Hick and Newbigin. Essentially, my point here is that experiences have brought to my attention three kinds of 'others' – those within my (or one's) particular tradition, worldview or tribe (often hastily generalized as 'us'); those of plural other traditions (generalized as 'them'); and those, in a more universal sense, who are invisible, pushed to or beyond the edges of each tradition or tribe, whose voices are being lost (who barely appear on the radar of 'us' or 'them'). In other words, our 'identity' is invariably more compound than we imagine; our 'differences' are more nuanced; and we often opt for a more limited version of 'solidarity' than we might.

The Church and Docetic Christology

As a theological tutor on Congregational and ecumenical courses, I see hints of these same issues in the life and witness of churches. In each case, though admittedly I am generalizing on the basis of anecdotal experience, I see these things as being related to the dominance of docetic christologies, ones in which the humanity of Jesus is only 'apparent'. It is arguably even docetic in those traditions which seek to affirm his humanity more than the divine presence, since the socially constituted nature of his humanity – to which I am committed – is invariably overlooked, thus he only appears human. I explain this further below. In essence, he is idealized; his 'shadow side' is suppressed;[10] he is objectified so as to distinguish him from the rest of us. That is, he is 'othered' in the extreme. As I see it, this contributes to three problems in the (Western) Church, related to the issues of identity, difference and solidarity; the problems are: insularity, indifference and impotence. My alternative vision is of a 'shaken' Jesus, a fully human being, who can shake the Church out of its insularity, indifference and impotence, and enable it to re-engage constructively with a whole world of 'others'. So how do I see this docetic christology affecting the Church?

Firstly, there is the (Western) Church's insularity. Bewildered by such a fast-changing world, anxious about the intellectual challenges of post-Enlightenment

---

[8]   See Colin Hines, *Localization: A Global Manifesto* (London, 2000), p. 5, on the difference between 'globalization' (a systematic reduction of protective barriers, pitting community against community) and 'internationalism' (a global flow aiming to rebuild sustainable local communities).

[9]   Min, p. 135.

[10]   See, for example, Werner Ustorf, 'The Emerging Christ of Post-Christian Europe', in Thomas F. Foust, George R. Hunsberger, J. Andrew Kirk, Werner Ustorf (eds), *A Scandalous Prophet: The Way of Mission after Newbigin* (Grand Rapids, MI, 2002), p. 138, and Stephen Pattison, 'The Shadow Side of Jesus', *Studies in Christian Ethics*, 8/2 (1995): pp. 56–7.

culture, and shocked by the relative weakness of the Church in the face of assertive secularism, the Church can appear deeply insular and defensive. The privatization of faith, as Newbigin argues too,[11] in conjunction with an over-dependency on preachers and pastors, and a resignation to some elements of relativism, have left many of us nervous about expressing faith in public. While there is a good deal of devotion to the Church, and a desire to be compassionate towards others, it is taken for granted that we know our purpose and that we are like-minded. There is little basis for both assumptions, however, since we struggle to act so purposefully, and our like-mindedness is presumptuously oversimplified, neglecting the diversity of 'others within'.

In terms of how this anxious insularity manifests itself in relation to others, there are conflicting but related trends. For the relatively 'liberal', the difference between 'them' and 'us' must be minimized, so as to emphasize our normality and make it seem easier for others to imagine themselves joining us. There is an implicit relativism here, indifferent to the differences between my truth and yours, because of an eagerness to affirm common ground. The point of Jesus, in this view, is to be the ultimate bridge-builder between us and them, to make hospitable space possible. However, our lack of confidence in our particularity, feeding our anxious insularity, sees us reliant on a Jesus who is beyond exemplary. Thus, even if we claim to affirm his humanity, he is still idealized, as a figure somewhat divorced from our human experience. (For example, when our church was wrestling with the fascinating case of Jesus' inability to do 'a deed of power' (Mark 6:5), one member made a point of reasserting that 'Jesus was Son of the Almighty God', as though we must be misreading this apparent inability of his.) For Jesus is seen as one who leads a way we do not expect to be able to follow, as though he is beyond our human anxieties and ambiguities.

However, the more 'conservative' emphasize the substantial difference between 'us' (Christians) and 'them' (non-Christians), rooted in the belief in Jesus' absolute difference as the ultimate gate-keeper between insiders and outsiders. Although this can inspire the desire to tell others about his absolute difference, for their own sake, still there is an insularity: for the Church's purpose may be asserted clearly, but it is taken deeply for granted, anxiously resisting the Church's infection by any worldly ideas. Again, an idealized Jesus is divorced from human ambiguities. So, whilst liberals like Hick may underplay the difference between Christian faith and the otherness of modernity, relative conservatives like Newbigin seem to exaggerate the distinction. In both cases, however, the tradition itself is thereby oversimplified, by suppressing the others within Christian identity. Anxiety and insularity lead to a denial of internal diversity, exacerbated by a commitment to an idealized Jesus – a figure immeasurably more different from us than we are from each other.

---

[11] Lesslie Newbigin, *Foolishness to the Greeks: The Gospel and Western Culture* (London, 1986), pp. 15–17, 36–8.

As briefly indicated, such anxiety and insularity feeds the Church's indifference or inattentiveness to the subtleties and concreteness of 'others beyond'. After all, liberals would rather belittle the differences and emphasize common ground, so as to avoid conflict. This is fed by a grasp of Jesus as the truly nice man, who wants everyone to live in harmony. This is, however, an idealized Jesus, an unreal caricature of a much more awkward historical figure. Meanwhile, conservatives are not so interested in the array of differences because they detract from the ultimate difference: Jesus is Lord, and no-one else is. To re-encounter a more grounded Jesus is to be prompted to attend concertedly to difference as a God-given reality, to recognize and engage its nuances.

Although this is not immediately apparent in conservative Christianity, with its confident acting in the world, nor in the social activism of some liberal Christianity, nevertheless the idealized Jesus who underpins the Church's insularity and indifference also generates a certain kind of impotence. It is partly about a weary resignation in the face of apparently intractable global problems, and partly a long-term disempowerment brought about by the clericalization of the Church's ministry. However, there is also a theological commitment to Jesus' work being the potent work, which renders our own acts apparently, or relatively, impotent. Only Jesus, the exemplary God-man, can truly make a difference, calm storms, raise the dead; we can simply celebrate his achievements. The alternative is a Jesus whose solidarity *of* 'others' inspires us to demonstrate such transformative solidarity: for we shall do greater things than he (John 14:12).

It is, I suggest, the vision of Christ as part of his Body's 'solidarity *of* others' who thereby enables the Church to overcome its insularity and indifference, seeing its otherness within and beyond, and to rediscover the potency of its corporate potential.

Resisting Objectification

Constructing a Shaken Christology

How, then, might we understand Jesus Christ in relation to 'others'? This book is an attempt to do christology differently, both in terms of its understanding and in engagement with Christian discipleship. It not only attempts to describe christological reality and relatedness in a distinctive way, but aims to help Christian communities with reflections and resources for their mission. In particular, it offers a vision of more constructive engagement with the contemporary 'problems' of identity, difference and solidarity, by virtue of its alternative approach to christology.

In this context, Hick and Newbigin are significant and worthy dialogue-partners, because their writings emerge from contexts experiencing considerable upheaval with regards to the three problems of identity, difference and solidarity. Rooted in similar church backgrounds, which resonate also with mine, it is illuminating that their contrasting approaches to these problems reflect the tensions and polarities within churches, and discussion of their related errors (which I describe as 'partial shakenness') gives rise to my constructive proposal of Jesus as 'the Shaken One'.

At the heart of this proposal is the concern to resist objectification – both of Jesus himself and of each other. Drawing on the insights of Wink, Benhabib and Žižek, I demonstrate the nature of this resistance, culminating in discussion of shakenness.

It is Wink's identification of the 'integral worldview' which resists objectification, since this worldview insists that 'everything interpenetrates everything else'.[12] The point is that reality's 'outer forms' and 'inner spirituality' interpenetrate each other, with ambiguous consequences; for the 'good' but 'fallen Powers' (the social practices, institutions, traditions and structures of the world's social fabric) both distort the connectedness, such that we objectify each other, and facilitate our ethical resistance to objectification itself.[13] In other words, neither the powers nor we are simply good or simply evil, but live with both potentialities by virtue of this interpenetration of reality. Our task, then, is to *engage* the powers – including our own religious tradition and that of others – in such a way as to resist the objectification of self and other, and to energize our mutual realization of each other's humanity. Of course, our powers of analysis are themselves interpenetrated by these ambiguities, so we must be as self-critical as possible in our challenges to objectification. Jesus himself was and is embedded in such ambiguities – the tendency to objectify and the processes of othering – so christology is subject to these powers. Nevertheless, it is a Christian conviction that Jesus Christ also enables our liberation from these distorted relations – and he does this in and through relationship with, or by virtue of generating a solidarity of, 'others'. For his primary concern is the *basileia* of God, an alternative empire exposing and overcoming 'kyriarchy'[14] (the lordship by some over others), such as Roman military and economic power. This alternative reality is concertedly social (it is about human relationships), inclusive (it is for 'the least' and 'the last'), and transformative (it impacts all of life).

Seyla Benhabib's critical distinction between 'generalized' and 'concrete others' further underpins my critique of our objectification of the other.[15] In essence, the 'generalized other' is the result of our abstraction or 'disembodying' of the other from real contexts. We assume 'they' are like 'us' in particular ways on the basis of

---

[12]   Walter Wink, 'The New Worldview: Spirit at the Core of Everything', in Ray Gingerich and Ted Grimsrud (eds), *Transforming the Powers: Peace, Justice and the Domination System* (Minneapolis, MN, 2006), pp. 21, 23. See also Walter Wink, *Engaging the Powers: Discernment and Resistance in a World of Domination* (Minneapolis, MN, 1992), p. 10.

[13]   This is an elaboration of Wink, *Engaging the Powers*, p. 10.

[14]   Fiorenza explains the term 'kyriarchy' in *Jesus – Miriam's Child, Sophia's Prophet*, p. 14.

[15]   Seyla Benhabib, *Situating the Self: Gender, Community and Postmodernism in Contemporary Ethics* (Oxford, 1992), pp. 152–69, as follows.

minimal experience, generalizing about them for our own convenience. It allows us to oversimplify any dialogue, since we are effectively satisfied with what we already 'know'. In contrast, to see the 'concrete other' is to attend more carefully to the particularity of context, the embedded nature of identities, the nuances of our interrelatedness, and the possibility of being in solidarity – or affirming the common humanity – of those who are genuinely different from us. It is, Benhabib says, 'a vision of moral maturity that views the self as a being immersed in a network of relationships with others'.[16] To generate this 'enlarged mentality', we need principles, institutions and procedures 'to enable articulation of the voice of the "others"'.[17] In that light, Wink is right to argue for engagement with, not retreat from, the powers – including religious traditions. Although they are themselves infected by generalizing and objectifying tendencies, we should not presume to step out of corporate traditions, since they offer tools for resisting the objectification of the other. For me, though he is (as we are) inseparable from these ambiguities, Jesus Christ's vision and practice of God's *basileia* offers such tools with particular power. This does not mean he should be objectified as the idealized God-man, or that the Christian community should idealize itself, since both Christ and his Body remain subject to the ambiguities and unintended consequences of reality's interpenetration: thus 'the Shaken One' equips us to be self-critical and ever open to further shakenness.

Slavoj Žižek, too, illustrates the danger of distorted relations between different kinds of 'others', or between humans, the powers (including religious traditions) and God. Žižek argues that where two 'others' meet, there is a 'traumatic encounter', since the 'hard kernel' of one cannot be symbolized or translated into the other's terms; each must simply deal with the difference and distinctiveness of the other.[18] There are, again, three kinds of other.[19] First, the 'imaginary other' is 'other people "like me", my fellow human beings', including Benhabib's 'generalized' and 'concrete' people. Secondly, the 'symbolic "big Other"' is 'the "substance" of our social existence, the impersonal set of rules', akin to Wink's powers, or social practices, including religious traditions. The third other is 'the impossible Thing, the "inhuman partner"', with whom 'no symmetrical dialogue ... is possible'. God exemplifies this kind of otherness, 'the unfathomable abyss of radical Otherness'. The task, as Žižek proposes, is to recognize each 'other', so as not to distort the relationalities.

So, to elaborate his point: first, were I to lose a sense of the impossible Thing, that which defines what is genuinely distinctive and other about this tradition, I would retreat into relativism. I must therefore affirm the impossible Thing – the scandalously universal claims of Christian particularity; that is, I must affirm the identity of what is genuinely particular about this tradition, but in and through relationships with 'others' within this tradition. (This entails re-owning

---

[16] Ibid., p. 149.

[17] Ibid., p. 168.

[18] Žižek, p. 58.

[19] Ibid., pp. 163–5.

the 'shadow side' of our history, as well as the good news.) Secondly, were the relations between my fellow humans to break, such that we could not see each other as concrete others, only as generalized others, then I would lose the ability to differentiate between them (in all their differences) and me. The symbolic Other, the rules of the game, would dominate me, since the imaginary others would have collapsed. All I would have would be 'the tradition', my symbolic Other, which I would thus see as the impossible Thing. In response, I must engage critically but constructively in dialogue with plural others, to distinguish this tradition from the universal Thing once more, to see that there are real and valid differences. Thus I must learn to see the others not on my terms, but as concrete others. (This entails some defiance of my own tradition's finalities, to see the divine presence in 'the other'.) Finally, were the symbolic Other to become dysfunctional – that is, the fallen powers are not 'engaged' – then some imaginary others would fill the vacuum, acting like an impossible Thing, dehumanizing others and evading rigorous dialogue. In response, I must reaffirm external structures, social practices, religious traditions – powers bigger than myself, solidarities capable of holding the dominant to account and of liberating the oppressed. (This entails commitment to the corporate Body of Christ, a solidarity of others, in pursuit of ever greater solidarity.)

This attentiveness to the other/s, which Žižek encourages, is not only about affirming an appropriate relationality between the particular (identity), the plural (difference) and the universal (solidarity), but is also about resisting the idealization of the other. He argues that Christian love for the other is because of what they lack; we love imperfect others, just as we are imperfect too.[20] (This underpins the reciprocity of the love, since each is loved in its imperfection.) Thus the other is not to be idealized – or objectified at all, since the hard kernel of the other is untranslatable, ensuring that the other is always 'more than' a known object, and because the other is constituted partly by its relations to other kinds of other. However, Žižek does not go as far as speaking of *Jesus*' enigmatic kernel, his 'shadow side' or his 'lack', whereas Ustorf encourages us to see Jesus as more fully rounded.[21]

Thus, Wink's integral worldview asserts the interrelatedness of all things. If we are to avoid objectifying each other, we need social resources and traditions to help us. We cannot be sufficiently self-critical on our own. Benhabib agrees. We need corporate traditions to enable us to nurture the vision of our complex interrelatedness, to see and relate to each other as concrete, not generalized, others. So, too, for Žižek. To manifest healthy, not distorted, relations between different kinds of 'others', we should attend to our differences in the light of 'symbolic others', social practices capable of regulating and transforming our tendencies to objectify. I argue that christology is such a tradition, a social practice particularly capable of effecting our resistance to objectification; but it needs to be focused

---

[20]   Ibid., p. 57.
[21]   Ustorf, 'The Emerging Christ', pp. 134–41.

on Jesus 'the Shaken One'. So what is the relation between shakenness and the christological tradition?

Shakenness is, as Shanks puts it, about 'anti-ideological thoughtfulness'.[22] Ideologies tend to make us sentimentalize, idealize, demonize or suppress any dissonant experiences, to paper over the cracks or ambiguities which raise unwanted questions about reality. On the other hand, when we are 'shaken', or traumatized by an encounter with an other, we are urged to resist any such captivity or closed-mindedness, being confronted with a common humanity shared by deeply different people. This is because, as we explore 'shakenness' now, what is involved here is 'the condition of being, to some extent, *un*-tied from the constraints' of a culture, its imperialism, its particularism.[23] As Shanks thus puts it, 'An ethos celebratory of shakenness is necessarily therefore an ethos for all' – that is, it is concerned with genuine universality (hence he affirms the 'grand narrative', as we see below). For Shanks later explains:

> the best theology of all is that which most explicitly seeks to serve the universal *solidarity of the shaken*, as such. An alliance, that is to say, embracing all comers. The solidarity of those shaken – out of complacency, out of inertia, out of numb despair – into a serious pursuit of true Honesty. Solidarity conceived strictly on the basis of that shared shakenness, and without any further limitation whatsoever.[24]

'Honesty', I explain further below, is Shanks's ultimate kind of 'truth', distinct from the 'sacred ideology' of 'truth-as-correctness' which is more limiting.[25] First, though, I must outline the roots of 'shakenness' and its relation to my overall argument.

Shanks's notion of 'shakenness' comes originally from the term 'solidarity of the shaken', first used in Czechoslovakia under Soviet rule. It was Jan Patočka's image of being shaken out of life 'within a lie', with its 'unquestioned prejudices', and of being prompted 'into a genuinely open-minded thoughtfulness', an 'openness to transcendence'.[26] It is about the way in which people are compelled to respond to 'historic trauma' or 'grimly disturbing experiences … by a determined attempt to rethink one's whole moral attitude to the world'.[27] Such shaken people cannot claim

---

[22]   Shanks, *God and Modernity*, p. 5.

[23]   Ibid., p. 19.

[24]   Andrew Shanks, *The Other Calling: Theology, Intellectual Vocation and Truth* (Oxford, 2007), p. 18 (his italics).

[25]   Andrew Shanks, *Faith in Honesty: The Essential Nature of Theology* (Aldershot, 2005), p. 2.

[26]   Shanks, *God and Modernity*, p. 5, citing Jan Patočka, *Heretical Essays on the Philosophy of History*, the final chapter of which is translated into English as 'Wars of the Twentieth Century and the Twentieth Century as War', *Telos*, 30 (1976–77). (See also Andrew Shanks, *Civil Society, Civil Religion* (Oxford, 1995), chapter 3.)

[27]   Shanks, *God and Modernity*, p.5.

to be a 'moral authority' in themselves, but that they reinforce 'the awareness that a higher authority does exist'.[28] As for this 'higher authority', Shanks speaks of it as that 'to which all shakenness ... bears witness. And to which, moreover, *nothing else, except shakenness*, bears witness. The authority of that which shakes.'[29] Not all who are shaken will believe in God, however, though for those who do, every response we make to each cultural shake-up or historic trauma constitutes 'the same ... story about God: God as one who shakes'.[30] Shanks's particular concern, there, is the way social movements (such as Amnesty International) can constitute 'solidarity of the shaken', not by leading people to specific answers, but by begging profound questions about how we take for granted the nature and inevitability of certain social realities. This, in turn, begs questions of the Church, and whether we too demonstrate such solidarity with people who are being shaken, or are we ourselves trapped within closed-mindedness and self-authenticating practice?

The point of shakenness, with regards to Christian theology, is to energize the dialectic between the tradition itself and its wider purpose. After all, I understand the Christian tradition to have a purpose, and good news, beyond its own constituency – not least because, as McFarland suggests, its constituency is defined by those on the 'outside' ('the last') at least as much as 'insiders' ('the first').[31] Thus, as Shanks explains:

> As a Christian theologian, what I am interested in trying to develop is, thus, a grand narrative whose central theme would be the historic emergence of the possibility of the solidarity of the shaken – a church which would explicitly identify its own vocation as a kenotic contribution to that larger ideal.[32]

This does not mean that shakenness takes priority over the tradition as such, since Shanks's understanding of shakenness is itself shaped by the tradition. The relation is reflexive, because shakenness is rooted in the life of God, as the one who shakes. For he speaks of 'the shaking power of revelation'[33] and suggests 'true "unconcealment" [revelation] comes, precisely, from shakenness – the shaking away of that which conceals'.[34] That shakenness opens us to transcendence also demonstrates that it has much to do with the life of God, who is transcendent; but

---

[28]   Ibid., pp. 5–6, citing Jan Patočka, 'What Charter 77 Is and What It Is Not', in H. Gordon Skilling, *Charter 77 and Human Rights in Czechoslovakia* (Winchester, MA: Allen and Unwin, 1981), p. 219.

[29]   Shanks, *God and Modernity*, p. 6 (his italics).

[30]   Ibid., p. 15.

[31]   Ian McFarland, *Listening to the Least: Doing Theology from the Outside In* (Cleveland, OH, 1998), pp. 80–97.

[32]   Shanks, *Faith in Honesty*, p. 104.

[33]   Andrew Shanks, *What is Truth? Towards a Theological Poetics* (London and New York: Routledge, 2001), p. 144.

[34]   Shanks, *God and Modernity*, p. 36.

it is also christological, since Shanks proposes, for example, that the Beatitudes signify Jesus' affirmation of shaken people, that they can in fact be summarized as 'how blest are the shaken', and that Jesus' whole ministry reflects such a focus.[35] The point is, for Shanks, that Jesus is a community-builder, not in the conventional sense of boosting the status of 'insiders' and reinforcing the pre-existing boundaries of a traumatized group, but 'the absolute opposite to a sectarian',[36] shaking those barriers in solidarity with 'others', so creating new possibilities of being, thinking, relating and acting.

In this sense, shakenness affects and shapes our three problems: for Christian identity is shaken by the others within; this tradition is shaken by the fact of different others beyond;[37] and we are shaken so as to be in solidarity with those who suffer the powers of domination.[38]

Constructing a Social Christology

Having argued that there are problems in the (Western) Church arising from the dominance of docetic christologies, it is necessary to demonstrate further the connection between christology and ecclesiology, between our vision of the person of Christ and our vision of his corporate Body. This is fundamental, also, to my proposal that Jesus is 'the Shaken One', since his shakenness implies his deep relatedness with and attentiveness to 'others'. Thus it is integral to this constructive christology that Jesus Christ is inseparable from the discipleship community, because all human beings are constituted socially, including Jesus of Nazareth. As Barnes puts it: 'To be is *to be in relation*.'[39] Ultimately, this will lead me to articulate the Christian mission in terms of 'mutual humanization',[40] that is, the task of enabling each other to be more fully human.

---

[35]   Ibid., pp. 16–17.

[36]   Andrew Shanks, *What is Truth? Towards a Theological Poetics* (London and New York, 2001), p. 21.

[37]   Shanks, *God and Modernity*, p. 43: 'Non-pluralist theology (whether exclusivist or inclusivist) may be deeply shaken, but the solidarity it affirms is still not the solidarity of the shaken as such; it is the solidarity of shaken Christians.'

[38]   Shanks, *Faith in Honesty*, p. 105: 'The solidarity of the shaken ... may be for any sort of emancipatory political purpose – purely and simply, to begin with, on the grounds of a shared trans-ideological commitment to primal shakenness.'

[39]   Michael Barnes, *Theology and the Dialogue of Religions* (Cambridge, 2002), pp. 75–6 (his italics).

[40]   The term is originally from Paulo Freire, *Pedagogy of the Oppressed*, rev. edn (London, 1996), p. 56, in relation to the educational process, but I am giving it a wider meaning: for I see Jesus in particular as one who enables us to humanize one another mutually.

As Wink outlines,[41] there are clear biblical connections between the individual Jesus and the corporate 'body of Christ'. For, in Paul's terms, 'we, who are many, are one body in Christ and individually we are members of one another' (Romans 12:4–5). These images of our interpersonal connections not only have Old Testament roots, but speak of and to something innate to being human. As Wink insists, 'We are one body, not just as a church, but as a species', hence the language of the Christian's being 'in Christ' and of Christ's indwelling in us. So, too, for McFarland, Jesus' identity and the Church's identity are inseparable.[42] Crucially, though, as McFarland argues, Jesus demonstrates this relation to be 'from the outside in', that is, the connection between the individual and the community is meant to be inherently transformative of dominant social relations. For Jesus identifies with those on or beyond the margins of the social and religious community, those regarded as 'other', indicating that God 'undermines any claim to theological authority that is not made from a position of solidarity with those at the margins'.[43] To reaffirm Jesus' sociality is to relocate the focus of religion from interior, privatized spirituality and personal salvation to Wink's 'interpenetration' of reality and the interpersonal purposes of God. It is also to confirm Shanks's understanding of a grand narrative, a universal vision, in terms of the ongoing quest for an ever greater solidarity of others; that is, the Christian particularity demonstrates that it is even for those regarded as 'beyond redemption'.

This fundamental emphasis on Jesus' sociality thereby binds christology with ecclesiology and ecclesiology with a mission beyond its own frontiers. It is underpinned further by the interaction between two frameworks, as we shall see – that of Peter C. Hodgson regarding christology in a postmodern context, and that of Andrew Shanks concerning the 'virtues' of the Church (and the nature of theology *per se*).[44] That their frameworks deeply interrelate is further indication of the connection between Christ and his Body. Also, their criteria, as outlined below, speak directly to the three dimensions of otherness which reflect the 'problems' of identity, difference and solidarity.

Firstly, there is the problem of the identity of the Christian tradition itself. This is partly explained by Christ's Body viewing him in different ways, many of which involve denying the authenticity of the other's view – that is, as we have begun to see, 'the other within' is objectified and suppressed. Secondly, there is the problem of difference and the Church's struggle to attend constructively to

---

[41]   Walter Wink, *The Human Being: Jesus and the Enigma of the Son of the Man* (Minneapolis, MN, 2002), pp. 209–11.

[42]   McFarland, pp. 19–39, 58.

[43]   Ibid., pp. 5–7, 33–4, 36, 38–9, 79–82, 86–97.

[44]   Hodgson, *Winds of the Spirit*, p. 243 (I shall explain my understanding of 'postmodern' shortly); Andrew Shanks, *A Theological Context for Urban/Industrial Mission*, privately circulated paper, cited by Malcolm Brown, *New Government, New Community?* Second Andrewtide Lecture, 26 November 1997, published in association with The William Temple Foundation, p. 16.

the nuanced relations between its tradition and that of others – that is, 'the other beyond' is objectified in one of several ways. (While I elaborate this argument when discussing theologies of religions in Chapter 6, the point is not to offer a comparison between Jesus and other religious figures, but to explore the causes and effects of different Christians' visions of religious diversity.) Thirdly, the problem of solidarity is the question of ethical commitment. We might celebrate Jesus' solidarities with those 'othered' by dominating powers, but in our practice do we collude with such objectification and oppression or transform it? In that respect, this is a political theology, not identical to the campaigning nature of liberation theology *per se*, since this project also has a mediating purpose, to enable the different to dialogue peaceably with each other, but it is certainly coloured by the liberationist bias towards those 'othered' as outsiders. It is a quest for a greater solidarity of others.

It is the application of Hodgson's and Shanks's frameworks to these problems which gives this christology its distinctive shape and purpose, by leading me to envisage Jesus 'the Shaken One'.

Constructive Christology: Shaped by Postmodern Concerns and Criteria

Hodgson offers criteria for christology which pertinently speak to the experiences and problems we have been unfolding. I shall outline them shortly, but first it is necessary to explain the way in which he understands his criteria as being appropriate for the 'postmodern' context. This project is located on the boundaries between the modern and the postmodern, since 'objectification (of the other)' is largely a modernist problem – concerned especially with the dichotomy between the subject and the object, amongst other dichotomies, to which we shall return – and the problematic of 'otherness' is more a postmodern concern. I see Hick and Newbigin also as being theologians on this boundary, between the modern and the postmodern, but, in accordance with Hodgson's analysis, I believe they each make a wrong postmodern turn. For Hodgson argues for what he calls a 'late' modern, or 'critical postmodern' approach.[45] This is about properly valuing the inheritance of post-Enlightenment modernity – its pursuit of emancipatory meta-narratives, as opposed to the suspicion and deconstruction of all such possibilities,[46] and its affirmation of 'individuation', believing in the worth and integrity of each human being, but not its distortion into 'individualism', which presumptuously separates the individual from social relations. Thus its 'critical' dimension problematizes the modern legacy of false dichotomies, the vision of reality as 'either/or', and argues instead, as Min does, for 'liberating totalities' but by way of 'a dialectic of

---

[45]   Peter C. Hodgson, *Theology in the Fiction of George Eliot: The Mystery Beneath the Real* (London, 2001), p. 151.

[46]   Shanks, *Faith in Honesty*, pp. 90–91. We saw he defends the 'grand narrative'.

totality and infinity [of the other] in the interest of solidarity of others'.[47] That is, as I interpret it, any narrative with ambitions of totality must consciously be open and attend to the presence of others – the forgotten others within, the different others beyond, and those who are sociopolitically othered (marginalized, oppressed) by distorted relations.

This means that Hodgson's late modernism, which prioritizes a 'revisionist' approach to theology, as opposed to 'renewal' or 'deconstruction',[48] aims to affirm aspects of the modern but also to recognize that its tasks are unfinished; thus it is a never-ending commitment. This contrasts with the approaches of Hick and Newbigin. Although their theologies can also be defined by reference to the totalizing discourse of post-Enlightenment modernity – that is, they cannot help but engage with Western modernity, even as Hick does so far less critically than Newbigin – their interests and trajectories point to different kinds of postmodernism. To use Hodgson's terms, Newbigin represents not the 'late modern', but the 'counter-modern' approach, or 'renewal',[49] by way of his reaction against Western modernity and his desire to revive older meta-narrative orthodoxies in the face of the Enlightenment's distorting effects. Hick, on the other hand, while being generally very much committed to Kantian modernism, as we shall see, incorporates elements of the more 'radical' postmodernism, or 'deconstruction', by which a truth cannot really be said to be any more valid than another truth. (These two positions can co-exist in Hick's theology, since it can be read as both a first-order discourse, or prescription, by which he effectively argues for a universal ethical religion, along similar lines to Kant, and a second-order discourse, by which he seeks simply to explain reality's ambiguous relativity.) In essence, though, these contrasts are what distinguish their respective forms of 'partial' shakenness from the potential for further shakenness in a 'critical postmodern' christology.

Philosophically, the three dimensions of otherness can also be understood with reference to three dichotomies rooted in the modern epoch. Each contributes to the way in which our visions of Jesus are shaped. My response to them is to attempt to reaffirm the human subject. Whereas Kant's modern turn to the human subject is a turn to an idealized individual, an objectified figure, so feeds our own objectification of the other, this instead is a postmodern turn, resistant to the false dichotomies of modernism.

First, this postmodern turn resists the dichotomy between the subject as detached observer and the object being observed or defined. The dichotomy is problematized because the observer's very presence, methods and interpretations (being historically constituted and ideologically laden) themselves define, distort and disrupt the field of observation.[50] In the christological field, this means 'I' cannot presume to isolate 'Jesus' for study: for Christian traditions and social

---

[47]   Min, pp. 7–8, critically adapting the terminology of Levinas.
[48]   Hodgson, *Winds of the Spirit*, p. 55.
[49]   Hodgson, *Theology in the Fiction*, p. 151; Hodgson, *Winds of the Spirit*, p. 55.
[50]   Wink, *Human Being*, p. 7.

histories mean that 'he' comes to 'me' not in some pure, singular form. He is not an 'object', but a real subject; that is, he is (as I am) both an active agent, and subject to others' stories and perceptions. Our histories condition our vision, though we need not be imprisoned by our histories if we are alert to the assumptions we make. Thus, if we are committed to understanding Jesus' identity we must engage in conversation, as 'others within', to help each of us to see the factors shaping our vision, and to reaffirm the intersubjective nature of human identity, including Jesus'. It is about affirming the *particularity* of Jesus. This demands sensitivity to the never-ending, reflexive relationship between the impact of Jesus' vision on us and the impact of our contexts on our visions of him.[51]

Secondly, there is the dichotomy (or the so-called 'scandal of particularity') between the particular (with its 'accidents' of history) and its relation to the universal: how can the former bear any true relation to the latter? How can one historical narrative speak of and to the totality of history? This modern question, about the audacious Christian conviction that Jesus Christ can be *the* key to all of history, presumes that the focus of attention must be the connection between the particular and the universal. This focus is problematized, however, in postmodern minds, by the fact of *other* convictions apparently competing with this one. The point is that ours is not the only tradition to connect its particulars with the universal. Nor do these different traditions speak completely independently of each other; rather, they intersect with one another, in terms of both their contexts and resources (for example, Jesus the Jew is foundational for Christian faith and is the Great Prophet in Islam) and their comparable ethics (such as between Gautama Buddha and Jesus of Nazareth[52]). Thus the dichotomy between particularity and universality, which defines the 'scandal of particularity', is problematized by this further dynamic – the 'scandal of *plurality*'. For we cannot do christology, or grasp the identity and role of Jesus, without regard for those 'other' particularities and their vision of the universal. Such otherness is concrete and complex.

Thirdly, there is the modern dichotomy between the self and others, or between the individual and the community – and in effect, between an internalized, personal religion, and an externalized, social religion. This must be problematized, so to reaffirm the sociality of the human being, and thus, for christology, the sociality of Jesus, as Fiorenza does by exploring his maleness and Jewishness.[53] As I have argued, the Christ and the Body of Christ are interrelated, which is confirmed also in the breakdown between subject and object. To problematize the dichotomy

---

[51]   Albert Schweitzer noted this relationship, in *The Quest of the Historical Jesus*, 3rd edn (London, 1954), which Theissen puts in these terms: 'For what is historical scholarship, if not an ongoing conversation about the past in which no one has the last word' (*Shadow of the Galilean* (London, 1987), p. 55).

[52]   See Marcus Borg (ed.), *Jesus and Buddha: The Parallel Sayings* (Berkeley, CA, 1997).

[53]   Fiorenza, *Jesus and the Politics*, pp. 12–13, 18, 24–5, 119–22, 137–44, 145–9, 153–8.

between self and others is to become more consciously political. Since it is arguable that Jesus demonstrates this relation as being 'from the outside in', or, in the terms of liberation theology, since Jesus embodies a preferential option for the poor, this shapes our quest for solidarity of others. For it is about affirming the *universality* of the quest for solidarity, recognizing and affirming our common humanity, not least with those most 'othered' by the System.

These problematizations are thus interrelated: for the intersubjective correction of the subject/object dichotomy indicates also that any objectified individual, including an idealized Jesus, is a distorted construction, who must be re-located in community. So, too, the particular – whether a particular subject, object, individual, tradition, community, or, for that matter, modern dichotomy – is problematized by plural other particularities and their diverse, interconnected relations to the universal. In the face of all this, Hodgson's suggestions for an appropriate christology appear to give voice to such interrelatedness.

For him, in our postmodern climate, christology must:[54] 1) appropriate and release 'the considerable saving resources of the Christian tradition' – that is, it must engage with the others within its particularity, within its identity, to ensure an appropriate degree of interrelatedness between Christ and the (whole) Body of Christ; 2) be open to the diversity and plurality of mediations of 'divine saving presence' – that is, it must engage with the genuinely different others beyond the particular; and 3) 'be genuinely committed to the project of human liberation' – that is, it must express the solidarity of universal humanity, especially for the sake of marginalized others. In contrast, any tradition, including a christology, which claims universal scope without engaging in both constructive dialogue with the 'others' within its own tradition or the 'others' of different traditions and liberative practice is, in my terms, a 'universal pretender', a self-deceiving ideology, insufficiently shaken out of its dishonesties.[55]

This critical postmodern dynamic, an ongoing quest, is rooted in the life of the living God, the one who shakes us into greater solidarity with others. It is thus a christological dynamic concerned with these three dimensions: In what way do Jesus and his communal vision and practice of God's *basileia* constitute the Christian tradition's particular contribution to the healing of history and our mutual humanization? Secondly, in what way do Jesus and his communal vision and practice of God's *basileia* facilitate honest dialogue with those whose contributions (and resistance) to our mutual humanization differ from our own? Thirdly, in what way does this (presumed) universal quest for mutual humanization undermine what Wink calls the 'Domination System',[56] the idolatrous complex of powers which nurtures our objectification and dehumanization of each other,

---

[54] Hodgson, *Winds of the Spirit*, p. 243.

[55] McFarland, pp. 9–10: the Church's self-definition or identity is to be reshaped by pluralism and theologies of liberation (empowering those normally suppressed by the dominant). Regarding 'dishonesties', see below, p. 23–4.

[56] Wink, *Engaging the Powers*, p. 9.

affirming instead that such 'fallen' powers can be redeemed through our mutual solidarity with all who dream of liberation? These concerns, or criteria, are not separate, nor are they objective: but they shape my vision.

Constructive Christology: Shaped by Virtues and Dishonesties

Andrew Shanks also sees the connection between the individual and the community as essential for a new ecclesiology. His three 'virtues' of the Church,[57] together with his conception of radical 'Honesty', can be understood as taking Hodgson's christological criteria further. Firstly, 'sanctity' (which, for Shanks, is a formal rather than material category) is the virtue of embodying, of being true to, the values of one's (Christian) culture – that is, in Hodgson's terms, of appropriating the saving resources of the tradition. It is the concern with the particular, and the question of identity (who are we?), which entails attentiveness to 'others within'. Secondly, 'transgression' is the virtue of crossing the boundaries between one's own and another's culture or tradition; not trespassing where one is not welcome, but readily transgressing one's own complacencies and apparent finalities, to be changed by the consequent encounter – that is, of being open to God's saving presence in other traditions. It is the concern with the plural, and the question of difference (who are they?), which entails attentiveness to 'others beyond'. Thirdly, 'solidarity of the shaken' is the virtue of being committed to 'anti-ideological thoughtfulness' and action – that is, as I see it, of working for liberation through solidarity with those who suffer the effects of 'kyriarchy' and domination. It is the concern with the universal, and the question of solidarity (with whom should we be in solidarity?), which entails attentiveness to those othered by sociopolitical powers.

While Hodgson's christological criteria nudge us towards openness to the other, Shanks's ecclesiological virtues are more radical, and it is the reality of 'shakenness' which explains this. The difference between them is as follows. Hodgson essentially 'orientates' us, such that we *recognize* the fact of otherness – with regards to the breadth of voices within our tradition, the reality of God's presence in other traditions, and the need for action for the sake of others who are the victims of injustice. To a certain extent, this recognition problematizes our own identity: we are prompted to understand ourselves in and through our relations with these others. There remains a possibility, though, that we could still objectify the other, seeing them in our generalized terms without being deeply shaken by them. However, Shanks's concept of 'sanctity' urges us, further, to recognize the very otherness *of* our identity: we have a story, which shakes others, just as it is also susceptible to being shaken. Secondly, we must not simply accept God's presence in other traditions, but actively 'transgress' our own finalities: it is of the very nature of the Christian tradition to undertake such risky humility, to allow for 'their' shaking of 'us'. Thirdly, our concern for justice is part of a bigger concern for solidarity – not

---

[57]   Shanks, *A Theological Context*, p. 16.

'with' others, but a solidarity 'of' others, in which we rigorously attend to each other's otherness.

Shanks does not recommend shakenness for its own sake, however, but sees it as that which serves the pursuit of Honesty. As he puts it: 'What "shakes" the "shaken" ... is the sheer imperative of Honesty.'[58] The capital 'H' represents its radicality, not mere frankness (truly saying what one thinks) nor mere sincerity (truly meaning what one says), but 'being truly *open to what other people may have to say*'.[59] Such radical truth-as-Honesty, the focus of authentic theology, never finished, 'is a quality of sheer conversational *receptivity*', which contrasts with 'truth-as-correctness', the concern of 'sacred ideology', which is 'impatient with the pursuit of truth'. That is, where a tradition succumbs to sacred ideology, it claims already to possess truth-as-correctness, to know *enough*; in contrast, truth-as-Honesty is ever open to being shaken further. So, for Shanks:

> The highest cause is the cause of Honesty, and, in organizational terms, what Honesty requires is the solidarity of the shaken, a solidarity, purely and simply, on the basis of shared shakenness, a shared commitment to Honesty.[60]

In other words, in organizational terms, a tradition is required to manifest and energize this shared commitment, and Shanks articulates the way in which the *trinitarian* tradition does indeed manifest such commitment. For each of the three 'persons' is said to represent (but not exclusively) the Christian responses to three dishonesties.[61]

First, there is 'dishonesty-as-disowning', the dishonesty which is about a tradition evading responsibility for its chequered past. A 'boastful community', or, at its most brutal, a 'destructive mob', will refuse to see its 'shadow side'[62] – the harm it has done due to its sectarianism. In response, what Shanks calls Third-Person theology's 'flair for tradition', epitomized by the Holy Spirit, shakes the Church out of its sectarianism, enabling it to re-appropriate even those parts which we dishonestly disown for their uncomfortable reminder of our shadow side. That is, such shakenness alerts us to the others within – within our particular identity – so causing us to review our partiality, constantly. (As I shall argue, both Hick and Newbigin are more sectarian, and guilty of more disowning, than they would admit.)

Secondly, there is 'dishonesty-as-banality', the dishonesty of remaining 'trapped in the present moment: swept along by routine ... the sheer low-key unreflectiveness, or spiritual indolence, of those who are content just to belong'.

---

[58]   Shanks, *The Other Calling*, p. 27.

[59]   Shanks, *Faith in Honesty*, p. 2 (his italics).

[60]   Ibid., p. 148.

[61]   Ibid., pp. 11, 47, 54 (as follows).

[62]   The term 'shadow side' is also used by Ustorf, 'The Emerging Christ', pp. 137–42, and Pattison, pp. 54–67, as noted above.

It is, in essence, 'the dishonesty of the herd' – the unthinking indifference to other herds and their truths. In response, First-Person theology's 'decisively transcultural generosity', epitomized by God the Father of all peoples, asserts the possibility of learning from the different. That is, such shakenness alerts us to the others beyond – plurality as such. (It is questionable how well both Hick and Newbigin truly value plurality *as plurality*.)

Thirdly, there is the 'future-oriented dishonesty' which sets out to manipulate; the 'dishonesty of a gang' or ideology. It is the dishonesty of the Roman Empire, the deceit that authorized violence and scapegoating bring social order, the lie that the ways of the world are inevitable. In response, Second-Person theology's 'free-spiritedness', epitomized by God the Son, exposes the ideological dishonesties of establishment dogma. The lies are reversed: for the Crucified One is shown not to be worthless; the last are shown to be first; those outside are welcomed in; those othered and dehumanized by the system are cherished as part of the *basileia* of God.[63] That is, such shakenness alerts us to those othered by powers of domination. (Again, I question the extent to which Hick and Newbigin shake us out of the oppressive effects of ideology.)

Thus, the quest is as follows: especially in an age in which issues of identity, difference and solidarity call for our engagement, christology needs to be attentive to 'the other'. I suggest that the arguments of Hodgson, Žižek and Shanks might collectively offer a framework by which we could assess existing christologies and even construct an alternative vision of the person, and Body, of Christ. It has to do with the sociality of being human, which includes the sociality of Jesus, and his relatedness with 'concrete others' – those within his or our tradition, those beyond the tradition, and those effectively invisible to the traditions. It is 'shakenness' which particularly drives this constructive approach, since it is an experience which prompts attentiveness to and a solidarity of others; that is, Jesus' being shaken by the other causes his, and our, engagement with and commitment to those who are different from him, and us.

---

[63]   Andrew Shanks, in *Hegel's Political Theology* (Cambridge, 1991), pp. 2–6, argues that Hegel's understanding of Christian faith properly addresses the problem of ideological 'kitsch' and its destructiveness. The point is that 'kitsch', as Kundera describes it, is 'the absolute denial of shit' (Milan Kundera, *The Unbearable Lightness of Being*, (London, 1984), p. 248), and that, when it infects a tradition, it causes us to name certain others as shit or worthless, worthy of being excluded or crucified. This infection can take the form of populist brutality or even sentimentality. In contrast, for Shanks, Hegel sees Christian faith as *not* denying shit, since the Crucified One is resurrected, so God denies that the individual is worthless and reasserts the worth of all, not least those *regarded* as the least. This connection fails if a gulf between Jesus and the rest of us is emphasized, so it is necessary to affirm his humanity. It is the same in Sölle's understanding of Jesus as our 'representative' rather than our 'substitute', for a substitute replaces us, so denies us a role, whereas representation is only temporary, so we are worthy of following (Dorothee Sölle, *Christ the Representative: An Essay in Theology after the 'Death of God'* (London: SCM, 1967), pp. 102–5, 130ff). This is expanded in Chapter 8.

Christ and the Other: The Essential Criteria

As will be already apparent, this book is not a systematic study or comparison of the theologies of John Hick and Lesslie Newbigin as such. Rather, they are dialogue-partners in a more constructive enterprise. Nevertheless, since I am concerned with resisting objectifying and dehumanizing tendencies, I endeavour to take seriously the distinctiveness of Hick and Newbigin, in their respective and related contexts, without turning them into mere ciphers for the main argument. Similarly, it may seem unfair to judge them by a framework which was not their concern, *per se*. The point, though, is not to test them and find them wanting, in their own right, by virtue of their partial shakenness, but is to address them as significant players affecting the christologies of Christian communities. Thus, whilst I bring to bear on them some postmodern criteria which were not explicitly on their theological landscape, it is appropriate to show why their approaches – which are present within churches – should be surpassed by Jesus 'the Shaken One'.

Helpfully, they not only resonate with my own ecclesial experiences, but their differences reflect a polarity between two well-established christological categories. Newbigin's christology reflects the more dominant, and more orthodox, 'constitutive' christologies: that is, Jesus is said to constitute the very means by which God changes the course of reality, being embodied in history and objectively making a salvific difference. Hick's christology, on the other hand, reflects the 'expressive' christologies: that is, Jesus is said to express God's general intentions towards us, not necessarily being embodied in history uniquely, nor objectively making a salvific difference, but rather subjectively making a difference in one's experience. My problem with this polarity, which I shall develop, is the priority it gives to the expectation that Jesus should reveal his relation to the divine. What, instead, of the expectation that Jesus should reveal, and constitute, the fullness of humanity to us – neither objectively nor subjectively, but intersubjectively, that is, through relationship with 'others'? Or what of the relationality between God and humanity, not in an idealized individual, but in human community? For Jesus in community expresses *and* constitutes the very means by which the fullness of humanity is revealed to us.

I will thus ask how well Hick and Newbigin attend to others within (within the particularity of Christian identity), others beyond (amongst the plurality of religious identities), and the sociopolitically othered (in solidarity with those on the margins). My finding is that Hick prioritizes the plural over the particular, and Newbigin prioritizes the particular over the plural, but both make a shared mistake: they both universalize, or generalize, their visions of Jesus on the basis of partial shakenness. That is, rather than allowing Jesus to speak and act as a particular human in community, with a distinctive dynamic to contribute to the whole, he is apparently made to represent universal pretenders. This is because of the priority given to the expectation that Jesus must be revealing to us his relation to the divine, whether in a constitutive christology or an expressive christology, rather than the expectation that he should demonstrate the fullness of humanity. (While I will argue that Jesus' fullness of humanity is itself a reflection of God's humanity, I maintain that it makes a difference – to Jesus and to each other – whether we look firstly for his relation to the divine or his revelation of human wholeness.)

Specifically, the questions for Hick and Newbigin, and for any christology today, are these: firstly, how well do their christologies demonstrate sanctity to the breadth of the Christian tradition? In other words, how well do they affirm the tradition's identity, its untranslatable otherness or scandalously universal claims, while at the same time re-owning its shadow side, the way in which its sectarian tendencies have suppressed others within itself? Secondly, how well do their christologies distinguish their tradition from the universal? In other words, to what extent do they transgress the tradition's herd-mentality, to see others not as generalized ciphers or demonized 'others', but in their complex concreteness and interrelatedness? And thirdly: how well do their christologies enable corporate solidarities to liberate those whose humanity is particularly threatened by the 'Domination System'? In other words, do their visions of Jesus, in community, energize an ever greater solidarity of others, in resistance to the powers of domination, so as to transform the predicament of those especially 'othered' by such forces?

In short:

1. Is Jesus envisaged as one who shakes us out of our convenient streamlining of this particular tradition, that we might rediscover the real distinctiveness together with the awkward diversity of our identity?
2. Is Jesus envisaged as one who shakes us out of our impatient generalizations of other traditions, that we might rediscover deep dialogue with others with whom we are related?
3. Is Jesus envisaged as one who shakes us out of our treatment of particular groups as though they are invisible to us, that we might act in solidarity with each other in our common humanity?

So we turn to the work of Hick and Newbigin, in turn, to see how they fare and to develop the features of this quest.

Chapter 2

The Christology of John Hick:
Partially Shaken

We turn to Hick to see how his christology fares: to what extent is his vision of Jesus attentive to others within the tradition, others beyond the tradition and those others invisible to the traditions? The first three sections are outlines of the main features of Hick's approach – his emphasis on experience, the language of myth, and a common ethic in response to one transcendent reality. Then, in the following three sections, his overall christological vision is measured against the criteria I have been constructing. His sensitivity to the fact of plurality is acknowledged, but the partial shakenness of his approach – also evident in churches – prevents deeper engagement with the otherness of Christian identity, religious difference and sociopolitical solidarity.

It is not irrelevant that Hick's childhood (born: 1922), which was coloured more by his mother and grandmother than his conservative father, consisted of religious exploration, including encounters with Spiritualism and theosophy (which mingles Hindu and Western concepts).[1] While he was acutely aware of God's reality, he found the local Anglican church dull and was not convinced by Christian faith. His Quaker schooling taught him the importance of 'the individual', and prompted him to be a conscientious objector in the Second World War, so he worked for the Friends' Ambulance Unit, including in Egypt where he was disturbed by British attitudes of superiority over the Egyptians. At university he first studied law, but detoured into philosophy. He experienced an evangelical conversion into a deeply conservative and christocentric faith, which led him to train for Presbyterian ministry, though he continued to explore philosophy, not least the work of Immanuel Kant, Bertrand Russell, A.J. Ayer and Ludwig Wittgenstein (but not, interestingly, the Continental traditions of existentialism, transcendental analysis or hermeneutics[2]). After three years in ministry he held academic appointments and became professor at Birmingham University in 1967. In the 1970s, he was active in resisting the National Front's aggression towards people of minority faith communities. Over many years his 'pluralistic hypothesis' has provoked controversy, but even his strongest critics recognize that he raises

---

[1]   John Hick, *John Hick: An Autobiography* (Oxford, 2002), pp. 16–40.

[2]   Gavin D'Costa, *John Hick's Theology of Religions: A Critical Evaluation* (Lanham, MD, 1987), p. 7.

important questions.[3] Though his thought has developed, certain foundations have stayed firm.

Hick's Experiential Reading of Christology: 'Seeing-as' is Believing

A number of key factors coalesce in Hick's biography: his doctoral thesis, which became his first book *Faith and Knowledge*,[4] was concerned with the relationship between the two – how can 'faith' be rooted in 'knowledge' without being wholly determined by it? Hick's theological training is relevant here, being informed first by H.H. Farmer, whose Gifford Lectures epitomized the naturalistic approach to religion, deploying Kant's use of reason.[5] However, it was the next Principal of Westminster College, John Oman, who had a greater impact, both by way of his more global perspective, including non-theistic traditions, and because he was a translator of Schleiermacher, whose thinking underpins Hick's theology of experience.[6] For, as with Schleiermacher, Hick maintains that it is the realm of human experience which mediates faith-knowledge. Whilst for Kant, God is a postulate of morality, for Hick, on the other hand, God is a postulate of religious experience.[7] The twin giants of Kant and Schleiermacher shape Hick's theology, not least his christology, as follows.

It was Kant's 'Copernican revolution', by which the human mind becomes the centre of cognition, which fascinated Hick. He saw it in terms of 'critical realism' – the understanding that there is a reality beyond our minds, but that we perceive it through our senses and conceptualizations.[8] Thus, for Sinkinson, whose doctoral research was on the work of Hick, this Kantian view means that even apparent objectivity is conditioned by the mind.[9] Both for Kant and Hick, the fundamental distinction is therefore between the 'noumenal' reality – the thing as it really is, which cannot

---

[3]   For example: Gregory H. Carruthers SJ., *The Uniqueness of Jesus Christ in the Theocentric Model of the Christian Theology of World Religions: An Elaboration and Evaluation of the Position of John Hick* (Lanham, MD, 1990), p. 2.

[4]   John Hick, *Faith and Knowledge* (New York, 1957).

[5]   Christopher Sinkinson, *The Universe of Faiths: A Critical Study of John Hick's Religious Pluralism* (Carlisle, 2001), pp. 106–7. (See H.H. Farmer, *Revelation and Religion* (New York, 1954).)

[6]   See Hick, *John Hick*, pp. 84–5; D'Costa, *John Hick's Theology*, pp. 9–10. (See John Oman, *The Natural and the Supernatural* (Cambridge, 1931), and *Grace and Personality* (Cambridge, 1917).)

[7]   See Sinkinson, *Universe of Faiths*, p. 72; John Hick, *An Interpretation of Religion: Human Responses to the Transcendent*, 2nd edn (Basingstoke, 2004), p. 243.

[8]   Hick, *John Hick*, pp. 68–9.

[9]   Sinkinson, *Universe of Faiths*, p. 36.

be directly experienced – and the 'phenomenal' – the thing as it is experienced.[10] Such is the prevalence of this distinction, that even in Hick's earliest theology (as in *Faith and Knowledge*) experiential awareness or the 'interpretative' nature of religious faith takes precedence over any supposedly objective understanding of doctrinal claims.[11] It is the dominance of this epistemological issue, informed greatly too by Schleiermacher's emphasis on religious experience, which begs the question: is Hick's theology a first-order discourse, proposing a new religion in its own right, as it reshapes the contours of orthodoxy, or is it basically a second-order explanatory framework within which religious experience and traditions may be understood?[12] Hick later argues that his perspective simply takes seriously the ambiguous nature of the universe, the fact that it can be 'read' in very different ways.[13]

In this light commentators have debated whether experience or philosophy is the primary motor driving Hick's theological developments. The fact of his anti-fascist activism in solidarity with people of minority religious traditions in the 1970s, and his conviction that such Hindus, Muslims and Sikhs were no less moral than Christians,[14] suggests real experience did inform his increasingly pluralistic affirmation of the validity of diverse 'phenomenal' responses to the one 'noumenal' reality. Philip Barnes, however, sees this development as being essentially continuous with Hick's underlying epistemology;[15] that is, Hick reads his experience in the light of the conviction that reality is interpreted by the culturally-conditioned mind. With Twiss, though, I want to qualify this, since Hick's epistemology is inseparable from his *ethical* concerns;[16] but as we shall see, his moral framework is itself greatly shaped by Western (Kantian) assumptions about what is universally just. Certainly this suggests that the 'otherness' between Christian faith and the modernism of Kant's conceptual dichotomy (noumenal/ phenomenal) is minimized by Hick, whereas Newbigin's theology views the

---

[10] Hick, *An Interpretation*, p. 241, citing Kant, *Critique of Pure Reason*, B69: 1958, p. 88.

[11] Sinkinson, *Universe of Faiths*, pp. 29, 48. (See also Hick, *An Interpretation*, pp. 158–60.)

[12] Sinkinson, *Universe of Faiths*, p. 48; D'Costa, 'Foreword', in Gavin D'Costa (ed.), *Christian Uniqueness Reconsidered: The Myth of a Pluralistic Theology of Religions* (Maryknoll, NY, 1990), p. vi; David Cheetham, *John Hick: A Critical Introduction and Reflection* (Aldershot, 2003), p. 6.

[13] Hick, *An Interpretation*, pp. 74, 124, 129.

[14] See Sinkinson, *Universe of Faiths*, p. 7; Eleanor Jackson, 'Reviews', *British and Irish Association for Mission Studies*, 22/6 (March 2004): p. 7; John Hick, *The Metaphor of God Incarnate* (London, 1993), pp. 8, 88.

[15] L. Philip Barnes, 'Continuity and Development in John Hick's Theology', *Studies in Religion*, 21/4 (1992): pp. 395–402.

[16] Sumner B. Twiss, 'The Philosophy of Religious Pluralism: A Critical Appraisal of Hick and his Critics', *The Journal of Religion*, 70/4 (October 1990): pp. 533–68.

otherness of Western modernism like a looming, destructive force.[17] (It is, broadly, the contrast between 'idealizing' and 'demonizing' an other.) Essentially, as D'Costa sees it, Hick's intellectual openness, commitment to joined-up thinking, and relative inattentiveness to church tradition and the Bible mean that his preference for (Western) 'philosophical theology' dominates his development.[18]

Hick's 'critical realism' means the propositional claims of a religious tradition do indeed refer to a reality, but, as in Wittgenstein's understanding of language, our claims are culturally-conditioned ways of expressing what is of soteriological or ultimate value.[19] In Žižek's terms, our tradition's 'symbolic Other', or language, cannot grasp the most asymmetrical other, 'the impossible Thing'. Thus, because our language cannot authoritatively represent or give real access to the radical, impossible otherness of the tradition's particularity, we risk falling into relativism – a problem to which I will return. Whilst, for postliberals, the language conditions the experience, for Hick, on the other hand, the experience trumps the propositions; the words are understood to be culturally-specific ways of describing the religious experience.[20] Faith is thus about 'experiencing-as', or 'seeing-as', in the sense that the interpretative ambiguity of things gives us freedom to 'experience' and 'see' the same reality in varied ways.[21] Thus there is a distinction between the reality and the particular experience of it, or between the true meaning and the linguistic interpretation of it.[22] It is the popular modernist contrast between a religion's core and its cultural dressing or conditioning.[23]

Experiencing Jesus' Significance

With regards to the person of Christ specifically, this distinction between truth and interpretation affects Hick's thinking in two stages. Initially, Hick seeks to affirm the orthodox *intentions* of the tradition of Chalcedon, that Jesus is genuinely

---

[17]   See below, pp. 50–52. 67–9.

[18]   D'Costa, *John Hick's Theology*, pp. 6–7.

[19]   Twiss, pp. 567–8.

[20]   Ibid., p. 534; Cheetham, p. 6. That is, our religious language does not describe the metaphysical reality, but our inner experience of it: see Sinkinson, *Universe of Faiths*, pp. 120, 123–4; Hick, *An Interpretation*, p. 348.

[21]   John Hick, *God and the Universe of Faiths* (London, 1973), pp. 37–52; Hick, *An Interpretation*, p. 12; John Hick, *The Rainbow of Faiths* (London, 1995), p. 24 (citing Wittgenstein, *Philosophical Investigations*); Barnes, 'Continuity and Development', pp. 398–401.

[22]   Below, p. 45–6, we see Shanks arguing that this is a conflation of two problematics – language and experience.

[23]   See Sinkinson, 'Is Christianity Better than Other Religions?', *The Expository Times*, 107/9 (June 1996), p. 261; Sinkinson, *Universe of Faiths*, p. 136.

unique in kind, but that the language needs contemporary re-expression.[24] The manner of this re-expression, however, already indicates that he does more than he realizes: for he argues that Jesus has just one nature, that of a human, but that the 'identity' of Jesus with God consists in the 'continuity' between the divine *Agapé*ing (God's loving-towards-us) and the human *agapé*. He argues that the language of a shared 'nature' or 'substance' fails us, whereas *homoagapé* – an identity of love – communicates in today's world. Jesus is thus the finite (temporary) 'inhistorization' of God's infinite *Agapé*ing, the one whose love is the same as, by virtue of being 'continuous with', God's love, and who thereby prompts us to participate in such movement-towards-others.[25] Whilst this is meant to affirm the orthodoxy of Jesus' uniqueness in kind, its paradoxically allusive way of describing the identity between God and Jesus paves the way for Hick's subsequent emphasis on the metaphorical nature of the achievement in Jesus. It is understandable that Hick should question the language of 'substance' for its seemingly static, perhaps we can say 'objectified', notion of the God/human identity,[26] but it is debatable whether *homoagapé* either provides the contemporary clarity he intends or avoids the trap of christologies-by-degree (whereby Jesus is 'only' different 'by degree') which Hick means to avoid. After all, what is the distinction between God's nature

---

[24]   John Hick, 'Christology at the Cross-roads', in F.G. Healey (ed.), *Prospects for Theology: Essays in Honour of H.H. Farmer* (Welwyn, 1966), pp. 137–66.

[25]   There is, then, a direct causal connection between what God's love is doing and Jesus' love towards other human beings; his love is the same-loving as God's loving-towards-us. Thus he constitutes God's means of salvifically changing the course of history, by 'inhistorizing' – realizing in history – God's initiative. (Note: 'inhistorization' is originally from H.H. Farmer, 'The Bible: Its Significance and Authority', in *Interpreter's Bible* vol. 1 (Abingdon, 1952), p. 12, where it conveys the centrality of the Incarnation; but Hick uses it to express the paradox of the continuity between God's general acts in history *and* the discontinuity of God's act, in Jesus, 'into' history.)

[26]   Hick fails to mention other twentieth-century theologians who also offer critiques of '*ousia*'. For example: Barth focuses on 'time' instead of 'substance', R.H. Roberts, *A Theology on its Way? Essays on Karl Barth* (Edinburgh, 1991), p. 63. Bonhoeffer suggests Chalcedon is primarily an expression of the more relational 'who?' question than an answer to the more mechanical 'how is it so?' question: see Dietrich Bonhoeffer, *Christ the Centre*, trans. E.H. Robertson (New York, 1978), pp. 101–2. Moltmann argues that God is a subject, rather than substance (Jürgen Moltmann, *The Crucified God* (London, 1974), p. 88) and that God's subjectivity is communicated as we do God's will, to demonstrate his Lordship: see Jürgen Moltmann, *The Way of Christ: Christology in Messianic Dimensions* (London, 1990), p. 43. Meanwhile, postmodern philosophy critiques the modernist grasp of concepts such as 'nature', which claims to isolate and objectify an 'essence'; whereas by contrast postmodernism's 'de-centred' intersubjectivity points to the fluidity (and 'deferred' meaning) of all (such) concepts: see, for example, Anthony Thiselton, *Interpreting God and the Postmodern Self: On Meaning, Manipulation and Promise* (Edinburgh, 1995), p. 85.

or substance and God's loving-towards-us, and how can one put limits 'in kind' on the nature of love?[27]

In the light of those problems and further experiences of plurality, Hick comes to see Jesus as the primary actor, rather than God acting in him.[28] Jesus manifests vibrantly the human potential for reflecting God's love, and Hick understands this as being expressed metaphorically, or mythically, in terms of his being 'God incarnate'. This development has more to do with our *experience* of him *as* a person of unique significance, that is, more to do with *our* consciousness of and response to Jesus' historic achievement than with any presumed awareness by him of God's unique act in him. As a result of our vision of him in such evocative terms, and our tendency to project upon an 'other' our deepest longings for meaning and purpose, the Christian tradition has thus 'deified' him,[29] or 'othered' him to such an extent that he has become our Lord – or inspiration. I shall discuss the adequacy of this christological interpretation below, but for now, suffice to say that it evidently relies on Hick's theology of experience, the primacy given to the consciousness of one's phenomenal experience. The effect of experiencing or seeing Jesus *as* such a lively instance of God's presence, such that we 'project' on to him our ideals and deify him with our language, is more than a merely second-order explanatory discourse; for, as we shall see, Hick hopes that we might undo the literalized God-man to rediscover the spiritually responsive human who has been religiously othered to the extreme.

Hick's Mythological Reading of Christology: Changing Attitudes

Now, on the one hand, Hick is characterized by others as 'empiricist', in his desire for an evidential basis for religious claims and his association with an emphasis on historical discovery. For instance, Coventry believes Hick's *Myth of God Incarnate* mistakenly prioritizes the historical critical method over the claim of God's self-revelation in Christ.[30] Loughlin, too, suggests Hick and his colleagues surrender the truth of Jesus to questions of historical criticism.[31] Rooted in the empiricist distrust of 'mystery', as Loughlin sees him, Hick thereby caricatures the tradition of the incarnation, sharply distinguishing literal from metaphorical

---

[27]   See, for example, Carruthers, pp. 2, 132, 308–10; and Gerard Loughlin, 'Squares and Circles: John Hick and the Doctrine of the Incarnation,' in Harold Hewitt Jr (ed.), *Problems in the Philosophy of Religion: Critical Studies of the Work of John Hick* (London: Macmillan; New York: St. Martin's Press, 1991).

[28]   Hick, *Metaphor*, pp. 12, 27ff.

[29]   John Hick, 'Jesus and the World Religions', in John Hick (ed.), *The Myth of God Incarnate* (London, 1977), pp. 167–85.

[30]   John Coventry, 'The Myth and the Method', *Theology*, 81/682 (July 1978): pp. 253–4, 257.

[31]   Loughlin, 'Squares and Circles', pp. 185–90.

understandings, thus betraying the influence of logical positivism on his thinking – the idea that words ought to mean exactly what they say.[32]

To an extent, Hick accepts that he is empiricist: but not in the sense that the scientific method works alone to uncover all truths, since he believes we know things by virtue of our experience.[33] That is, as with Kant and Schleiermacher before him, the external authority of any supposedly special revelation in history is displaced by the internal authority of personal religious experience.[34] Experience can trump history. Thus, on the other hand, others accuse Hick of holding history far too lightly, since subjective interpretations are pivotal to his religious hypothesis.[35] It is as though Hick fears to delve into history too deeply, in case it uncovers too much complexity or conflict: for it is essentially his view that, behind all the ambiguity, there is an ultimate simplicity. For example, he suggests the contrast between Christianity and Islam is largely a matter of whether or not Jesus was crucified.[36] The historical differences are not as significant as they appear, since the basic reality behind them all is far more important, and whilst we cannot access it as such, Hick presumes – by way of 'eschatological verifiability' – that the time will come when it will be verified.[37] The words, specific to each tradition, point in their own way to the one transcendent reality – which is discussed below.

Essentially, though, we see here that, whilst *experienced* reality (the world of phenomena) may be ambiguous and complex, the *noumenal* is presumed to be simple. This is influenced by logical positivism's demand for straightforwardness in language and Hick's belief that the literal can be separated from the metaphorical: for we ought to know what we mean by the words we use. This distinction is thus also symptomatic of his widespread tendency to polarize – whether between truth and interpretation, reality and appearance, external authority and internal experience, or the noumenal and the phenomenal – and all such dichotomies share their roots in a modernist mentality.[38] Hick is therefore very interested in the question of religious language, believing for a long time that the nature of the

---

[32] Hick, *John Hick*, pp. 18, 33; Hick, 'Christology at the Cross-roads', p. 156.

[33] John Hick, 'Reply', in Hewitt Jr (ed.), *Problems*, p. 206.

[34] See Sinkinson, *Universe of Faiths*, p. 115.

[35] See Daniel W. Hardy, 'Theology through Philosophy', in David F. Ford (ed.), *The Modern Theologians: An Introduction to Christian Theology in the Twentieth Century*, vol. 2 (Oxford, 1989), p. 56.

[36] Hick, *Rainbow*, pp. 55–6. Whilst in Hick, *An Interpretation*, pp. 362–76, he acknowledges that there are conflicting truth-claims, he argues that they are not ultimately as they appear – one Reality is behind them all.

[37] Hick, *An Interpretation*, pp. 178–80; Hick, *Rainbow*, p. 72.

[38] In postmodern thought, by contrast, 'interpretation' can be *both* a potential safeguard against 'manipulation' of truth (as expounded by Betti, Gadamer and Ricoeur) *and* a potential means of truth's manipulation (as expounded by Rorty, Derrida and Lyotard): see Thiselton, *Interpreting God*, pp. 41–2.

'object' to which it refers is a critical issue in religion and theology.[39] Crucially, he understands the 'mythological' nature of religious language in a particular way:

> a myth is a story which is told but which is not literally true, or an idea or image which is applied to something or someone but which does not literally apply, but which invites a particular attitude in its hearers. Thus the truth of a myth is a kind of practical truth consisting in the appropriateness of the attitude to its object.[40]

In other words, this understanding of the mythological and metaphorical nature of language focuses on experience: so the incarnation, as myth, is 'experienced as' the case, by virtue of the appropriate attitude it 'evokes' in us towards Jesus, rather than being 'literally' the case.[41]

Hick does not, however, simply want us to see how our religious language generates meaning and purpose in us; he wants us to 'demythologize' it. Bultmann understood demythologizing to be concerned with *interpreting* the role of myth, the way the divine interacts with human life. It was about unearthing the (objective) *kerygma* or message of Christ, enabling us to see what is not visible to modern 'objectifying thinking' – that human existence is grounded in a transcendent reality.[42] His point was that, by demythologizing our religious language, we are confronted again with the hidden power of God's self-revelation: the *kerygma* demands a response. In contrast, Hick's demythologizing is about exposing as myth that which has been literalized; it is simply about rediscovering the presumed intentions behind our language, how they mean to evoke certain attitudes in us. He understands these hidden intentions as being essentially pluralistic – in the sense that different culturally-conditioned language systems allude broadly to one reality in different ways – whereas Bultmann understood the hidden nature of the *kerygma* as being christocentric. The contrast, though, between the ethical being and action demanded by the *kerygma* and Hick's 'attitudes' is illuminating: for whilst attitudes *ought* to flow into action and shape one's being, Hick's approach seems more interior, more a matter of one's personal experience.

His point is that the mythological or metaphorical understanding of language makes more sense of the ambiguous nature of the universe – the way in which it can be 'read' freely in different ways – whereas a literal understanding would seem to demand that there is only one way of reading reality. (He does not explain his

---

[39]   Hick, *God and the Universe of Faiths*, Chapter 1.

[40]   Hick, 'Jesus and the World Religions', p. 178.

[41]   See ibid., pp. 172, 175–80.

[42]   See Rudolf Bultmann, 'New Testament and Mythology', in H.W. Bartsch (ed.), *Kerygma and Myth*, vol. 1 (London, 1953), p. 10; Rudolf Bultmann, 'Jesus Christ and Mythology', in Roger Johnson (ed.), *Rudolf Bultmann: Interpreting Faith for the Modern Era* (London, 1987), p. 291; David Ferguson, *Rudolf Bultmann* (London and New York, 1992), p. 108, citing Rudolf Bultmann, 'On the Problem of Demythologizing', in Schubert Ogden (ed.), *New Testament and Mythology and Other Basic Writings* (London, 1985), p. 99.

understanding of 'literality', however, even though its meaning is also culturally constituted.) So, for him, the mythological understanding of the incarnation of God in Jesus makes more sense of Christian experience, since it explains the way in which a certain attitude of faithfulness, a desire to follow and imitate Jesus as our 'saviour', is evoked in us, without requiring us to believe the ontological peculiarity of God and Jesus sharing 'substance'.[43] The matter of contention for Hick is not, as such, the mythological language, but the way in which we come to misread it as a literal or ontological fact: the idea that God's incarnation in Jesus is more than an expression of Jesus' openness and obedience to God's loving presence, and actually constitutes a new being. As we noted above, this shift in our interpretation of the language represents the 'deification' of Jesus, which itself is fuelled by the ambiguity of religious 'images'.[44] The New Testament was the canvas on to which the Early Church painted its 'projections' of Jesus, being a 'tightly-knit' Body living under threat of persecution which intensified its 'devotion and loyalty' – that is, the Church idealized its inspiration, partly to justify its distinctiveness and suffering. Although it is an oversimplification of the language and the situation, as Carruthers notes, Hick understands this deification as resulting from the cultural acceptability of the idea of a deified figure, the disciples' need for a way of making sense of their experience of God's closeness in the light of Jesus' death, and the tendency of the human mind to exalt a figurehead (as in Buddhism too).[45] (Hick might claim to connect Jesus' *idealization* and the Church's *insularity*, even *impotence* – and yet the Church acted quite bravely, not impotently, and with purpose beyond itself.)

Hick's fundamental point is to establish that a constitutive christology, by which God's incarnation in Jesus is understood to be ontological, is 'optional', because of its roots in a specific religio-cultural context, and 'mythological', because its literal content is not persuasive.[46] Rather than describing Jesus' consciousness of himself, Hick's mythological interpretation of incarnational christology is asserting instead that the consciousness of Jesus' disciples is being described.[47] In other words, Hick's demythologized Jesus is not uniquely the other of Žižek's 'impossible Thing' (for the Church mistakenly projected such radical otherness on to Jesus); but even the 'symbolic Other' of Christianity's language system is a misreading of the reality (for the language has not clarified but distorted Jesus' identity). Instead, our visions of Jesus are more the ideals and projections of 'the imaginary other', other disciples 'like me'. If Hick is right to read christology this way, how does he guard against relativism? If he remains committed to the existence of transcendent reality, how does his christology not collapse into

---

[43]　See Hick, *God and the Universe of Faiths*, pp. 167–72.

[44]　Hick, 'Jesus and the World Religions', pp. 167–74.

[45]　Ibid.; see Carruthers, *Uniqueness*, pp. 80, 83.

[46]　Hick, 'Jesus and the World Religions', p. 168.

[47]　Carruthers, *Uniqueness*, p. 87.

personal immanence? What criteria determine the 'appropriateness' of the attitudes evoked by such a mythological understanding of Jesus' distinctiveness?

Hick's Ethical Reading of Christology: Illustrating a Universal Ethic

On the one hand, the fact that Hick comes to view the different religious traditions as culturally-conditioned responses to the one transcendent reality, or 'the Real',[48] might suggest that he offers no criteria for judging the adequacy of a tradition's truthfulness or the quality of its goodness. For if Jesus is simply one human response amongst others, what is the basis for any discriminating judgments? We should note, however, that it is partly because of Hick's ethical unease with regards to any Christian superiority, and the 'repugnance' he feels for the idea that most people might not be 'saved' simply by virtue of their being born outside Christendom, or despite their behaviour being no morally worse than most Christians', that his myth of God Incarnate finds its voice.[49]

Thus, on the other hand, he does offer criteria to determine the appropriateness of the attitudes evoked by the myth of God Incarnate: in fact, they are rooted in the very oneness of the Real. That is, because the Real is one, the appropriate attitudes evoked by its culturally-conditioned responses are also, in essence, one: for Hick sees in all ethical religious traditions a commitment to be transformed from 'self-centredness' to 'Real-centredness', which is demonstrated by the broadly common Golden Rule, 'Do to others as you would have them do to you', and that to participate in this transformation is to be 'saved/liberated'.[50] This hybrid term reflects the diversity of religious language systems, and the transformation it describes is, in Christian terms, about 'saintliness': for our understanding of Jesus as God Incarnate, in the sense that *his* obedience to God's loving presence generates *in us* a desire to imitate his example, inspires us to move from self-centredness to centredness in the transcendent. In other words, if a tradition does not evoke such a transformation in one's attitude or behaviour, it does not signify an authentic response to the Real. I shall further interrogate the paradox in this hypothesis later in this chapter – namely, Hick's focus on interior religious experience seems to

---

[48]   Hick, *An Interpretation*, pp. xix–xx, 10–11; Hick, *Rainbow*, p. 11.

[49]   Hick, *God and the Universe of Faiths*, pp. 122–3; Hick, *Metaphor*, p. 8; John Hick, 'On Grading Religions', in Paul Badham (ed.), *A John Hick Reader* (London, 1990), pp. 182–3.

[50]   Hick, *An Interpretation*, pp. 36–54, 299–314. Incidentally, he acknowledges the potential danger of expecting some, namely the belittled, to move beyond 'self-centredness' before others have truly affirmed their 'self'; that is, self-realization should precede Real-centredness: Hick, *An Interpretation*, pp. 52–4. I would suggest that the language of 'mutual humanization' is therefore preferable, since it affirms the relational nature of one's realization in the other.

contrast with the notion of being centred in transcendence; but it needs a little more explanation.

First, it is relevant that Hick's Christian theism sought not only to revise more orthodox assumptions but to resist more assertive humanism. As a critical realist, he affirms the existence of transcendence, but accepts that propositions concerning it are rightly open to criticism.[51] As humanists questioned Jesus' own faith, Hick's theism is as much a moral conviction as an intellectual one: for what right does a humanist have to belittle the genuine experience of believers? For Hick, the very ambiguity of the universe demands that Christian orthodoxy and atheistic humanism ought to be reasonable enough to respect the other's vision. However, in Shanks's terms, both seem convinced of their own truth-as-correctness and of Hick's incorrectness. This does not mean Hick is a natural advocate of truth-as-Honesty, as opposed to truth-as-correctness: for his pursuit of truth is itself impatient and ideological in its partiality, as we shall see. Nonetheless, he is free to criticize others whose religious or anti-religious claims are also partial. As such, he identifies anti-Semitism, Western colonialism and 'patriarchalism', as well as Christianity's dominant and dismissive approaches to people of other traditions, with its 'literal' incarnation.[52] After all, if our tradition alone was initiated by 'God in person', it can claim a theological and moral authority over all others,[53] with the consequent generalizing and objectifying of – or indifference to – 'them' and our corollary self-aggrandizement in the light of Jesus' ultimate idealization. (Of course, as we shall see in Newbigin's theology, Hick need not automatically identify Jesus' unique status with a Christian superiority-complex, since Jesus not only produces saints but justifies sinners; that is, the tradition invites us to boast only in Christ's self-giving. Arguably, however, Hick is suggesting it is humanly very difficult for Christians to accentuate Jesus' definitiveness without also seeing themselves as definitive of faith.[54])

---

[51]   Hick, *Christianity at the Centre* (London, 1968), p. 16; Hick, *An Interpretation*, pp. 174–5.

[52]   Hick, *Metaphor*, pp. 80–85: he cites Rosemary Radford Ruether and Mary Daly for their critiques of the connection between a unique incarnation in Jesus and the damaging history of Christian particularism.

[53]   John Hick, *God Has Many Names* (London, 1980), p. 26.

[54]   There are, of course, many ways in which christology and morality interrelate: for instance, Gunton suggests the mistreatment of others is more closely associated with *divergence* from traditional christology (Colin Gunton, *Yesterday and Today: A Study of Continuities in Christology* (London, 1983), p. 182); and Williams argues that incarnation is about God's judgment on and grace for a world of idolatry and oppression (Rowan Williams, *On Christian Theology: Challenges in Contemporary Theology* (Oxford, 2000), p. 81 (and chapters 6, 7 and 15)). For Cupitt, by too readily uniting God and humanity, as Williams also notes, incarnation can weaken the 'ironic disjunction' or juxtaposition perceived by Jesus between God's ways and the world's ways; but this can be overcome by rediscovering the 'deabsolutized' Jesus/Christ present in the New Testament's diversity (Don Cupitt, *The Debate about Christ* (London, 1979), pp. 139–46). Sobrino too affirms

Secondly, he argues that his understanding of the common ethic flows from real experience of other traditions.[55] That is, it is not implied from above, but is encountered from below.[56] This would make Hick's hypothesis more a second-order explanatory framework, accounting for the plurality of religious experiences and languages, than a first-order discourse prescribing the direction in which religion should travel. Although this is not convincing, as I shall argue, it relates to the developments in Hick's version of the 'Copernican revolution'.[57] The traditional 'Ptolemaic' map consisted of all heavenly bodies orbiting the Earth. In religious terms, Jesus was the salvific centre of the universe. Hick's first revolution located God as the central Sun, and Jesus orbited God. Increasingly, though, he would attend to nontheistic traditions, positing 'the Real' as the centre. The various theistic and nontheistic traditions which orbit it are simply diverse responses to it. However, their respective interpretations of the 'personal' or 'impersonal' nature, or even the 'goodness', of this transcendent reality are not mediated by the Real; it transcends all such conception.[58] We can only say each of the religious responses, whether the Trinity, Brahman, Yahweh, or Allah is its object, is *an appropriate response to* the Real; not that the Real 'causes' such responses.[59] It is not, then, that the Trinity (as 'known' by Christians) is actually the economic Trinity and the immanent Trinity (as it really is) is in fact the Real; rather, the Trinity (whether economic or immanent) is simply one culturally-conditioned linguistic response to that which cannot be known or mediated. To fail to see the limits of our language is to make it idolatrous, as though the words encapsulate the reality. Since idolatry has unethical consequences, which Hick deems manifest in the superiority-complex associated with the 'literal' incarnation, he sees all such language-systems as partial but authentic responses to the one transcendent reality, a reality which cannot and must not be limited to any particularity.[60] For it would not be fair for ultimate reality to be more accessible to, or for moral transformation to be more likely amongst, some than others. This reflects his experience, too, of the comparable morality of people of ethical traditions.

---

the need for 'deabsolutizing' Jesus, to unmask the needs of the oppressed (Jon Sobrino SJ, *Christology at the Crossroads: A Latin American View* (London, 1978), pp. xvii–xix. This is developed in Chapter 8 below).

[55] Hick, *Metaphor*, pp. 8, 88.

[56] Hick, *An Interpretation*, pp. 1–3 (this method is also implied in his 'Introduction to the Second Edition', pp. xl–xli).

[57] Hick, *God and the Universe of Faiths*, pp. 120–32; also Robert Cook, 'Postmodernism, Pluralism and John Hick', *Themelios*, 19/1 (1993): p. 10.

[58] Hick, *An Interpretation*, pp. 246–9; see also Sinkinson, *Universe of Faiths*, pp. 77, 82.

[59] Hick, *Rainbow*, pp. 46, 75–6; see also Philip L. Quinn, 'Religious Pluralism and Religious Relativism', *Scottish Journal of Religious Studies*, 15/2 (1994): p. 81.

[60] Christopher Insole, 'Why John Hick Cannot, and Should Not, Stay Out of the Jam Pot', *Religious Studies*, 36/1 (March 2000): p. 32.

Thirdly, then, we see how Hick's ethical criterion, proposed as the response to one Reality, may also be read as a first-order discourse, essentially re-expressing Kant's universal ethical religion.[61] Since special revelation would work against the universality and self-consistency of the transcendent reality, as indicated by Hick's insistence that the Real cannot be deemed to 'cause' the responses to it, so the transcendent is not revealed – it can only be a 'postulate', in Hick's case, of religious experience. For it is a Kantian tenet of faith that revelation would limit freedom, and since the freedom of the individual's religious experience is paramount to Hick's ethical religion, it is natural that God is not revealed in Jesus Christ.[62] Instead, for Hick, Jesus' reflection of God's loving presence is indicative of an appropriate response to the transcendent reality, in that this 'mythological' incarnation inspires us, as his followers, to be transformed from self-centredness to Real-centredness. Jesus is thus a Kantian 'archetype', a representation of what is possible, at the core of our tradition, if we do good freely; whereas the literalized interpretations of incarnational language are no more than cultural conditioning.[63]

Hick and the Other within the Tradition: Streamlining Christian Identity

There are two elements to this: firstly, what of Hick's regard for the otherness *of* the tradition, that is, its scandalous particularity; and secondly, what of his regard for otherness *in* the tradition, that is, its internal diversity and nuances? On both accounts, his caricature or reduction of the tradition works against the potential of the Christian tradition to foster a solidarity of others; it instead becomes a solidarity of liberals.

The Otherness of the Tradition

First, Hick is surely right to attend to the cultural conditioning of our religious propositions. This shows some shakenness on his part. There is a radical otherness to the nature of God, and the limitations of our language give the lie to the prospect of words fully capturing human experience of the divine.[64] Hick is aware that a tradition probably points to 'more' than its words can demonstrate. In that light, it appears paradoxical that he should expect words to be used more precisely, as I argue with regards to his simplification of 'myth' and 'metaphor' below, but this is explained by the cultural conditioning within which he operates. For he basically reformulates Kant's universal ethical religion.[65] It conditions his

---

[61] See Sinkinson, *Universe of Faiths*, pp. 88–95, 98–100.

[62] See Sinkinson, *Universe of Faiths*, pp. 138–62; see the next section below.

[63] Ibid., pp. 88–9, 96–8.

[64] See, for example, Tillich's 'the God above the God of theism': Paul Tillich, *The Courage to Be* (New Haven, CT, 1952), p. 189.

[65] See Sinkinson, *Universe of Faiths*, pp. 90–94.

philosophical theology, including his christology, as follows: he commits not only to take all major religious traditions into account, when trying to interpret religious experiences, but also to locate them within one comprehensive interpretation.[66] He insists this is the result of an 'inductive' approach, and is offered as the 'best explanation' of the evidence, rather than being imposed from a 'privileged vantage-point'.[67] However, such is the extent of his re-visioning of the Christian tradition (and others, as we discuss in the next section) that it is difficult not to interpret his framework as a universal pretender: a tradition insufficiently attentive to the distinctions between its particularity and universal truths. His 'tradition' is instead the (culturally conditioned) universal ethical religion, a new particularity, or renewal of Kant's older one. It is premised on the basis of the appropriateness of responses to the Real; appropriateness being judged by the ethical criterion: is there a movement from self- to Real-centredness? In effect, this is not simply a second-order discourse 'explaining' the plurality of traditions, since the common ethic becomes the lens – the first-order discourse – through which he interprets and judges the traditions. It prevents him from affirming the otherness and particularity of the Christian tradition, its 'impossible Thing', not least because it denies the possibility of meaningful revelation. After all, what is Hick's notion of the transcendent reality? For Sinkinson, just as Kant can only speak of God as a 'postulate' of reason, Hick cannot claim anything of the Real (except that it is).[68] The dichotomy between the noumenon and phenomena is so absolute, it is arguable that the Real is all but empty[69] – though Hick is personally committed to theistic faith. Hick must therefore maintain that the Real must be *real*, not an illusion, otherwise we return to the problem of judging between the conflicting truth-claims of diverse particularities;[70] whereas, for him, if they are culturally conditioned responses to one ineffable reality, the conflicts are only temporary misunderstandings. However, Hick's Real cannot reveal itself to us: so *is* it real,

---

[66]   Hick, *Rainbow*, pp. 69–71.

[67]   Ibid., pp. 49–51. In response to D'Costa's criticism of Hick, which sees him as perpetuating the Enlightenment's totalizing agenda, as though from a neutral vantage-point (*The Meeting of Religions and the Trinity* (Edinburgh, 2000), pp. 27–30), Hick replies again that his method works from the ground upwards: John Hick, 'The Possibility of Religious Pluralism: A Reply to Gavin D'Costa', *Religious Studies*, 33/2 (1997): p. 164.

[68]   Sinkinson, *Universe of Faiths*, pp. 73, 77, 82. In Hick, *Rainbow*, p. 46, he acknowledges that Kant might disapprove of his use of Kant's complex concepts, but maintains that the distinction between a tradition's partial propositions and the genuine transcendence and unknowability of the Real is paramount (pp. 57–69).

[69]   See, for example, D'Costa, 'John Hick and Religious Pluralism', p. 7; Sinkinson, *Universe of Faiths*, p. 84, citing, Gerard Loughlin, 'Noumenon and Phenomena', *Religious Studies*, 23 (1987), p. 505: 'At the centre of Hick's universe of faiths there is an "empty space".'

[70]   Hick, *Rainbow*, pp. 67–9.

or is Hick's notion of transcendence not actually empty and reduced to personal immanence?[71]

Sinkinson roots this problem in Hick's deep indebtedness to Kant, with reference to four themes.[72] Firstly, like Kant, he is committed to libertarian freewill: for if we are to do the good freely, there must be no compulsion, not even any real grace taking the initiative towards us: thus it is only 'by our fruits that we shall be known'.[73] Secondly, as with Kant, Hick reinterprets historical particularities, including Christ, viewing him as a representative 'archetype', demythologizing the miraculous and focusing on 'core' universal meanings.[74] Thirdly, then, universal religion is affirmed as opposed to external, cultural, particularistic trappings, placing emphasis on ethical criteria or 'moral transformation'. The point is Kant's: that all people must be able to participate in it freely, so the universality of moral religion supersedes the particularity of religious forms. Fourthly, as with Kant's general thesis about the development of religion, despite his anti-Semitism, so with Hick's view of history, doctrine, ritual – they are all provisional stages towards a higher universality. Ultimately, that Kant and Hick share an epistemology leads to very similar theologies.

As Sinkinson sees it, Hick's Kantianism causes him to reject revelation:[75] First, the Kantian dichotomy between the noumenon and phenomena renders revelation impossible. The noumenon effectively exists only as a postulate to explain the diversity of phenomena, so any remaining revelatory language (such as 'influence') is misleading. Not only can 'it' not be discovered by us, but 'it' cannot tell us about itself. Thus D'Costa suggests Hick's alternative religion is 'not unlike deism'.[76] (Hick might well respond that he personally believes in a God who has structured the universe with such ambiguity so as not to restrict our interpretative freedom: but this suggests a modernist model of freedom concerned with freedom from interference, whereas, as we saw in Chapter 1, Hodgson sees God's freedom and

---

[71]   Sinkinson, *Universe of Faiths*, p. 121.

[72]   Ibid., pp. 86–103.

[73]   Hick, *An Interpretation*, p. 312: morality can be separated from metaphysical beliefs.

[74]   Regarding Hick's reinterpreting: for example, the atonement, see *Metaphor*, p. 115; *Rainbow*, p. 130; on the Trinity, see *Metaphor*, p. 149 ('three ways … God is humanly thought and experienced').

[75]   See Sinkinson, *Universe of Faiths*, pp. 145–56. He argues (pp. 138–44) that, with reference to Dulles's five models (Avery Dulles, *Models of Revelation* (London, 1992)), Hick's approach is against revelation: he even avoids 'revelation as inner experience', since the Real does not reveal itself as having any real content to us. As for 'revelation as new awareness', Sinkinson does not see this as necessitating revelation of the divine, rather of our surroundings, so although Hick might fit here, the scope of this model's openness resists particular revelation.

[76]   D'Costa, 'Foreword', p. vi.

relationality as being inseparable.[77]) Secondly, the fact that relational or personal qualities cannot logically be attributed to the Real, such that no manifestation of 'it' is any more or less true than any other, leaves us with a wholly non-revealed, *im*personal transcendent reality. Thirdly, following Kant, any particular revelation privileges a particular community, so compromises the cognitive freedom inherent to religious experience; that is, if faith is to be a genuine virtue, revelation must be absent. Fourthly, religious language simply orientates us soteriologically, instead of telling us about God, so any 'revelation' is only about the world, or us. (The only exceptions to this are that our language tells us there is a Real, there is life after death,[78] and selflessness is a moral virtue.) Finally, then, as Sinkinson interprets Kant and Hick, the history of the universe is the history of our self-consciousness, not of divine reality.

It is evident that Hick requires the human value of doing good to be freely chosen. Arguably, this non-revealed human value is effectively regulating, even limiting, the nature of the divine. In fact, D'Costa argues that the notion of the 'appropriateness' of responses to the Real implies that Hick actually presupposes and privileges a particular ethical norm, and that by projecting it on to all others, he is in fact 'inclusivist', not 'pluralist'.[79] D'Costa even suggests Hick might be 'exclusivist', since his hypothesis defines 'them' in 'his' terms without tolerating genuine division or dissent.[80] Thus, although Hick sees this norm in all traditions, it cannot have identical status in them all, so he projects its centrality on to 'them'. In essence, these observations about Hick's Kantianism demonstrate his resistance to revelation and the modernist conditioning of his own particularity – a universal ethical religion. These leave his vision of the otherness of the tradition, not least the otherness of Jesus, somewhat minimized. Even though Jesus epitomizes the ethical criterion, as a distinctly Real-centred rather than self-centred person, this is an idealization of the individual Jesus. After all, this vision involves a streamlining of the personhood of Jesus, stripping away to a 'core' religio-cultural norm which can be inoffensively universalized, without real engagement with the awkwardness of Jesus' sociality. So we turn to the question of relatedness and otherness within the tradition.

The Otherness within the Tradition

Regarding otherness within Christian identity: on the one hand, Hick's willingness to criticize the tradition demonstrates sensitivity to its 'shadow side' and its suppression of particular others throughout history (notably, the suppression of the metaphorical tradition). However, on the other hand, his criticisms rely

---

[77]   Peter C. Hodgson, *Winds of the Spirit: A Constructive Christian Theology* (London, 1994), p. 84.

[78]   Sinkinson, *Universe of Faiths*, p. 159.

[79]   D'Costa, *John Hick's Theology*, p. 102.

[80]   See also Sinkinson, *Universe of Faiths*, pp. 170–73.

on a modernist caricature of the tradition, which distorts it. This distortion is epitomized, in particular, by his desire for linguistic precision and his polarization of metaphorical and literal interpretations.[81]

In effect, Hick believes metaphor needs decoding, seeing it as an evocative way of saying what can be said 'literally'. For him, the problem with the tradition is that its metaphorical language has been misread as literal truth, and that this misreading has suppressed others within. However, I see Hick's understanding of metaphor as a misreading which itself suppresses otherness within the tradition. The point is that his focus on the *experiential* meaning of myth and metaphor is rooted in a confusion of the partiality of religious propositions and the partiality of culture-specific experiences.[82] That is, his conflation of language and experience allows him to detract from a more sophisticated understanding of myth and metaphor – both their 'interplay' and sociality. In Ricoeur's terms, it is only metaphor which makes possible the 'interplay of resemblance' between the 'is' and 'is not' of 'identity and difference', or between truth and untruth, which a literal interpretation of language denies.[83] So Hick claims it is a *mistake* to think 'myths [and metaphors] can express deep truths that cannot be expressed in any other way',[84] as though (according to his modernism) there is a universal language that can state everything. This is an impoverished view of language.[85] Hick treats religious language as effectively 'only about how we should behave',[86] simply functioning as prescription of appropriate attitudes. This means, for Sinkinson, that Hick's theology is 'experiential-expressive': religious language is only testable by the inner experience of believers, which suggests that, however much he insists on the transcendent's reality, his immanence supersedes it.[87] D'Costa understands this as 'transcendental agnosticism', since we cannot say what it is to which our words refer. Whilst Cheetham, on Hick's behalf, states there is a difference between refusing to decide the nature of the transcendent and simply recognizing that we cannot know it or express it, Sinkinson argues that Hick's religiously ambiguous universe means that his epistemic agnosticism takes priority over his personal theism.[88] Shanks criticizes such agnosticism, in general, for its failure 'to confront

---

[81]   For Hick, a myth is 'a much extended metaphor' (Hick, *Metaphor*, p. 105), so he treats them almost synonymously.

[82]   Andrew Shanks, *God and Modernity: A New and Better Way to Do Theology* (London, 2000), pp. 44–7: discussed further in the following section.

[83]   Paul Ricoeur, *The Rule of Metaphor: Multi-disciplinary Studies of the Creation of Meaning in Language* (Toronto, 1977), pp. 247–8.

[84]   John Hick, *The Fifth Dimension* (Oxford, 1999), pp. 230–31.

[85]   Sinkinson, *Universe of Faiths*, p. 128.

[86]   Ibid., p. 130.

[87]   Ibid., pp. 120–24, referring to 'experiential-expressivists' in George Lindbeck, *The Nature of Doctrine: Religion and Theology in a Postliberal Age* (London, 1984), pp. 21–55.

[88]   D'Costa, 'John Hick and Religious Pluralism: Yet Another Revolution?', in Hewitt Jr. (ed.), *Problems*, p. 7; Cheetham, pp. 140–41; Sinkinson, *Universe of Faiths*, pp. 55, 77.

sacred ideology', and its effective 'withdrawal from conversation'.[89] Whilst Hick
would deny that he withdraws, believing he is committed to dialogue and intending
his hypothesis to be only a second-order interpretative framework which simply
enables the traditions to see how their languages are working, his reductionistic
approach to language at least implies a new first-order system, which works against
the tradition's creative ambiguity – or its otherness within.

In contrast, Ricoeur insists that metaphorical language relates to reality, that
the 'meaning' of a narrative is not confined to what is 'inside' the text but consists
of a 'web of relationships' with what is also 'outside'.[90] In fact, reminiscent of the
triad of particularity, plurality and universality, Ricoeur's hermeneutic consists of
a threefold mediation: between self-understanding (a human's relation to self),
communicability (between humans), and referentiality (between humans and the
world). Essentially, for Ricoeur, a metaphor does not represent a 'clash' between
pertinent and impertinent (literal) readings, but *solves* the enigma.[91] The point is
that metaphor is not claiming what is literally untrue, but that it simultaneously
claims truth and untruth.[92] By bringing two (or more) sets of associations into
relationship creatively,[93] it is a much richer reality than Hick suggests. Were we
to overlook the 'is not' implicit in a metaphor, the element of untruth, we would
surrender to 'ontological naivete', a prematurely concrete notion of language
and reality, but were we to exclude the 'is', the element of truth, we would deny
metaphor's distinct power.[94]

On the one hand, Hick does appear to appreciate a degree of interplay, recognizing
that metaphor depends upon 'a common reservoir of shared associations ... Indeed
it is a very plausible view of the function of metaphor that it serves to promote
community.'[95] On the other hand, despite this awareness of its social constituency,
he demands that we should distinguish sharply between literal and metaphorical
readings of our tradition, thereby imposing a modernist dichotomy on to both
religious language and the Body of Christ as the tradition's interpretative community.
After all, by characterizing the dominant tradition as a set of propositions which

---

[89]   Andrew Shanks, *Faith in Honesty: The Essential Nature of Theology* (Aldershot,
2005), pp. 6–7.

[90]   Paul Ricoeur, *Figuring the Sacred: Religion, Narrative and Imagination*
(Minneapolis, MN, 1995), pp. 239–41. For Soskice, too, the claims about Jesus must not
merely prescribe attitudes but describe something of his reality: Janet Martin Soskice,
Metaphor and Religious Language (Oxford, 1985), p. 191; see Loughlin, 'Squares and
Circles', p. 193.

[91]   Ricoeur, *The Rule*, pp. 152, 156, 214.

[92]   Wendy Doniger, *The Implied Spider: Politics and Theology in Myth* (New York,
1998), p. 3: 'real and unreal'.

[93]   Soskice, p. 49.

[94]   Ricoeur, *The Rule*, pp. 248–9, 255, 318.

[95]   Hick, *Metaphor*, p. 100. Doniger, p. 2, argues that myth works like this, too: 'a story
sacred to and shared by a group of people who find their most important meanings in it'.

are mistakenly understood literally *as opposed to* metaphorically, he caricatures it as a one-dimensional ideology (with a superiority-complex); but his mythological/metaphorical reinterpretation is also one-dimensional, since it relies on a simplistic understanding of metaphor. Whilst the diverse community of the Christian tradition might not itself fully appreciate the 'interplay' of metaphor, Hick's modernist re-reading of it is inattentive to its fluidity and creativity. Not only the tradition in general, but christology in particular, is better able to hold together its radical otherness and its openness to diversity (within and beyond), when it embraces its metaphorical nature. For metaphor demands an appropriate attentiveness to the otherness within the tradition: both truth and untruth, both audacious particularity and an awareness of the limitations of our cultural conditioning.

There are other features of Hick's suppression of otherness within the tradition, some of which we encounter in Chapter 4, regarding the alternative biblical vision. The point here, though, is simply that Hick's particularity, while purporting to focus on a core commonality with 'others', is actually more sectarian than he admits. It builds, not a solidarity of others, with a sense of being repeatedly shaken, but a solidarity of moderns or liberals: those who impatiently caricature the tradition in order to replace it with a universal religion which suppresses the otherness of and within particularity.

Hick and the Other beyond the Tradition: Generalizing the Differences

Given these criticisms, what is the extent to which Hick sees other traditions as concrete, not generalized, others? How sensitive is he to the nuances between the particularity of Jesus and other particularities? Does his approach to such others foster meaningful dialogue? (Dialogue is discussed in more depth in Chapter 6, but I need to establish here whether an expressive christology helps or hinders the process.)

As we have already begun to see, in essence his Kantianism works against real attentiveness to the differences amongst others. We noted that Hick sees apparent conflicts between the traditions' truth-claims as only apparent; they will only be temporary; they are indications of the limitations of our language and knowledge. Here we see Shanks's point, that Hick conflates two concerns.[96] How we deploy our limited language to give expression to the inexpressible is not the same as being aware that our religio-cultural traditions are distinct from the transcendent reality. Shanks suggests that Hick conflates the two out of an impatience, to equate the partiality of our language (Brahman, Trinity, Yahweh) with the idea that our partial experiences or 'phenomena' are responding to the same noumenon. Hick seeks to negate exclusivist claims, reducing the Incarnation to the status of a propositional expression of the Christian's cultural-specific experience which merely points to That to which others also point. Thus, as with Kant, Hick's

---

[96]   Shanks, *God and Modernity*, pp. 44–7.

pluralism avoids the awkwardness of being tested by historical phenomena. He does not want, in effect, to deal with the problem of language and the problem of what our experience tells us as two separate matters. Both limitations are therefore deemed to be demonstrations of the same issue: only a pluralistic hypothesis can really make sense of the apparent contradictions amongst our language systems and our religious experiences.

For Shanks, this is not a proper ground for pluralism; in fact, he sees it as theological Esperanto, a merger of languages. Instead of Hick's 'dogmatic Kantian agnosticism', which cuts short the 'infinite restlessness of authentic thought', he would be better to risk genuine dialogue with 'others' – both within the tradition and beyond it. Basically, Hick demonstrates the temptation of truth-as-correctness:[97] an impatience with the pursuit of truth, which manifests itself in his case in a framework purporting to be comprehensive but which is actually as ideologically conditioned as the incarnational tradition he parodied and reinterpreted. Truth-as-Honesty, instead, is about recognizing the partiality of one's particular tradition, for better and for worse, but also being open to what others might have to say – not only hearing their voices as more similar than they would imagine, but hearing the genuine differences.

Hick would find this criticism astonishing – the very idea that he fails to be properly attentive to the otherness of other traditions – because his paramount concern, in reinterpreting the Christian tradition, his vision of Jesus, and in building a comprehensive pluralistic hypothesis, is to take seriously the religious experience of the various traditions. In essence, however, as we have been exploring, he cannot maintain that his hypothesis is simply a second-order discourse which merely explains the religious ambiguity of the universe and gives an account of various responses to one transcendent reality. Otherness itself resists such domestication, because too many elements of his thesis point to its own cultural conditioning as a universal Kantian religion: for it is a first-order discourse, a normative tradition which presumes and projects a common ethic, shaped by modernist assumptions about fairness and freedom. Such is its captivity to Western modernism that it fails to distinguish between its particularity and what is genuinely universal: thus it is a universal pretender.

As a consequence of this effective inattentiveness to the genuine otherness of other traditions, Hick's vision of Jesus does not foster meaningful dialogue amongst 'others', but rather pre-empts it and debilitates against its point. After all, if we already know that Jesus is simply one good instance of the moral transformation which signifies an appropriate response to the Real, what more could we learn through further dialogue and shakenness?

---

[97]   Shanks, *Faith in Honesty*, p. 2.

Hick and the Invisible Other: Impeding Liberative Solidarity

To what extent does Hick's vision of Jesus energize Christian solidarity with those othered by powers of domination? How does his mythological christology shake us, politically?

This is essentially the question of relativism: has Hick so emptied the Christian tradition, and Jesus in particular, of moral purpose, that it (or he) cannot effect real change for the sake especially of those who are marginalized or oppressed? Certainly, Hick's theology is universalist, otherwise he believes God is not omnibenevolent.[98] As he puts it, at one point: 'All that we know, if our big picture is basically correct, is that nothing good that has been created in human life will ever be lost.'[99] This can seem unhelpfully general and as though it comes from a place of relative luxury and security. We will return to such sensibilities in Chapter 7. However, like Sinkinson, I believe Hick denies relativism.[100] His demand for the divine nature's omni-benevolence is itself a sign that his theology is not indifferent or neutral; and while he suggests it is difficult to settle the balance of evidence concerning the moral impact of the major traditions,[101] he confirms that goodness is different from evil, selflessness is better than selfishness. After all, even though his Real cannot as such 'cause' responses, Hick presumes that appropriate responses to it involve moral transformation.

The problem, though, is relative: he may not be committed to relativism, as such, but is his Jesus relatively impotent, in accordance with much of the Western Church's apparent impotence? Or does his vision engender commitment to a solidarity of others, in the sense that Christ's Body is prompted to resist the dehumanizing effects of sociopolitical othering? As Surin sees it, Hick is part of the Western movement which relativizes all others within 'a world ecumenism ideology', the same ideology underpinning McDonald's hamburgers as 'the world food'.[102] This suggests Hick's Christianity in general, and christology in particular, is basically toothless: what can it offer in the face of overwhelming powers of domination and inequality? We shall return to the question of the Western captivity of notions of justice in Chapters 4 and 7; but it is interesting that Sinkinson believes Hick's resistance to God's self-revelation in Christ makes it harder for him to sustain the importance or content of his moral norms.[103] Hick's personal involvement with the struggle against British fascists in the 1970s and his focus on the ethical criterion by which responses to the Real are to be judged suggest a moral motivation, which

---

[98] See, for example, John Hick, *Evil and the God of Love* (London, 1966, 1977).

[99] Hick, *Fifth Dimension*, p. 224.

[100] Sinkinson, 'Is Christianity Better than Other Religions?', p. 262.

[101] For example, see Hick, *Rainbow*, p. 13.

[102] Kenneth Surin, 'A "Politics of Speech": Religious Pluralism in the Age of the McDonald's Hamburger', in D'Costa (ed.), *Christian Uniqueness Reconsidered*, pp. 200–201.

[103] Sinkinson, *Universe of Faiths*, p. 162.

in itself may be very real. However, apart from references to the damaging effects of the Christian tradition's 'literal' incarnation, and its superiority-complex, Hick is relatively silent on matters of liberation and justice. Of course, he believes his hypothesis encourages such concerns, but, partly because his sanitized vision of Jesus is disengaged from human sociality, his theology does not confront us with the political question: with whom should we be in solidarity?

In conclusion, though Hick sets out to do christology with generosity towards 'others', his own cultural conditioning in Kantianism determines that his intentions are shaken but only partially. For he belittles the otherness of the Christian tradition and the otherness of other traditions, in accordance with the demands of universal ethical religion, and does not energize the Body of Christ much to be in solidarity with those othered by the 'Domination System'. His approach is thus not a strong basis for building a solidarity of others in the Church or the world.

Chapter 3
The Christology of Newbigin: Partially Shaken

A comparison between John Hick and Lesslie Newbigin is particularly worthwhile because of interconnected experiences and themes in their biographies and work. For instance, both realized they had quiet, devoted mothers, but neither was especially sensitive to gender politics.[1] Both were educated in Quaker schools, which, as with Hick, led to Newbigin's initial pacifism.[2] Thus their politics were similar – on the liberal-left, concerned about rampant capitalism.[3] What is most striking, though, is that, while their early scepticism regarding religious faith would be transformed partly due to extraordinary conversion experiences, their oddly similar paths would then diverge increasingly. Hick's initial evangelicalism would evolve, as we have seen, influenced by Kant's universal ethical religion; whereas Newbigin's initial liberalism would metamorphose into a conservative stance dependent on the 'objectivity' of the atonement.[4] So, whilst Hick's modernist framework would come to emphasize tolerance (though ironically suppressing dissent), non-discrimination (though ironically discriminating in favour of Western presuppositions) and the universal ethic of self-lessness (though ironically overlooking the particularity of this norm and obscuring its own individualism), Newbigin, by contrast, would emphasize God's self-revelation in Jesus Christ, its finality as the clue to the meaning of all history, and its 'elected' missiology by which God chooses the particular to bear witness to God's acts for the sake of others.

How should we understand these divergences? It may be relevant that Newbigin was born in 1909, Hick in 1922, so the collapse of nineteenth-century liberalism in the face of the Great War and the rise of Nazism was more present for Newbigin. Although Hick's education was stalled by the Second World War, he studied further in the optimistic post-war years and read philosophers who predated the existential

---

[1]   Regarding Hick, see John Hick, *John Hick: An Autobiography* (Oxford, 2002), pp. 19–20; Eleanor Jackson, 'Reviews', *British and Irish Association for Mission Studies*, 22/6 (March 2004): p. 7; and regarding Newbigin, see Lesslie Newbigin, *Unfinished Agenda: An Autobiography* (London, 1985), p. 3; Lynne Price, 'Churches and Postmodernity: Opportunity for an Attitude Shift', in Thomas F. Foust, George R. Hunsberger, J. Andrew Kirk, Werner Ustorf (eds), *A Scandalous Prophet: The Way of Mission after Newbigin* (Grand Rapids, MI, 2002), p. 108.

[2]   This would evolve in the face of Nazism: Newbigin, *Unfinished Agenda*, p. 36.

[3]   Jackson, 'Reviews', p. 7; Newbigin, *Unfinished Agenda*, p. 36.

[4]   Newbigin, *Unfinished Agenda*, pp. 30–31.

crisis. Thus, the Barthian path was more likely to shape Newbigin: the need for an objective response to the evils of the day; and he had been impressed by Barth's speech at the inception of the World Council of Churches.[5] Also, as a missionary in India for many years, Newbigin was part of a minority religious community – he was one of 'the others', and resisted the dominant (Hick-like) 'Hindu belief that all religions are equally valid paths to the one unknowable god',[6] which inspired Indians to inquire of his convictions. Whereas, in Birmingham, Hick stood in solidarity with minority religious communities – those who were 'other'. Also, both studied at Westminster College, and while Hick preferred John Oman's outlook, which encompassed nontheistic traditions, Newbigin enjoyed H.H. Farmer's approach (which, as Hick notes, was influenced by Hendrik Kraemer).[7] J.H. Oldham affected them both, too – in Newbigin's case, not least for his making the Edinburgh World Missionary Conference (1910) 'a real turning-point in the history of the Church', while Hick was influenced by Oldham's working 'on the frontiers of the debate on religion'.[8] Thus, while Newbigin would come to be a great critic of the Western Enlightenment, the contours of both his and Hick's theologies are shaped by Western discourse and debate. It is, then, to these contours and frontiers that we turn first of all; after which, we outline his emphasis on Christ's radical discontinuity, and his approach to difference – both within and beyond the Church. Then, as with Hick, we examine his christology in three regards, finding limitations on each count – his attentiveness to the other within, the other beyond, and the invisible other.

Newbigin and the Authority of Christology: The Gospel Confronts the West

Newbigin would come to be known for his critique of post-Enlightenment culture – partly by virtue of his returning to the UK, following many years as a missionary at the interface of 'gospel and culture' in India, so seeing his home turf with new eyes, as a 'pagan' culture,[9] but also by virtue of his faith convictions, especially regarding the authority of Jesus.

He identifies the existence of a 'plausibility structure' or 'fiduciary framework' in any culture or tradition, on the basis of his reading of both Michael Polyani's philosophy of science, and Peter Berger.[10] In essence, there is an element of

---

⁵   Ibid., pp. 115–16.

⁶   Ibid., p. 127.

⁷   Hick, *John Hick*, pp. 78, 84–5; Newbigin, *Unfinished Agenda*, p. 31.

⁸   Newbigin, *Unfinished Agenda*, p. 176; Jackson, 'Reviews', p. 7.

⁹   Newbigin, *Unfinished Agenda*, pp. 243, 249; Lesslie Newbigin, *Foolishness to the Greeks: The Gospel and Western Culture* (London, 1986), p. 20.

¹⁰   See Lesslie Newbigin, *The Gospel in a Pluralist Society* (London, 1989), pp. 12, 27–51, 243; Newbigin, *Foolishness*, pp. 10, 65–94; and Michael Polyani, *Personal Knowledge: Towards a Post-Critical Philosophy* (Chicago, IL, 1962); Peter L. Berger,

personal risk when building any system of knowledge: a presupposition must always be put beyond question, as the foundation for further questing and the gathering of evidence, because all quests begin with an act of trust. In the case of Christian faith, the basis for our system is 'in the name of Jesus'[11] – we can presume he bears all the authority we need, because he will ultimately be shown to be the clue to the meaning of all history. We can know this by virtue of God's self-revelation in him; that is, it is self-consciously an argument from revelation (we know it to be true because it will be shown to be true[12]), which cannot be second-guessed but must be accepted on trust. It is, specifically, the event of the cross-turned-resurrection which demonstrates this: 'the simple truth is that the resurrection cannot be accommodated in any [worldview] except the one of which it is the starting-point.'[13] In other words, it is because Jesus is raised from the dead that we know his authority in history is unique and that he can personally be the basis for a distinctive plausibility structure. There is risk in this, but that is the very nature of faith, which is the same with any other tradition: all are built upon presuppositions.

The contrast between the Christian plausibility structure and Western post-Enlightenment culture is that, while Christian faith affirms the risk of participating in it, Western culture strives to eliminate risk, purporting not to be built upon presuppositions but upon universally testable facts.[14] For Newbigin, this itself entails a presupposition: in particular, Western culture presumes that reality can be defined in terms of the scientific questions of 'cause and effect' rather than broader and deeper questions of purpose and meaning.[15] The very objectification of reality, by which it is reduced to the properties and behaviour of its constituent parts, is a presupposition: for reality is surely understood more authentically in terms of its relationality. Thus, whilst Newbigin proclaims Jesus Christ is the Lord of all time and space, not least because his experience is of Jesus' absolute claim

---

The Heretical Imperative: Contemporary Possibilities of Religious Affirmation (Garden City, NY, 1979). (It is debatable, however, whether Newbigin reads Polyani correctly: see Thomas Foust, 'Lesslie Newbigin's Epistemology: A Dual Discourse?', in Foust et al. (eds), *A Scandalous Prophet*, pp. 154ff, suggesting Newbigin conflates the 'tacit knowing' of assumptions needed to make further propositions with biblical 'faith'.)

[11] Lesslie Newbigin, *The Open Secret: Sketches for a Missionary Theology* (London, 1978), p. 16.

[12] Newbigin, *Pluralist Society*, p. 243; that is, like Hick, he believes in eschatological verification.

[13] Lesslie Newbigin, *Truth to Tell: The Gospel as Public Truth* (London, 1991), p. 11. (So, too, for Paul D. Molnar, *Incarnation and Resurrection: Toward a Contemporary Understanding* (Grand Rapids, MI, 2007), pp. 244–9, in his criticism of Hick's position: he insists that Christ's resurrection only has authority in its own terms.)

[14] See Foust, 'Lesslie Newbigin's Epistemology', pp. 154–60.

[15] Newbigin, *Foolishness*, pp. 23–38.

on him personally,[16] he describes how Western culture forces public and private realms apart. The public sphere is the place for consideration of objective facts, based upon empirical evidence, and heretics are those who resist the dominance of such fact-oriented orthodoxy. In the private realm, by contrast, people are free to express their subjective values – in fact, people are encouraged to resist any value-laden orthodoxy, because values are not based upon evidence, so we are happily diverse and must tolerate each other's private heresies. For Newbigin, such a dichotomy, between public and private, fact and value, is at the root of much meaninglessness, even violence, in the modern world;[17] and its effect on the Church has been the depersonalizing of God,[18] the privatizing of faith, and the consequent reticence of the Church to proclaim the Lordship of Jesus.

As several critics of Newbigin argue, discussed further below with regards to the other beyond the tradition, his diagnosis of the Western disease is too apocalyptic,[19] not least because he himself wrenches apart the gospel from modernity as though they are not themselves far more related than he supposes.[20] Nevertheless, for our current purposes his critique of Western culture is profound and is inseparable from the absoluteness of his christology: for his vision of Jesus, unlike Hick's, does not simply aim to transform the human tendency towards self-centredness, but has a much more concrete other to confront and convert.[21] For Newbigin sees Western culture as having become particularly adept at resisting the gospel of Jesus Christ, so it needs to be re-engaged missiologically. In effect, its whole worldview needs 'radical conversion'.[22]

That the Church in Western culture faces distinctive challenges is hard to deny – in fact, as one writer suggests, there is a sense of trying to build skyscrapers during an earthquake[23] – and it is pertinent that Newbigin returns to the UK with

---

[16]   Newbigin, *Open Secret*, pp. 16–19: 'I make this confession only because I have been laid hold of by Another.'

[17]   See Lesslie Newbigin, 'Response to David M. Stowe', *International Bulletin of Missionary Research*, 12/4 (1988): p. 152.

[18]   Lesslie Newbigin, *Honest Religion for Secular Man* (London, 1966), pp. 56–76: 'the Denial of the Other'.

[19]   See David R. Peel, 'The Theological Legacy of Lesslie Newbigin', in Anna M. Robbins (ed.), *Ecumenical and Eclectic: The Unity of the Church in the Contemporary World – Essays in Honour of Alan P.F. Sell* (Milton Keynes, 2007), p. 146.

[20]   See Bert Hoedemaker, 'Rival Conceptions of Global Christianity: Mission and Modernity, Then and Now', in Foust et al. (eds), *A Scandalous Prophet*, pp. 13–22.

[21]   See Charles C. West, 'Mission to the West: A Dialogue with Stowe and Newbigin', *International Bulletin of Missionary Research*, 12/4 (1988): p. 153.

[22]   Donald Le Roy Stults, *Grasping Truth and Reality: Lesslie Newbigin's Theology of Mission to the Western World* (Eugene, OR, 2008), pp. 154–6, citing Lesslie Newbigin, *The Other Side of 1984: Questions for the Churches* (Geneva, 1984), p. 53.

[23]   Brian McLaren, *Church on the Other Side: Exploring the Radical Future of the Local Congregation* (Grand Rapids, MI, 1998), pp. 15–16.

the vigour of a missionary and the experience of episcopal authority, not intending to demonize the culture as such, but to reinvigorate the Church with God's calling. However, his argument from revelation, though tempered by a humility we shall note below, frames his vision of Christ and culture in such a way that a stark dichotomy is established. For what of the role of reason in the Christian plausibility structure?[24] It looks as though his faithful presumption of the authority of Jesus prompts him to take a great deal more for granted: after all, he does not seem to allow historical criticism to raise questions about the bulk of evangelical orthodoxy, apparently taking as read not only the incarnation, atonement and resurrection, but the ascension, second coming, ultimate consummation of history, and doctrine of the Trinity.[25] Of course, it is of the nature of such audacious revelation, of God in Christ, that it will trump any debate or dispute; but as we shall discuss further, Newbigin does not seem to allow for the arguments about such orthodoxy, let alone its probable Western conditioning.

Newbigin and the Discontinuity of Christology: The Measure of All Others

For Newbigin, then, the self-revelation of God in Christ is absolute. He speaks of it as 'the interpretive clue'[26] for the meaning of all history, of 'the total fact of Jesus' and 'the absolute sovereignty of Jesus Christ'.[27] As provocative as he knows it seems to 'enlightened' minds, Jesus' life, death and resurrection have the authority of 'a single happening ... of decisive significance to all'.[28] As the manifestation of a victory, a victory out of defeat, the resurrection reveals that the Christ-event '*is* the true secret of universal and cosmic history',[29] fundamentally discontinuous with all other events, yet also a real part of (secular) history itself.[30] While on the one hand he insists that it is the person and event of Jesus Christ who is absolute and final, rather than any interpretation of him, on the other hand, Newbigin appears to be clear that God has revealed the true meaning, even if only

---

24 Peel, p. 144: 'Reason has a more fundamental part to play in Christian theology than Newbigin ever allows.'

25 Ibid., pp. 143 (Peel notes all the 'beliefs which Newbigin would have us accept on the basis of the testimony of others'), 146 (he suggests Newbigin is adhering to 'the Augustinian-Calvinist-Barthian wing of Reformed theology', without regard for the approach of Irenaeus, Schleiermacher, Oman).

26 See Lesslie Newbigin, *A Faith for this One World?* (London, 1961), pp. 46–53; Lesslie Newbigin, *The Finality of Christ* (London, 1969), pp. 65–87.

27 Newbigin, *A Faith?*, pp. 57, 60; *Pluralist Society*, p. 169.

28 See Newbigin, *A Faith?*, pp. 77–8; *Open Secret*, p. 57.

29 Newbigin, *Open Secret*, pp. 40–41; Lesslie Newbigin, *Christ our Eternal Contemporary* (Madras, 1968), p. 5: 'If Jesus died and rose again, then we are at the beginning of a new world, a new creation.'

30 Newbigin, *Finality*, pp. 46–9.

to those whom God has chosen.[31] This is explained in terms of the paradoxical relation between continuity and discontinuity.

Newbigin is aware of Western problems with the notion of 'finality'[32]: the scandalous assertion than an obscure corner of an obscure planet should give rise to the end itself; the fact that even scientists speak less now in terms of finality and more of the provisionality of knowledge; the cultural conditioning of every event relativizing them all; the observation that other religious traditions happen to offer some beliefs about reality similar to those of Christian faith; and he notes the 'bad conscience' of Westerners which can associate assertions of Christ's finality with a guilty history of imperialism. Recognizing that there is no 'unprejudiced' position from which to adjudicate between perspectives, and sensing the dominance of the Hindu-like insistence that everyone's personal experience points to universal truth, Newbigin does not purport to demonstrate finality but simply to explore its meaning.[33] Like Kraemer, he does not equate Christ's finality with Christianity itself, and is clear that any Christian's claim to have the whole truth would be a denial of Christ's finality.[34] For Christ is the end of all religion, including Christianity. So, for Newbigin, like Barth, there is an element to the Christ-event which is continuous with secular life, not least because religion itself is human activity and God's self-revelation does indeed appeal to and engage everyday human experience.[35] We see here that Newbigin implies there is a kind of universality about human experience and culture, a continuity which is confronted by a discontinuous gospel. Arguably, as we explore below, this perception of culture involves a Western objectification, insufficiently nuanced to the intersubjectivity of culture and gospel. As he sees it, in contrast to Jesus' continuity with and embeddedness within human experience and culture, the Christ-event is discontinuous with all other religious claims. For Jesus is not merely the epitome of general truths, but is the measure of all others; his cross-turned-resurrection is the means by which all – both Christian and non-Christian – are judged. Of course, it is for each of us to decide personally whether to respond to the ultimate authority of God's act in Christ – *has* God's kingdom come in him, or not? – but such is the nature of the event that it does indeed demand a response, one way or the other.[36] We are with Christ, or we resist him: though, like Barth, Newbigin does not want to second-guess the sovereign will of God, so leaves open the possibility of the salvation of non-Christians.[37]

---

[31]   See Newbigin, *A Faith?*, pp. 60–62; *Finality*, pp. 21–2; *Open Secret*, pp. 39–43.

[32]   Newbigin, *Finality*, pp. 9–15.

[33]   Ibid., pp. 15–21.

[34]   Ibid., pp. 22–5; Hendrik Kraemer, *The Christian Message in a Non-Christian World* (London, 1938).

[35]   See also Newbigin, *A Faith?*, pp. 20–28.

[36]   Newbigin, *Eternal Contemporary*, p. 28.

[37]   Newbigin, *Open Secret*, pp. 197–8; *Pluralist Society*, pp. 182–3.

Newbigin is utterly confident of the historicity, thus the public truth, of the 'central verities'[38] of the gospel – in contrast to the notion of their truth as merely inner experience or private *gnosis*[39] – but he does not strive to demonstrate evidence for their historicity. It is crucial to him that these events are part of history; that they are, in that sense, continuous with the experiences of history; but that they are, as Wiles understands Newbigin's view, of such a 'different order', that their historicity is beyond question.[40] Whilst theologians such as Pannenberg argue that it is possible, and necessary, to give evidence for the claims of faith,[41] Newbigin's overriding emphasis on God's self-revelation relativizes even the debates of history. He acknowledges that it may be more acceptable or reasonable to locate Jesus as one 'among' others, but insists on the genuine scandal of the Christ-event's discontinuity.[42] In Fackre's terms, to which we return in Chapter 6, Newbigin's approach is not akin to Rahner's, in which Christ finds 'hospitable territory' amongst 'underground forces'; that is, Christ fulfils the general work begun by allies through history, so draws others in to his embrace. Instead, as with Barth, Newbigin understands Christ's assault on the occupying forces as being possible only 'from beyond', and that its effects radiate outwards.[43] Christ is, therefore, the radical other, the impossible Thing, who cannot be measured by any other human terms, but is the event which intrinsically proves to be the measure of all others.

This outrageous break with history is located in the incarnation, atonement and resurrection, which together effect a new reality, brought about in person; that is, God's kingdom comes *in Christ*. How, then, does Jesus' personhood compare and contrast with that of others? Newbigin offers a comparison with Hindu concepts: for whilst the Hindu can accept Jesus as one of the *jeevanmuktas* (those who attain the full realization of the divine), or as *Swamy* (Lord), *Satguru* (true teacher), *Avatar* (incarnation) and even *Kadavul* (the transcendent God) who has become man, Newbigin insists that none of these captures Jesus' uniqueness – or otherness. It is the difference between a human achievement and a gift.[44] It is not clear whether Newbigin engages the Hindu notion of 'avatar' in its integrity, since some sources suggest it is God's act, not a human's achievement; nevertheless, an

---

[38]   Newbigin, *Pluralist Society*, p. 139.

[39]   Lesslie Newbigin, 'The Centrality of Jesus for History', in Michael Goulder (ed.), *Incarnation and Myth: The Debate Continued* (London, 1979), pp. 205–6.

[40]   See Maurice Wiles, 'Comment on Lesslie Newbigin's Essay', in Goulder (ed.), *Incarnation and Myth*, pp. 212–13. Newbigin, *Unfinished Agenda*, p. 57.

[41]   See Wolfhart Pannenberg, *Jesus – God and Man* (London, 1968), pp. 89, 98.

[42]   Newbigin, 'The Centrality of Jesus', pp. 208–10.

[43]   Gabriel Fackre, 'The Scandals of Particularity and Universality', *Mid-Stream*, 22/1 (1983): pp. 32–52.

[44]   Newbigin, *Open Secret*, pp. 20–21.

avatar is believed to have an apparent, not a real, body.[45] Crucially for Newbigin, though, is the distinctiveness of Jesus' personhood by virtue of his relation to the Father: 'It is God's kingdom [and] Jesus is the one who is sent as herald and bearer of [it]'; that is, it is a Son's obedience to his Father's calling, which is also anointed and energized by the Spirit.[46] Newbigin is clearly influenced by Barth, for whom God does not change, rather our apprehension of his dealings with us changes by virtue of God's self-revelation;[47] but his concern is not as such to explain this, simply to point to God's concern for and experience of materiality.

Intriguingly, in this context, he suggests churches are free to find 'new ways' to state 'the essential trinitarian faith' in different cultural settings,[48] but this is not the same as the freedom shown by Hick's reformulations of the tradition; it is more a matter of each culture being able to appreciate the gospel in its own terms. (Of course, this also indicates the implicit influence of Western modernism, as though the language of each culture might not actually colour the nature of the gospel. That is, he is evidently conditioned by Western constructs, but also criticizes them. For he employs Polyani's philosophy of science partly to challenge the spiritual/material dichotomy of Western rationalism: for our knowledge is constantly reworked in the light of our response to what is revealed to us – and what is revealed to us is that God is Father, Son and Spirit, thus our knowledge evolves in that light.[49] However, he does not allow that historical study might lead us to 'modify' our perspectives about revelation.[50])

In Newbigin's theology, the materiality of God's experience, by which a change is brought about in the course of history, is most vitally demonstrated on the cross: '[for] from the cross, faith sees the decisive event by which all things were changed, the powers ... which falsely claim absolute power were unmasked and disowned, and the reign of God was established'.[51] It is, as Newbigin sees it, Jesus' personal role, not to overcome the forces of evil, but to bear their weight; the message of the cross is, thus, not least to Western minds, a great mystery, a paradox, if not an outright secret. Just as Jesus taught in parables, both to illuminate and confound, so the cross acts parabolically:

> Here is the supreme parable: the reign of God hidden and manifest in the dying
> of a condemned and excommunicated man: the fullness of God's blessing

---

[45]   Klaus K. Klostermaier, *A Concise Encyclopaedia of Hinduism* (Oxford, 1998), p. 33; and Karel Werner, *A Popular Dictionary of Hinduism* (Richmond, 1994), p. 38.

[46]   Newbigin, *Open Secret*, pp. 23–5.

[47]   See Karl Barth, *Dogmatics in Outline* (London, 2001), p. 60.

[48]   Newbigin, *Open Secret*, p. 29.

[49]   Ibid., pp. 30–31.

[50]   Wiles, 'Comment on Lesslie Newbigin's Essay', pp. 212–13.

[51]   Newbigin, *Open Secret*, p. 56.

bestowed in the accursed death of the cross. Who could believe this unless it was given to him by an act of God's sovereign grace?[52]

Although it is not for us to claim to understand the secret, since comprehension of its foolishness is only in God's gift, nevertheless God does give us a part to play: to bear witness to the new reality which this event initiates. We do not in ourselves constitute the new reality, though we are instrumental in making it known.[53] There is no correlation, though, between our obedience or faithfulness, as witnesses, and any success we may or may not have in history: for the mystery of the message of the cross is that its way involves defeat and suffering. It is significant, however, that Newbigin understands the new reality in relational terms: for we are not only dependent on others for our growing understanding of what has been revealed to us, but the new reality brought about in person also generates a new community, or a community of communities. It is to these social relationalities that we now turn.

Newbigin and the Plurality of Christology: The Many Witness Partially to the One

This dimension of Newbigin's christology is fundamental to it and straightforward. Basically, it consists of these elements: firstly, as noted above, it is Christ himself, not any interpretation of him, which is final, thus Christians are called to engage in dialogue with each other, or in 'mutual correction',[54] so as to qualify and enrich our partial grasps of the fullness of the Christ-event. In this sense, Newbigin is deeply committed to ecumenism: the calling of the Church to reflect the gospel of reconciliation in its own life. Secondly, such is the authority and decisiveness of the Christ-event, particularly the cross-turned-resurrection, that any claims to self-righteousness are necessarily humbled, not only those of other traditions, but also those of the Christian tradition; thus Christians are called to be open to those insights of others which remind us of our common judgment and humility under the cross.[55] In this sense, Newbigin is committed to engagement with other traditions: the calling of the Church to reflect the gospel of reconciliation in its relationships with others. Thirdly, these two elements are underpinned by his doctrine of election: the idea that God chooses the particular to bear God's message and acts for the sake of others. It is not the election of favourites, but a calling to responsibility, to bear witness to the gospel on behalf of others, so as to demonstrate the relational nature of God's personhood, of human beings with

---

[52] Ibid., p. 39.
[53] See, for example, Newbigin, *A Faith?*, pp. 86–7.
[54] Newbigin, *Foolishness*, p. 9.
[55] Newbigin, *Open Secret*, pp. 203–12.

one another, and of the gospel itself.[56] In this sense, Newbigin is committed to one united narrative by which God effects change: through Jesus Christ and the calling of his Church in all cultures.

It is about the relation between the One and the Many. For there is one salvific narrative, one plausibility structure which is the measure of all others, one Christ who is the clue to the meaning of the united biblical narrative, which is itself the one text by which history can be understood;[57] but the people interpreting and chosen to bear witness to the one Christ are many, so the communities which bear his name are many, and the cultures in which his message is held are many. As Hunsberger demonstrates, it is an underlying doctrine of election, rooted in Newbigin's missionary passion, which holds these elements together. Heim interprets Hunsberger's analysis as follows:

> Election thus denotes the fact that God draws us toward communion through unique acts of some on behalf of others. The Christian life is marked by acknowledgement that we are the recipients of such witness by others and depend upon it, and also by acceptance of the calling to be part of the community, the church, which is called to bear that witness. This thread links all features of Christian faith, from the fact that the unique events of Christ's life, death, and resurrection have significance for all, to the belief that God works in accord with the nature of history (not outside or above temporal and particular relations), to the fact that each unique culture and community converted to Christ brings with it a new creation of the church, 'elected' to bear back a distinctive witness to the missionary church out of which it was born.[58]

For Hunsberger, this thread suggests that there is a 'latent' theme in Newbigin, which he names a 'theology of cultural plurality',[59] and he successfully illuminates its presence and effect in Newbigin's thinking and practice. In essence, as I see it, Newbigin believes the biblical narrative shows us God's election, firstly of a people, Israel, narrowing down through faithful remnants, ultimately in one person, Jesus, before re-opening through his Church, which is the chosen community bearing the witness of the Spirit, that is, the responsibility to convey on behalf of all people the message of the cross through which salvation is effected.[60] Then,

---

[56]   See George R. Hunsberger, *Bearing the Witness of the Spirit: Lesslie Newbigin's Theology of Cultural Plurality* (Grand Rapids, MI and Cambridge, 1998), pp. 54–8, 90–96.

[57]   Ibid., pp. 44, 46.

[58]   S. Mark Heim, 'Review of *Bearing the Witness of the Spirit* by George R. Hunsberger', *Theology Today*, 56/2 (1999): p. 266.

[59]   Hunsberger, *Bearing the Witness*, pp. 7–8.

[60]   See, for instance, Hunsberger, *Bearing the Witness*, p. 79; Newbigin, *Open Secret*, pp. 200–201.

as each embodiment of the gospel consequently encounters diverse cultures, it undergoes renewed conversion by divine grace.[61]

Initially, as identified by Hunsberger,[62] this was about the 'inner logic of salvation'. While Indians were arguing that history is a whole, and that they ought to be free to claim Hinduism as their Old Testament, resisting the offensive particularity of Christian faith, for Newbigin it is simply intrinsic to Christian faith that the gospel's concreteness and particularity – its objectivity – is necessary; it is only because of the historical actuality of *this* person and event that salvation is offered to all. For its chosenness is not arbitrary favouritism, but the manifestation of God's means and ends: after all, since humans are social, it would be an egotistical denial of our sociality were we to expect unmediated salvation; rather it comes to us through interpersonal transmission.[63] A gospel of peace and reconciliation must involve relationality: God engages us in our solidarity with each other. This is the nature of God's personhood, since God is no object nor the sum of consistent propositions, but a living personality.[64]

Later, in the face of rising secularism and the depersonalizing of God, Newbigin focuses on the chosenness of faith itself: not that one chooses faith, but that one is chosen: '[Jesus] has chosen us as witnesses and agents of his purpose.'[65] This no doubt feeds the 'unshakeable' nature of Newbigin's confidence:[66] for if our faith is given to us, who are we to question its content? While Hunsberger believes Newbigin's genius is his balancing of boldness and humility, Peel advocates a little more 'hesitancy', to which we shall return.[67] Hunsberger notes that Newbigin, like Barth, can be accused of 'revelational positivism', since he suggests that God's self-revelation as attested in scripture is effectively beyond debate, but Newbigin's targets are Hindus and Western liberals for whom the scandal of particularity is at the root of the problem.[68] Newbigin knows it is offensive, to certain mindsets, since it involves an irrational leap of faith, but it simply reflects his 'experience of being laid hold of by Another, gripped from his earliest days by the vision of That One's cross as that which alone gives meaning and purpose to the whole breadth of life and history'.[69] That is, as with Hick's confidence about the religious ambiguity of the universe, underpinned by an epistemology which prioritizes personal

---

[61]   Hunsberger, *Bearing the Witness*, p. 34; Newbigin, *Foolishness*, pp. 5–6.

[62]   Hunsberger, *Bearing the Witness*, pp. 50–58.

[63]   Newbigin, *A Faith?*, p. 79; Lesslie Newbigin, *The Household of God: Lectures on the Nature of the Church* (London, 1953), pp. 110–12.

[64]   Hunsberger, *Bearing the Witness*, pp. 56–8: he suggests this reflects Newbigin's attraction to Polyani's emphasis on 'personal knowing' and the impact of John Oman's 'personalism', by which there is no such 'thing' as grace, only a gracious God.

[65]   Lesslie Newbigin, *Behold I Make All Things New* (Madras, 1968), pp. 28–9.

[66]   Peel, p. 144.

[67]   Hunsberger, *Bearing the Witness*, p. 30; Peel, p. 144.

[68]   Hunsberger, *Bearing the Witness*, pp. 41, 69–71.

[69]   Ibid., p. 81.

experience, so too in Newbigin, ironically, the power of experience is a defining factor. Although their confidence is based on very different foundations, leading them in very different directions, there is a sense in which both of their attempts to attend to otherness and plurality are undermined by the 'grip' of their experience.

What we see here, though, is the priority given to God's self-revelation, contrasting with Hick's denial of it, and of its elected course. It affirms our relationality, however, by impressing on us our need for both the divine Other and human others, thus presenting us with a first-order discourse, the gospel of reconciliation, by which the One and the Many are related, as evidenced not least by the Body bearing witness to it. Though the Church does not exactly constitute the new reality brought about by God's acts in Christ, it is called to be God's chief instrument in proclaiming it and striving to embody it, even as we inevitably suffer and fail.[70] Having increasingly noted the trinitarian nature of this trajectory, by the time of writing *The Open Secret*, he explains:

> The Father is the giver of all things. They all belong rightly to the Son. It will be the work of the Spirit to guide the church through the course of history into the truth as a whole by taking all God's manifold gifts given to mankind [*sic*] and declaring their true meaning to the church as that which belongs to the Son.[71]

Thus the Spirit, active in all cultures, is judging the Church for its failures to witness faithfully to the new reality of reconciliation brought about by God's acts in Christ, but is also renewing and empowering us to fulfil our calling to unity, to be God's chief instrument by which the world may see that Christ alone is the source of true unity.

Newbigin and the Other within the Tradition: Streamlining Christian Identity

On the one hand, it is clear that Newbigin is very focused on the otherness *of* the tradition: he is aware that some people understand the particularity of Christian faith as scandalous and offensive, but insists that it is only 'in the name of Jesus' that we have a plausibility structure of such unshakeable confidence, one which makes it possible to judge the subjectivities of our partial, divided claims and provides the only true source of reconciliation. Of course this looks like revelational positivism, as Newbigin does not allow for any way of testing the adequacy of such a narrative: it is simply revealed, if only to those whom God chooses. His point is that, in contrast to other standpoints which also rely on presupposition and which are deluded about their capacity to effect peace and unity, *this* clue to the meaning of all history is given by God: in fact, it *is* God, acting in Christ, to reconcile the

---

[70]   Newbigin, *Open Secret*, pp. 39–43.
[71]   Ibid., p. 203.

world to himself. The Christian tradition is, then, the ultimate other, so different from anything and everything else, not because its participants or proponents fulfil their calling perfectly, but because its narrative focus is the One and Only, the first and the last, the person/event by which God acts objectively.

On the other hand, it is the emphatic nature of this otherness which undermines Newbigin's attempts to attend to otherness *within* the tradition. Although he is concertedly ecumenical, intentionally and practically, his theology is only partially shaken: particularly with regards to christology, his revelational positivism places limits on the acceptability of Christian others. It is not that he denies the 'shadow side' of the Christian tradition, since he is insistent on our need for humility and on the inevitability of human frailty: the cross exposes and judges us all. However, he does pay scant attention to the real damage done by Christian faith through history, its violence and prejudice, being somewhat more inclined to identify the damage done by other traditions, both Western rationalism and other religious traditions, which we discuss further in the next section.[72] More significantly, with regards to others within, is the way in which his presumption of biblical unity and evangelical orthodoxy fosters an inherent resistance to those whose Christian faith is experienced, expressed and practised *too* differently from his.

We shall look further at alternative biblical visions in Chapter 4, but here we note the effects of Newbigin's approach to history. The problem, in short, is that his whole fiduciary framework relies on the presumption that orthodoxy is settled; that is, his faith convictions allow him to determine the contours of the historicity of the primary events, because it is of the very nature of his experience of faith that God's self-revelation in Christ simply, objectively, *is*. For Foust, the point is that Newbigin conveniently deploys a 'dual discourse' between knowledge and faith.[73] On the one hand, perhaps to humble the dominance of scientific positivism in Western modernity, Newbigin allows for the postmodern relativist perspective that all knowledge is subjectival, determined by the lenses given by culture, so effectively adopts Polyani's 'from below' epistemology; but on the other hand, he argues that history does not derive its meaning from the forces within it but from the goal promised to it – the crucified and risen Christ who is the true measure of everything. Foust thus suggests that Newbigin should not be understood through the lens of his epistemology at all, since he effectively leaps to an objective 'from above' position whenever the questions of knowledge and cultural relativism 'from below' become too difficult. Instead, Newbigin is to be understood as a missionary activist, who, like Barth, starts from scripture and the presumption that its truth comes 'from outside'. Newbigin is, as Foust notes, happy to engage in the debate, but does not expect the basis of orthodox systematic theology to be shaken by it.

---

[72]   See p. 64–9.

[73]   Foust, 'Lesslie Newbigin's Epistemology', pp. 155–61, referring for example to Newbigin, *Pluralist Society*, pp. 103–15.

The question of shakenness and the historical tradition re-emerges in Chapter 5, but I simply note here the limitations of Newbigin's position. Greene's defence of it is illuminating: he is right to criticize any contemporary preference for 'atomistic individualism', especially for its resistance to the idea that a particular revelatory event might genuinely hold the clue to the meaning of all history;[74] for it is possible that a particularity speaks of and to the universal reality and it is important to affirm human relationality. (After all, I am arguing from a particularity with claims to universality, but which more thoroughly seeks to root it in human relationality, as demonstrated by 'the Shaken One'.) However, it is arguable that Newbigin's attempts to distinguish between the finality of that particularity and the tradition's plural interpretations of it fails, especially since he appears to define the particular Christ-event in terms of historicity which is not as settled as he implies. In other words, is he properly wary of the danger of universalizing his own interpretation of Christ's particularity, or is his christology actually a universal pretender, suppressing others within? McFarland, for instance, states *both* that Christ is the measure of the Church's claims *and* that the Church is charged with evaluating what is meant by Christ – and that this is to be done 'from the outside in', that is, with particular regard for those lacking the formal power to make such judgments.[75] Now, whilst Newbigin affirms the interpretative role of the Church, being one of the first to argue for unity amongst not only Catholics and Protestants, but 'Pentecostals' too,[76] I maintain that his determined focus on the otherness *of* the tradition is inadvertently impatient with otherness *within* the tradition; the Church's freedom to evaluate what is meant by Christ is more restricted than the tradition's ongoing debates about history suggest it should be.

This is indicative of Newbigin's apparent difficulty with the mediation of revelation. It is part of the necessarily paradoxical nature of his perspective. While his christology seeks to emphasize God's affirmation of materiality (for God *is* present *in* creation: in Christ), Newbigin is simultaneously suspicious of materiality, as we see in relation to culture in the next section also. After all, he insists that God's self-revelation in Christ is absolute, but that our human grasps of it are problematically partial; that is, its mediation through our experiential and cultural filters involves its distortion or diminution. Of course, he means this to require our positive engagement with each other, as social and relational beings, mutually correcting one another in the light of the criterion given us through revelation; but the outcome is more negative. For our mutual corrections of one another are so conditioned by the distorting subjectivities of our cultures, that

---

[74]   Colin J.D. Greene, 'Trinitarian Tradition and the Collapse of Late Modernity', in Foust et al. (eds), *A Scandalous Prophet*, p. 71.

[75]   Ian McFarland, *Listening to the Least: Doing Theology from the Outside In* (Cleveland, OH, 1998), pp. 5–7, 20–28.

[76]   See Walter J. Hollenweger, 'Towards a Pentecostal Missiology', in T. Dayanandan Francis and Israel Selvanayagam (eds), *Many Voices in Christian Mission: Essays in honour of J.E. Lesslie Newbigin* (Madras, 1994), p. 74.

there appears to be no alternative but to accept the 'from above' reliability of the fiduciary framework he outlines.

In Hick's Kantian terms, is Newbigin actually presenting the gospel of the Christ as the incontestable 'noumenon' beyond our direct experience, whilst our partial visions of it are merely 'phenomenal' experiences? This is not quite so, because he claims to have experienced Jesus personally, but there is certainly a stark dichotomy in Newbigin's christology, described by Foust in terms of a 'dual discourse', as there is also in Hick's approach. Just as Hick supposes his framework is a second-order discourse, simply describing the ambiguous nature of our phenomenal experiences, whilst it acts more like a first-order discourse, so Newbigin supposes he is affirming interaction between different phenomenal expressions of Christ, whilst implying that Christ's objective reality is distinct from culture and is essentially just as the evangelical tradition discerns it. That is, both Hick and Newbigin differentiate too sharply between a truth and its appearance, in modernist terms, whereas – if we are to take seriously the sociality, not only of his disciples, but of Jesus himself – we must engage more deeply with the intersubjective relationship between his being and the experiences of him. While Hick empties christology of Jesus' being, focusing instead on the experience of his disciples, Newbigin also implies a polarity between Jesus and our interpretations of him. (The point is that both Hick and Newbigin cannot escape their modernist captivity. Even Newbigin's 'counter-modernism' illustrates his fixation with Western modernity, with its polarizing of reality and its notion that some things can be 'objective', which he applies to the atonement.) What, instead, of the authentic interrelatedness between Christ, his Body and culture?

By virtue of the 'integral worldview' by which 'everything interpenetrates everything else', Wink suggests we should neither idealize nor demonize that which conditions our perspective, including our christology, but should 'engage' such powers or cultural mediations. For the social fabric, or the religious tradition, which inevitably contributes to the distortions of our visions of Christ, is also necessarily involved in resisting the objectification of what God is revealing.[77] It could be the Holy Spirit, in particular, which is pivotal here, in terms of energizing our engagement with that which conditions our partial grasps of a broader, deeper tradition. To put it another way, the Spirit is potentially that part of the Christian language-system and living tradition which especially helps us to resist our objectification of Christ: for, as we shall discuss further in Chapter 6, the Spirit reminds us that the Christian tradition is more than Christ and that Christ is more than an isolated individual. Jesus, the Christ, is part of a matrix of relationships, both human and divine. Thus it is of the very nature of the transcendent God, to whom both Christ and the Spirit are opening us, that God is both the radical other with whom nothing can be directly compared *and* interrelated with the social fabric or cultural mediations through which revelation comes to us. Shanks, for instance, suggests that what he calls Third-Person theology (epitomized by

---

[77] See Chapter 1, pp. 11,13.

the Spirit's 'flair for tradition') is especially attentive to the tradition's potential for sectarianism and the need to re-own those parts of our tradition we would rather deny.[78] Newbigin, however, appears to adopt a functionalist pneumatology whereby the Spirit merely acts as the means by which the Church is enabled to give all the glory to Christ.[79] This is not a sign of attentiveness to the distinctions within the tradition – neither between Christ and the Spirit, nor between different visions of the trinitarian tradition, to which we return.

The thing is, Newbigin's commitment to ecumenical dialogue suggests he is shaken by the awareness that the Church itself is not final in any of its cultural manifestations. Nevertheless, as we shall see further, he is implicitly advocating a solidarity of shaken Christians, rather than shaken people more generally, but specifically a solidarity of Christians who share a broadly similar view of history and tradition, as determined by evangelical faith. Although Hick's identification of himself as Christian is not universally accepted, it is obvious that Newbigin's solidarity of others leaves little room for Hick. His particular understanding of the tradition's radical otherness restricts his ability to accept the genuine diversity of its internal otherness.

Newbigin and the Other beyond the Tradition:
Generalizing the Differences

This dimension is about being attentive to the danger of our failure to distinguish between the particular and the universal, especially to the neglect of other plural particularities each making their own claims. It is about 'transgressing' the supposed finalities of one's tradition, so as to see others beyond one's tradition not as generalized, or demonized, but as concrete others in whom the divine may be present and active. So to what extent does Newbigin's vision of Jesus Christ foster such engagement? Again, though we explore dialogical theology more explicitly in Chapter 6, we note here two issues: firstly, the way in which Newbigin's affirmation of other religious traditions is restricted, and secondly, the way in which he polarizes the gospel and Western culture so as to demonize it as the ultimate other.

The Religious Other

By way of an introduction to these themes, it is worth outlining Kenneson's appreciative interpretation of Newbigin's work.[80] He suggests that, if the trinity is

---

[78]   See Chapter 1, p. 23.

[79]   See, for example, Newbigin, *Open Secret*, p. 212; also Hunsberger, in *Bearing the Witness*, pp. 212–13, acknowledges that Newbigin's trinitarian claims are a little laboured.

[80]   Philip D. Kenneson, 'Trinitarian Missiology: Mission as Face-to-Face Encounter', in Foust et al. (eds), *A Scandalous Prophet*, pp. 76–83.

viewed, not so much as an object to be believed in (and taken for granted), but as the 'grammars' shaping how we think and talk of God, then Newbigin is *implicitly* offering a new approach. As Kenneson notes, affirming the integral worldview, there is a growing consensus about what it is to be human: that it involves being-in-relation and *perichoresis*, that is, interpenetration or mutual indwelling, the self being not only influenced by the other but that they 'dwell in' each other.[81] By way of this relational ontology, identity entails a circulation of gifts, which would happen naturally but for sin. The resultant obstruction of our giving and receiving amongst each other causes damage to our identity and relatedness, so we need the self-donating (crucified) God to effect restoration.[82] While Jesus Christ is the exemplary paradigm of such self-donation, the Spirit enables others to join the cycle of mutual giving. For Kenneson, it is because of this that Christians have more reasons, not fewer, to stay open to the otherness of the other; not merely to facilitate conversation or practise tolerance, but because this is the nature of the God who helps us humbly to receive from each other. Kenneson suggests, then, that Milbank identifies God as being able to arrange our diverse responses into a 'harmony of differences', much like we have seen Min identify the Body of Christ as a solidarity of others, or a solidarity of the different.

While Kenneson is not explicit as to whether the trinity is a doctrine or model particularly capable of handling difference constructively and peaceably, or the only source of such reconciliation, his engagement with Newbigin is illuminating. He believes Newbigin is right to question Western culture's dichotomies, between public and private, and between subject and object, but suggests Newbigin does not offer a determined picture of the intersubjective nature of reality. For Kenneson, although Newbigin rightly holds 'knowing' and 'doing' together, he fails to resolve the issue because he resorts to 'conventional metaphors', even Western models of thought, which cannot fully reflect the relational nature of 'the truth as a way'. New language is thus required, which will mean our vision of reality is constructed differently.

Young, too, commends Newbigin's grounding of mission in the Trinity.[83] She sees it as taking God seriously, rather than reducing mission to a merely human or ecclesial concern; but she identifies his trinitarianism as 'economic'. She thinks Newbigin views the debate about the immanent Trinity as too speculative or abstract, whereas she understands it in terms of 'appropriate recognition of our

---

[81]   This suggestion is derived partly from Miroslav Volf, 'The Trinity is our Social Program: The Doctrine of the Trinity and the Shape of our Social Engagement', *Modern Theology*, 14/3 (July 1998): p. 408. Kenneson, however, does not explore whether this ontology is necessarily morally preferable: for perichoresis could be harmful.

[82]   Kenneson cites John Milbank, 'Postmodern Critical Augustinianism: A Short *Summa* in Forty-Two Responses to Unasked Questions', in Graham Ward (ed.), *The Postmodern God: A Theological Reader* (Oxford, 1997), p. 271.

[83]   Frances Young, 'The Uncontainable God: Pre-Christendom Doctrine of Trinity', in Foust et al. (eds), *A Scandalous Prophet*, pp. 84–91.

creatureliness, about the quality of proper humility before the divine mystery'. While it is arguable that she undermines her own emphasis on the immanent Trinity by emphasizing how the doctrine 'emerged' only gradually, nevertheless she rightly criticizes Newbigin for effectively taking the doctrine for granted. For his trinitarianism focuses on Christ and on mission, in contrast to Young's conviction that trinitarian doctrine is concerned with God's uncontainable nature and our creatureliness. We must, then, be humble in our claims, and open to others' insights, since we cannot simply 'add up' God's 'activities' to reach three, but must recognize with 'a certain degree of agnosticism' that we do not grasp God's being. Like Kenneson, she is commending Newbigin for going so far, but sees his approach as restricting a proper degree of openness to the otherness of the other. It is the nature of his focus on Christ's finality which feeds this restriction.

The point is that Newbigin does accept the divine presence in the religious other; he emphasizes that Christians must be humble in our dealings with others, since they are charged with reminding us of our common judgment under the cross; but essentially his theology limits their validity to the extent that they serve the purpose of the gospel. As we have seen, he is careful to insist that God's election of some is not a mark of favouritism, but a call to responsibility, since there is always the warning that those who think they are 'closer' to God may actually be misunderstanding the exercise of God's grace.[84] For God wills to break open our egoism and self-righteousness by demonstrating to us how those who seem 'far off' may be the ones through whom God works to effect our own reconciliation. As it was for the Jews, reconciled in Christ through God's election of Gentiles, so it is for the Church in relation to other religious traditions: 'they' can be the agents of God's message, to the extent that they evoke in 'us' due humility before them and gratitude for God's reconciling work. We see here that Newbigin believes in the mutuality and relatedness of human beings; that there is a genuine sense of our interdependence; and that this is underpinned by his commitment to an essential unity, not between religious traditions, but in terms of a single historical narrative.

For him, the particularity of God's chosen means by which salvation is brought about, in world history, for the sake of the whole, is a united meta-narrative, attested to in the coherence of the biblical witness. The problem with this is not as such the awkwardness of supposing that all of history can be understood and transformed from one centre, but that Newbigin effectively 'generalizes' about the others, reducing them to functions of his vision of the gospel. Those parts of other traditions which claim something distinctive from the Christian claim, specifically where they purport to relate their particularity to universal truth, must be mere human religion, misguidedly 'absolutized'.[85] In contrast, the Christian claim about Christ's finality is unarguably absolute, and to the extent that 'the others' point Christians to this truth, they are signalling the gospel. Their reality

---

[84]   Newbigin, *A Faith?*, pp. 78–9; *Open Secret*, pp. 81–90.

[85]   Newbigin, *Truth to Tell*, p. 80: 'that which is good and proper at its own level is corrupted when it is absolutized.'

is thus generalized; their concreteness is belittled; and our readiness to be shaken by their concreteness is clearly limited, because Newbigin's emphasis is on their ability to confirm, not to problematize, our vision.

The Cultural Other

Newbigin's tendency to generalize about the other, with the negative consequence that 'it' is demonized and its relatedness to the gospel is distorted, is epitomized most starkly in his appraisal of Western culture. Of all 'others', it is the one which causes him most concern, as a missionary returning to it and seeing the Church's relative weakness in the midst of it; but while he might have paid more attention to the Church's mistakes,[86] he instead targets 'the culture' for most of the blame. Price, for instance, is frustrated with his excessive negativity towards the Enlightenment, accusing him of parodying its ambiguities and echoing the Church's initial resistance to modernity.[87] In particular she is concerned with Newbigin's suggestion that the Church should clarify its gospel before addressing the culture, as though the two dialogues can be arranged sequentially. She is right to discern this suggestion in Newbigin, because, even as he attempts to insist that the Church should constantly engage its many cultures, he certainly believes that the 'given' gospel is absolute over and against any cultural manifestation of it: the one precedes the other. As Hoedemaker argues, this is itself a sign of a Western trait, as though 'culture' can be objectified.[88] Specifically, to pinpoint Western culture as a culture is to misread the complexity:

> rather, it is the cradle and the reflection of a complicated global process in which so-called cultural identities are permanently created, projected, disputed, recaptured, 'cobbled together'. In this process the project of modernity is at work, but it also meets its limits in the widespread 'local' resistance against it. Perhaps one should say that it is modernity itself that has produced and keeps producing the 'clashing of cultures' and the emergence of 'new histories'.[89]

In fact, Newbigin's use of rational discourse and his construction of a clearly defined competition between the meta-narratives of Christianity and modernity are themselves utterly modernist dispositions, which overlook the symbiotic kinship and rivalry between the two ongoing processes of Christianisation and modernisation.[90]

---

[86] See Werner Ustorf, 'The Emerging Christ of Post-Christian Europe', in Foust et al. (eds), *A Scandalous Prophet*, pp. 128–32.

[87] Price, 'Churches and Postmodernity', pp. 107–14.

[88] Hoedemaker, 'Rival Conceptions of Global Christianity', pp. 13–22.

[89] Ibid., p. 18: 'cobbled together' coming from Robert J. Schreiter, *The New Catholicity: Theology between the Global and the Local* (Maryknoll, NY, 1997), p. 59.

[90] Hoedemaker, 'Rival Conceptions of Global Christianity', pp. 18–21.

Newbigin claims, for instance, 'Almost everything in the "plausibility structure" which is the habitation of our society seems to contradict this Christian hope.'[91] Peel argues that this assessment is 'unnecessarily pessimistic and apocalyptic'.[92] It is a 'simplistic' and 'polemical' account of the Enlightenment, which sees only its relativism, pluralism, individualism and narcissism, and which undermines Newbigin's own claims to be thankful for the benefits of modernity and to be receptive to ongoing learning.[93] After all, while Newbigin is right to criticize the polarizing between fact and value, and the damage done to faith and discipleship by the public/private dichotomy, he says little of modernity's responsible critiques of religion. Ustorf, for one, points to ways in which Western modernity sustains a public space for faith and religion: people's openness to some guidance, their interest in Jesus, and appreciation of the role of myths.[94]

However, Newbigin is focused on the secularization of Western society, which is a mark of what we now call 'globalization'. Taber, essentially adopting Newbigin's outlook, argues that we need not a 'modern' or 'postmodern' perspective to respond to such developments, but a 'gospel' perspective.[95] For whilst a modern approach homogenizes the world, being eager 'to overcome the destructive effects of divisions and particularisms', and a postmodern approach criticizes such an unacknowledged exercise of power, but without grappling with the reality of sin, only the gospel truly diagnoses the disease and provides the remedy – a self-sacrificing love.[96] Jeffrey retorts that there is 'no such thing as *the* gospel perspective', rather that religion can be traditionalist, revisionist, or prophetic *vis-à-vis* the world it encounters.[97] The issue is: perhaps inadvertently, Newbigin oversimplifies and polarizes the nature of the relationship between the gospel and the (Western) culture, because he is rooted in a particular experience and vision of the gospel tradition and has a particular vision of the culture to which he returns.

---

[91]   Newbigin, *Pluralist Society*, p. 232.

[92]   Peel, p. 146.

[93]   Ibid., pp. 145–7; see Newbigin, *Truth to Tell*, pp. 34–5.

[94]   Ustorf, 'The Emerging Christ', pp. 133–4.

[95]   Charles R. Taber, 'The Gospel as Authentic Meta-Narrative', in Foust et al. (eds), *A Scandalous Prophet*, pp. 182–94.

[96]   This positive appraisal of Newbigin's approach is shared by David Kettle, 'Gospel, Authority, and Globalization', in Foust et al. (eds), *A Scandalous Prophet*, pp. 201–14. He argues that there is no contest between the historically conditioned authority of Western rationality and the gracious initiative of God in Christ, which alone has the power to face and forgive the prevalence of sin, precisely because it is victorious when it *looks* as though it has failed: on the cross.

[97]   Robert M.C. Jeffrey, 'Globalization, Gospel, and Cultural Relativism', in Foust et al. (eds), *A Scandalous Prophet*, p. 196, referring to Richard H. Bliese, 'Globalization', in K. Muller and T. Sundermeler et al. (eds), *Dictionary of Mission* (Maryknoll, NY, 1997).

This problematic relation is illustrated by the contrasting criticisms of Graham and Walton, on the one hand, and Reader, on the other.[98] Graham and Walton, like Newbigin, are profound critics of the Enlightenment, but whilst they see Newbigin's critique as being focused on epistemological distortions, their concern is with its power relations. Thus they see Newbigin as being nostalgic for a time when truth was more straightforward and the authority of 'the Father' held sway, before the complications of rationalistic critiques; whereas they prefer the many voices of postmodern pluralism, since such a world is better able to resist the Many's oppression by the One. Reader, however, sees Graham and Walton opting for a grand narrative no less than Newbigin, though theirs is postmodern and his is, in Hodgson's terms, 'counter-modern'; but both grand narratives rely on a rejection of a parodied Enlightenment. Reader argues instead for the interdependence of the modern and the postmodern, since it is appropriate to be hopeful about the liberating power of a meta-narrative but only if we are also committed to constant reappraisal of each narrative and tradition.

In other words, we could say, what is required is a meta-narrative of shakenness: one which has a sense of universal applicability, concerned with shaking all people out of the unquestioned assumptions about reality, but which entails constant revision and re-engagement with each 'other'. As in Hodgson's late modernism, or critical postmodernism, the tasks of Western 'culture' are in process and the tasks of Christian faith are also ongoing: so any attempt to define one (the gospel of the Christ) over and against the other (Western culture) must attend to the kinship, rivalries and nuances of their intersubjectivity. Newbigin, by contrast, idealizes one and demonizes the other; his vision of Christ is central to this dichotomy. He is resistant to being shaken by that which he deems to be an unwelcome other; and to be shaken, or humbled, only by those others who confirm one's fundamental vision is not really to be shaken at all.

Newbigin and the Invisible Other: Impeding Liberative Solidarity

Finally, what of Newbigin's attentiveness to those who suffer sociopolitical marginalization and oppression? Is his christology sensitive to such forces? That is, does his vision of Christ enable a liberative solidarity of others, a Body energized to transform the predicament of those rendered 'the least'? We shall return to the questions of justice in Chapters 7 and 8, but we note here briefly the apparent contrast between Newbigin's theology and practice. Arguably, this is evident in many churches, where good work may be done but without particular

---

[98]   See Elaine Graham and Heather Walton, 'A Walk on the Wild Side: A Critique of *The Gospel and our Culture*', *Modern Churchman*, 33/1 (1991): pp. 2–7; John Reader, 'Theology, Culture and Post-Modernity: In Response to Graham, Walton and Newbigin', *Modern Churchman*, 34/5 (1993): pp. 58–63.

authorization by the dominant theology, or where the theology may be intentionally transformative but action does not seem to flow from it.

After all, we have seen how Newbigin sought to affirm the role of Indians in India, resisting the imperialism in which he as a white man would have been conditioned, and argued for local theologies, by which 'the others' (of relative powerlessness) would become responsible for making the gospel resonate in their communities. On returning to the UK, we must recognize his outspokenness from within a 'public theology' tradition, inspired by the likes of Barth, engaging in debates about the Welfare State and the effects of market capitalism.[99] However, as Forrester notes, Newbigin's public theology is better at the principles than the practicalities, lacking any clear guidance about application except with regards to the Church's own life.[100] For our current purposes, however, it is the critique implied by Sobrino which is most pertinent, since he suggests that liberation is impeded if rooted in an absolutized vision of Christ.[101] If we believe we know the 'absolute' of history, Sobrino claims, our interest in the 'non-absolutes', especially those who are oppressed, will tend to diminish. It is similar to my understanding of Min's insight that, while we need a claim to 'totality' in order for us to identify the damage done by powers of domination, this must be held dialectically with 'infinity', in Levinas's sense of everlasting openness to the otherness of the other; for infinity without totality is impotent, but 'totality without infinity is indeed oppressive and totalitarian'.[102] Now, of course, Newbigin's view of Christ's finality is tempered by his insistence on our common humility under the cross, reminding us of the nature of Christ's Lordship: he is not an oppressive force but a suffering and crucified servant. However, he notes that, because history 'will' turn out as Christian faith believes, 'finality becomes actual and threatening'.[103] While he means this in the sense that Christ simply demands a response, it begs further questions.

Sobrino suggests that, with regards to the Church's christologies, certain 'suspicions' are required. Firstly, he suspects that Christ can too often be reduced to a 'sublime abstraction', as though neutral in history, wielding his power to serve the interests of the *status quo*; whereas the historical Jesus was a partial figure on the side of the oppressed. Secondly, Sobrino suspects that Christ easily becomes the embodiment of 'universal reconciliation', as though not fully engaged in the conflicts of history; whereas Sobrino is clear that Jesus provoked conflict, and was killed for his pursuit of a domination-free order. In both regards, Newbigin's Christ is partial and 'threatening'; but his partiality is not clearly enough on the

---

[99]   See, for instance, Duncan B. Forrester, 'Lesslie Newbigin as Public Theologian', in Foust et al. (eds), *A Scandalous Prophet*, pp. 3–12.

[100]   Ibid., pp. 8–10.

[101]   Jon Sobrino, *Christology at the Crossroads: A Latin American View* (London, 1978), pp. xv–xxii.

[102]   Anselm Min, *The Solidarity of Others in a Divided World: A Postmodern Theology after Postmodernism* (New York and London, 2004), p. 8.

[103]   Newbigin, *Finality*, p. 87.

side of those who are poor, and whilst he identifies particular conflicts – including that of the gospel's confrontation with the West – his gospel of reconciliation does not engage so explicitly with the injustices of sociopolitical inequality. Arguably the same is true of Hick's Jesus who appears to be an embodiment of 'universal reconciliation'. In both cases, in effect, there is a weakening in the connection between matters of faith and matters of social justice. Neither Hick nor Newbigin means this to happen. However, as Sobrino's third suspicion implies, the problem is that a claim to absoluteness (whether Newbigin's absolute Christ or Hick's absolute noumenon) works against the interpenetration and intersubjectivity of personal and sociopolitical realities. For Sobrino suspects that the tendency to 'absolutize' Christ makes him the perfect corrective and correlative for the 'I' of each individual Christian; he becomes the One who alone satisfies all our needs and wants, whilst masking the perpetuation of oppressed people's needs and wants. We only arrive at the absolute through our contingent, conditioned histories, so the 'eschatological reservation' applies to all concrete mediations of God's kingdom; the work goes on, because for God the stuff of history has an absolute importance. Newbigin would respond by repeating his insistence that it is Christ, not any human interpretation of him, which is final and absolute, but Sobrino sees the emphasis on Christ's absoluteness as serving the interests of the *status quo*, because it detracts from the crucial connection between Jesus and the unfinished kingdom.

In my terms, the point is this: an absolutized Christ is a figure divorced from social relations, thus deprived of the fullness of humanity, because human beings are partly constituted socially. While Newbigin means his vision of Christ to be strong enough to undermine every power, to reverse every dishonesty by any manipulative Gang or System, and to embody God's victory-out-of-defeat, Sobrino implies that Newbigin's approach is only partially shaken – shaken by the dangers of 'other' universal pretenders, and of any Christian supposing that their own grasp is itself final, but not shaken by the concreteness of different others, their interrelatedness with one's own otherness, or the otherness of history's non-absolutes. In fact, Newbigin must realize that Jesus is more partial than he allows, in both senses. Jesus is partial, in that his interpersonal demonstration of God's new social order is incomplete, but the Body of Christ is charged with continuing the work; and Jesus is partial, in that his demonstration of God's new social order is much more explicitly biased: it is a dynamic 'from the outside in'. Such a christological affirmation is more likely to engender commitment to solidarity of others, *not least* those regarded or treated as 'the least', because it accentuates not only Jesus' connection with us in his outside-in Body but also his connection with a movement of social transformation, for the sake of those 'others' ignored by any universal pretender.

Chapter 4
An Alternative Vision: Biblically Shaken

The Myth So Far

It is evident that the christological approaches of John Hick and Lesslie Newbigin could shake each other, with regards to their different views of revelation and Western modernity, but since they are only partially attentive to the concreteness of others, their mutual shakenness is limited. Firstly, they both oversimplify, or generalize, the otherness of the Christian tradition, in the sense that Hick caricatures that which he seeks to re-express and Newbigin places a great deal of evangelical faith beyond debate; so they are only partially shaken by 'others' *within* the tradition. Secondly, they are both more indifferent to plural other traditions than they mean to be, in Hick's case by treating the differences as largely only apparent and in Newbigin's case by restricting the others' validity to the extent to which they serve the gospel; so they are only partially shaken by 'others' *beyond* the Christian tradition. Finally, the relative impotence of Hick's transformative ethic, simply advocating selflessness and tolerance, and the absoluteness of Newbigin's Christ, obscuring his connection with the unfinished *basileia* of God, impede their ability to act in solidarity with the *invisible* or marginalized others. Further shakenness is thus required.

These arguments have so far involved only brief engagement with scripture. Hick oversimplifies it, as the narration of people's religious experiences, and Newbigin streamlines its nature, as the witness to God's self-revelation. I am not about to outline an overarching theology of scripture, nor argue that there is a consistent narrative of shakenness. Rather, I seek to problematize their interpretations of biblical christology, while uncovering traces and hints of Jesus 'the Shaken One'. To begin, I note the diversity of New Testament christologies, including views through the lens of myth, before turning in particular to Wink's 'myth of the Human Being'. These themes will be developed in the light of the tradition's 'other-regard' and sense of justice. (David Horrell's Pauline scholarship identifies the theme of 'other-regard', and Glen Stassen's interpretation of Jewish traditions helps to illustrate the direction of the justice of Jesus.) I draw this chapter to a close with some specific signs of Jesus 'the Shaken One'.

Diversity in the New Testament: Constructing Christology

We noted briefly in Chapter 2 that Hick believes there was a general cultural acceptability for notions of a deified man, as though the meaning given by the Church to Jesus' divine Sonship should not be seen as particularly radical. However, the biblical scholarship of James Dunn suggests otherwise. There was something distinctive occurring, in the early Church's understanding of Jesus' personhood, which may well have been to do with Jesus' being seen as the Last Adam.[1] Nevertheless, Dunn is not convinced that ideas about the incarnation can be traced to Jesus' self-understanding; rather he sees it as 'an appropriate reflection on and elaboration of Jesus' own sense of sonship and eschatological mission'.[2] Of course, Hick seeks to exploit Dunn's identification of incarnational language as an 'elaboration', since he believes it suggests an unwarranted development.[3] However, Hick ignores Dunn's belief that the doctrine of the incarnation 'began to emerge' through the use of Wisdom imagery associated with pre-Christian Judaism which was developed by Paul, such that a pre-existent Christ could be conceived. Dunn suggests that this Wisdom-christology impacted on wider religious culture, and Johannine Christianity developed it.[4] Something more complex than Hick's account of deification was going on, which Dunn describes as follows:

> *the Christ-event defined God more clearly than anything else had ever done* ... 'Incarnation' means initially that *God's* love and power had been experienced in fullest measure in, through and as this man Jesus, that Christ has been experienced as God's self-expression, the Christ-event as the effective, re-creative power of God.[5]

The point is that, according to Dunn, the development of biblical christology is certainly a complex process, drawing on various resources and involving an interplay between religious culture or tradition and emerging religious ideas, but it cannot so easily be reduced to Hick's mythological account, by which the tradition deploys language which does not quite mean what it says. (In fact, Carruthers argues that the tradition sought to do precisely what Hick implies it could not have intended: it sought to prevent the Christian claim from being accommodated within existing worldviews, as though Jesus was merely a prophet or, conversely, a revelation of God only in human guise.[6]) For Dunn, the radicality of the early Church's imagery and metaphors, by which Yahweh's immanence was being

---

[1]   James D.G. Dunn, *Christology in the Making: An Inquiry into the Origins of the Doctrine of the Incarnation*, 2nd edn (London, 1989), pp. 22, 251–3.

[2]   Ibid., p. 254.

[3]   John Hick, *The Metaphor of God Incarnate* (London, 1993), p. 31.

[4]   Dunn, *Christology in the Making*, pp. 259–61.

[5]   Ibid., p. 262 (his italics).

[6]   Gregory H. Carruthers SJ., *The Uniqueness of Jesus Christ in the Theocentric Model of the Christian Theology of World Religions: An Elaboration and Evaluation of the Position of John Hick* (Lanham, MD, 1990), pp. 200–201. See also Michael Green, 'Preface: Scepticism in the Church', in Michael Green (ed.), *The Truth of God Incarnate* (London, 1977), p. 29.

related to Jesus personally, involve a reality and an effect more profound than the language of 'myth' can evoke.[7]

On the other hand, Theissen's biblical scholarship may suggest that Dunn's understanding of 'myth' is itself inadequate. For Theissen, we must recognize that each form of religion consists of a 'cultural sign system', and that Jesus must be understood within the 'Jewish sign language existing at the time'.[8] As he understands it, the Jewish 'myth' was largely about the coming of God's rule, by which God would be seen as the single reality determining everything else. He suggests that, in his parables and actions, Jesus 'historicized' this myth; that is, the myth of the end-time became a reality in the present, but his actions also, by their symbolic nature, were 'signs of a mythical reality which was not (yet) present'.[9] However, Jesus did not simply confirm pre-existing expectations about the end-time, but 'demilitarized it, in so far as he detached the hope for victory over the Gentiles and the subjugation of them from it. But he did not depoliticize it.' Arguably, it is this political dimension of 'myth' which is insufficiently addressed either by Dunn, on the one hand, or by Hick, on the other. After all, Theissen does suggest that Jesus was deified, but essentially by virtue of the interaction between religious sign systems and cultural/political factors.[10] For he argues, firstly, that the 'cognitive dissonance' between people's expectation of a victorious charismatic and the crushing fact of Jesus' death on a cross would need surmounting, and that Jesus' deification helps people to make sense of the dissonance. Secondly, people would need to affirm monotheism in the face of the apparent contrast between the earthly Jesus and the exalted, resurrected Jesus, and his deification fulfils this need. Thirdly, to compete with and outdo any rivals, the Lord Jesus needs to establish himself as a worthy contender.

So, unlike Hick, for whom deification seems largely to be a way of accounting for religious experiences through the creative deployment of mythological language, Theissen interweaves a political dimension: the claims of a religious tradition are also about its engagement with the powers of the world. Thus the business of doing christology is concerned not only with a religious person's or community's grasp of God's revelation (Žižek's 'impossible other'), but entails attentiveness to our varied grasps of it, as a community of diverse disciples (Žižek's 'imaginary other'), and to our relatedness with cultural and political forces (Žižek's 'symbolic Other'). Of course, Hick is aware of the connection between Jesus and his disciples – he suggests that Christians deify him because of our 'devotion and loyalty' to him[11] – but this means he identifies the relationship largely in terms of our

---

[7]   Dunn, *Christology in the Making*, pp. 262–3.

[8]   Gerd Theissen, *A Theory of Primitive Christian Religion* (London, 1999), pp. 2–6, 37.

[9]   Ibid., pp. 37–40.

[10]   Ibid., pp. 44–9.

[11]   John Hick, 'Jesus and the World Religions', in John Hick (ed.), *The Myth of God Incarnate* (London, 1977), pp. 173–4.

distortion of Jesus' reality. Theissen, however, sees the connection between Jesus and his community more positively: for he proposes that it is inherent to Jesus' transformation of traditional messianic expectations that 'a messianic collective', or the '*sym-basileia*' of disciples, should and does participate in God's promised power; that is, we are rightly engaged in the christological enterprise, not merely as viewers of Jesus' identity and action, but as participants in the vision. This is why I speak of christology in terms of people's 'vision' of Jesus Christ, because whilst a 'view' implies a relatively passive stance or glimpse of an other, a 'vision' alludes to our psychological and social contribution to what we 'see'. It is a dynamic and potentially 'shaking' experience, which entails relationality with 'others'.

By contrast, as Wainwright's summary of Newbigin's thesis suggests, Newbigin does not allow for such a creative psycho-social contribution *to the biblical witness*:

> The Christian faith offers ... the most comprehensive of clues to reality, for it proclaims that the divine Word which creates and sustains all things has been made flesh in Jesus Christ. The primary witness to this act of God, this fact ... is contained in the Scriptures; and the interpretative tradition is borne by the Church, which is part of the story that it carries on toward its conclusion.[12]

There is a recognition that the Bible is necessarily interpreted – that is, the Church must discern the meaning and implications of the witness, in each context and culture – but the Bible simply *is* the primary witness to God's acts. Whilst he acknowledges we must be open to mutual correction with one another, with regards to our partial interpretations of the biblical witness, and whilst the witness knows that the gospel was itself embodied in a culture,[13] Newbigin does not really engage with the constructive nature of the witness. The Church is simply called to play its part in acknowledging that the hermeneutical clue to the meaning of scripture will be shown to be reliable, since it is revealed to us by God. The narrative unity of the biblical witness thus supersedes all questions of its internal diversity or of its interrelatedness with cultural and political powers.

In essence, the problem with Hick and Newbigin is the extent to which they offer selective readings of scripture, without acknowledging that this is what they do.[14] It is not possible for any single interpreter to avoid selectivity, but it is wise for each of us to recognize that our engagement with biblical sign systems is inevitably more conditioned than we know, and that the Bible does indeed consist

---

[12]   Geoffrey Wainwright, *Lesslie Newbigin: A Theological Life* (New York, 2000), p. 49.

[13]   Lesslie Newbigin, *Foolishness to the Greeks: The Gospel and Western Culture* (London, 1986), p. 4.

[14]   See, for example, Stephen Davis, 'Critiques', in Stephen T. Davis (ed.), *Encountering Jesus: A Debate on Christology* (Atlanta, GA, 1988), p. 25; John B. Cobb, 'Critiques', in Davis (ed.), *Encountering Jesus*, p. 29.

of more sign systems and worldviews than we tend to realize. As illustrated by this brief discussion of the different approaches of Dunn and Theissen, christology in the New Testament is varied and is interpreted diversely. Since interpretation is thus intersubjective, it is understandable that Cobb suggests 'speculation' is always involved in our encounter with scripture, and that this is not something to fear but to affirm.[15] The difficulty, however, as Dunn notes, is that the New Testament witness has generally been read through one dominant lens, that of ontological incarnation, or through the lens of a unified creed,[16] as though all christological traces and signs can be forced into the same shape. The reality, instead, is that there is no 'latent orthodoxy waiting to be brought to light',[17] in terms of a biblical unity; arguably this problematizes both Hick's caricature and replacement of the ontological incarnation tradition and Newbigin's presumption of biblical coherence.

Theissen's approach is more fruitful; it seems more attentive to the nature of scripture, more adept at being 'honest' or open, in terms of the meaning of christology – its internal diversity, its engagement with 'other' traditions, and its political dimension. Jesus Christ should be understood as having radically 'historicized' the myth of God's end-time rule, while also being 'mythicized' in terms of his place in history, unlike in Hick's reductionist approach to myth and Newbigin's resistance to it. If christology entails constructive, ongoing engagement with scripture, how might we interpret the myth of Christ, and his Body, today? Myth, after all, is innately wary of objectification, since it is conscious that projection, speculation and imagination are inevitably involved in its interpretation, so it naturally provides for a dialectic between divine revelation and the human tasks of discernment and practice.[18] The important thing is for myth to be neither idealized, as though it is intrinsically the 'final' word on the matter, nor treated reductively as though it merely re-expresses what can be said more straightforwardly, but to be understood as relating to historical reality while fostering ongoing creativity. So we turn to the 'myth' outlined by Wink, which resonates with my approach.

---

[15]   Cobb, 'Critiques', p. 29.

[16]   Dunn, *Christology in the Making*, p. 265; James D.G. Dunn, *Unity and Diversity in the New Testament: An Inquiry into the Character of Earliest Christianity*, 2nd edn (London, 1990), p. 34.

[17]   Dunn, *Unity and Diversity*, pp. 204–5.

[18]   For more on the tradition's handling of 'myth', see for example Rudolf Bultmann, 'New Testament and Mythology', in H.W. Bartsch (ed.), *Kerygma and Myth*, vol. 1 (London, 1953); Rudolf Bultmann, 'On the Problem of Demythologizing', in Schubert Ogden (ed.), *New Testament and Mythology and Other Basic Writings* (London, 1985); Rudolf Bultmann, 'Jesus Christ and Mythology', in Roger Johnson (ed.), *Rudolf Bultmann: Interpreting Faith for the Modern Era* (London, 1987), as discussed briefly in Chapter 2.

The Myth of the Human Being: Growing in Humanity

Like many other commentators, Walter Wink observes that Jesus' preferred self-reference is 'son of (the) man', which he translates more inclusively as 'Human Being'. As a biblical scholar and peace activist, he brings a distinctive voice to the quest for humanization. He argues that Jesus' self-reference is not firstly an appropriation of Daniel's heavenly figure, but actually refers to Ezekiel's vision (in Ezekiel 1 and 2) in which God appears 'like a human' (though also with other faces, so as to resist too much anthropomorphism), and Ezekiel is addressed as 'son' of this 'Man' (*ben 'adam*).[19] God, then, is the only one who is *truly* human; we are but intimations of that humanity and must grow into it more fully, a journey trail-blazed by Jesus. While Wink values Feuerbach's critique of the human tendency to project our values on to God – a criticism we must heed if we are to avoid objectifying our claims – he nevertheless argues that projection can be truthful: that is, the reason why we see God in human terms is because God *is* truly human, yet so much more; therefore our projections teach us about who we are, or about who we are capable of becoming.[20]

Wink notes that Schweitzer believed nothing seems to teach us more about ourselves than our writing about Jesus: so each image of Jesus remains illuminating, not least because it reveals the need for ever more images. Of course, Newbigin acknowledges this need for mutual correction within the worldwide Church, since no individual image or christology contains the whole truth;[21] but there is a substantial difference between his understanding of mutual correction, which relates to the Church's partial glimpses of Christ's finality, and Wink's 'christology', which prioritizes those truths which expose the 'Domination System' and make the nurturing of our fuller humanity possible. Wink's approach is comparable with that of Fiorenza, for whom the 'anti-domination discipleship of equals' is the criterion by which to judge the world's 'kyriarchy'; that is, it is a matter of whether lordship over others is being transformed into equality.[22] As Wink explains it, '[Jesus] called people to repent of their collusion in the Domination System and sought to heal them from the various ways the system had dehumanized them.'[23] That is, as with Bonhoeffer, Wink's primary concern is not the theoretical basis for a 'christology', but its transformative purpose.

It is in this context that he speaks of 'the myth of the Human Being', as opposed to Hick's 'myth of God Incarnate', since Wink aims to affirm that, by his allusion

---

[19] Walter Wink, *The Human Being: Jesus and the Enigma of the Son of the Man* (Minneapolis, MN, 2002), pp. 25–9.

[20] Ibid., pp. 128–30.

[21] Lesslie Newbigin, *The Open Secret: Sketches for a Missionary Theology* (London, 1978), pp. 90–95, 177–9.

[22] Elisabeth Schüssler Fiorenza, *Jesus – Miriam's Child, Sophia's Prophet: Critical Issues in Feminist Christology* (London, 1995), p. 14f.

[23] Wink, *Human Being*, p. 14.

to the relation of *ben 'adam* as found in Ezekiel, Jesus understands himself as one especially addressed by the truly human God to reflect and embody such humanity in his life.[24] This is not about his becoming something we are not, but becoming what he truly is and we truly are – human.[25] Neither, as we shall explore further, is it about Jesus' being an idealized or perfected human, but one fully embodying the fragility and brokenness of human life, and being deeply integrated with 'others'. After all, as Wink demonstrates, Jesus does not accentuate his own goodness or uniqueness, but calls people to share with him in the world's brokenness, such that they/we may transform it together.[26] As Wink puts it, 'to see God as Human is to begin to become what one sees', but 'the Human Being must be corporate to further the human project, because we cannot become human by ourselves'.[27] Christology is thus not an intellectual exercise, in any sense in which one can stand 'outside' of the issues and simply claim to identify the person of Jesus in faith and history; it is instead an active process through which we are beckoned to participate in those dispositions and tasks by which we enable each other to become more fully human. It is about our mutual humanization.

Of course, this is to prioritize the human concern, resisting the normal emphasis in christology which presumes that it primarily interprets Jesus' relationship with God, either in constitutive or in expressive terms. Rather, I am suggesting that christology firstly interprets the way in which Jesus constitutes and expresses what it is to be human, then secondly that this may be explained in terms of Jesus' embodiment of God's humanity. (That the cross turns to resurrection certainly suggests God is deeply involved in this 'myth of the Human Being', not only exposing the hollowness of the 'Domination System' for its inability to contain or end God's humanity, but enabling the *basileia* – or, as Theissen expresses it, the *sym-basileia* – to continue and flourish.) In other words, if we look to Jesus primarily for what he reveals to us about being human, it implies the integral worldview in which everything interpenetrates everything: for what determines Jesus' full humanity, if not his relation to God, his relation to other human beings, and the way in which his personhood (christology) and his achievements (soteriology) are profoundly related? (That third dimension is a particular sign of the political dimension of his relationalities, since his personhood and achievements were bound up with his attentiveness to those on the margins, his movement being primarily 'from the outside in'.)

By contrast, the christologies of Hick and Newbigin partly impede this integral worldview, since they both universalize their particular visions of Jesus, instead of holding the varied visions of his particularity in tension with plurality and universality. For Hick's expressive christology, a reductionist version of Jesus,

---

[24]   Ibid., p. 7.

[25]   Ibid., p. 29.

[26]   Ibid., pp. 132–3: 'Jesus' sinlessness is not a datum of history, but a requirement of the myth of his divinity. [Instead] Jesus refuses to be idealized ….'

[27]   Ibid., pp. 31, 210.

is in effect no different from the totality of Hick's universal ethical religion (Jesus epitomizes its ethical criterion), and Newbigin's constitutive christology, a particularist vision of Christ, is intrinsically the clue to the whole (the others cannot qualify him or it, but simply remind us of the partiality of our understandings of the clue). It is preferable, instead, if we are concerned with the relationalities between identity, difference and solidarity, to attend as Wink does to 'the myth of the Human Being', with its constant engagement between Jesus and others. It is about being shaken, repeatedly.

It is a sensitivity we see in Ched Myers's scholarship, which we encounter further below, who speaks similarly of Jesus in terms of 'the Human One', and in the approaches of Hodgson, who stresses the 'social matrix' of God's being and relations, and Fiorenza, who consistently de-idealizes the individual Jesus and engages with him in his political context.[28] It is worth sketching two examples of Wink's insight, however, to expand on the historical myth.

Firstly, in Mark 2:23–8, Wink identifies such a radical trace of the Human Being that Matthew and Luke would exclude the phrase in question.[29] For, whilst they all have Jesus say, 'The Son of Man is lord of the sabbath', it is only in Mark that he says first, 'The sabbath was made for humankind, and not humankind for the sabbath'. In other words, as Wink sees it, there is a connection for Jesus between the Son of Man, or the Human Being, and humankind in general, such that the Human Being is the 'impulse' for the awakening of our mutual 'lordship' of the sabbath, especially if human welfare is in doubt. In a context of hunger, in which Jesus authorizes his disciples to pluck grain on the sabbath, it is as though he enables us to uncover our mutual humanity and allow human need to take precedence over apparently divine law. This authority over the law is, as Wink acknowledges, 'breathtaking', but it is intrinsic to the Human Being that nothing should 'obstruct the liberation of the human being'.[30] For our being human reflects God's humanity.

This involves no belittling of Jesus' authority, since he illustrates the Human Being's scandalous defiance of the law, but his authority is inseparable from that which he gives to others: the freedom to 'judge for yourselves what is right' (Luke 12:57), by virtue of that within us which is itself an image of God's humanity. Whilst we are, as was Jesus, embedded in the 'Domination System', such that the powers impede our freedom and our sensitivity to our mutual humanity, nevertheless Jesus acts as a catalyst by which we might give expression to that which is *not* 'the offspring of the Domination System'. Such is the power of the

---

[28]   Ched Myers, *Binding the Strong Man: A Political Reading of Mark's Story of Jesus* (Maryknoll, NY, 1998); Peter C. Hodgson, *Winds of the Spirit: A Constructive Christian Theology* (London, 1994), pp. 157, 258; Elisabeth Schüssler Fiorenza, *Jesus and the Politics of Interpretation* (London: Continuum, 2000).

[29]   Wink, *Human Being*, pp. 67–74.

[30]   Ibid., p. 73; he cites José Cárdenas Palleras, *A Poor Man Called Jesus: Reflections on the Gospel of Mark* (Maryknoll, NY, 1985), p. 22.

Human Being that we can share in its power, to become what we truly are. As such, we do not act as individuals, but by virtue of our human connection with a different part of the social fabric: the tradition, community and vision of the Human Being.

Secondly, Wink emphasizes that we are not only to be liberated from the powers; we are also healed in order that we too might help to heal others, in community with each other. That 'the Human Being came not to be served but to serve, and to give his life to liberate (or "ransom") many', as in Mark 10:43–5, illustrates this.[31] Wink argues that this was understood increasingly to be *about* Jesus, as the visions of his 'service' and 'ransoming' were associated in particular with atonement theologies. Similarly, any implications for 'us' were assumed to relate essentially to the Church. Thus the experience of his dying to the powers was turned into church sacraments, 'in which we repetitiously remember Jesus' dying for us without necessarily dying to the Powers ourselves'. By contrast, Jesus means us to understand ourselves as being related to the Human Being, such that we might participate, as Jesus does, in the (shaking) process of engaging with, exposing and ultimately transforming the powers.

The problem to which he is responding is not as such his disciples' dream of power, since we need power in order to effect change in the world; it is how they and we relate to power. Either we crave it, so to lord it over others; or, as we project so much power on to God, we wallow in our powerlessness, expecting to earn a reward from our powerful Master through our displays of self-negating service. Such mindsets can perpetuate unequal power relations; whereas the myth of the Human Being is all about subverting the powers of domination. Thus Jesus is not urging us to remain in bondage to, or complicit with, systems of oppression, but to know that the calling of true humanity is both to be free of such forces (that is, 'ransomed') and to work for others' freedom. We are therefore not to be humbly without ambition, but to be ambitious for a new world order, where the last are first and the first are last.

It is integral to this myth of the Human Being that the role of Jesus' death is to be seen quite differently: it is neither that Jesus' acts constitute God's very means of altering the course of reality, nor merely that Jesus' acts express what God generally intends to teach us. Rather, he embodies the myth of the Human Being to such an extent that the 'Domination System' exacts its violence on him, and its evil is thus exposed by his death, which also expresses compassion for and solidarity with its victims – those suffering poverty, exclusion, violence. Just as the Human Being came to seek and save 'the lost', and to suffer, so Jesus demonstrates the cost of becoming more human/e. There is no atoning 'transaction' as such in his death; instead his death reveals the awfulness of the System and his resurrection challenges its power. The point is that, as we discuss further in the next section, Jesus does not exclusively associate himself with the Human Being but beckons us to participate in its myth too, to believe we can also engage the powers and be

---

[31]   Wink, *Human Being*, pp. 92–7 and 98–111.

involved in each other's liberation from their grasp. Wink suggests that, if our christology is high and our anthropology is low, we will not see or realize our own potential to follow; and if our christology is low whilst we think highly of our own potential, we will arrogantly overlook our own collusion with the System. Instead, our christology and anthropology must be commensurate – whether as in the Eastern Orthodox tradition, which stresses Jesus' divinity and our correlative potential to be divinized, or as in Wink's approach, emphasizing that we, like the human Jesus, can grow into a fuller reflection of God's humanity within us.[32]

Solidarity and Other-Regard in the Body of Christ

Another piece of biblical scholarship which helps build the vision I am offering comes from David Horrell's *Solidarity and Difference: A Contemporary Reading of Paul's Ethics*. Not only does its title immediately indicate its relevance for my concerns, as it identifies 'solidarity' and 'difference' as the basis of a Pauline meta-ethic of inclusion, but its focus on Paul also usefully illustrates that my christological approach is not confined to the Gospels' narratives of Jesus' life. In fact, Horrell suggests that the concept of 'other-regard' is critical to Paul's vision of the *Body* of Christ and our ethical engagement with the world.[33] In other words, christology and ecclesiology are, again, inseparable, but neither discipline is to be seen as an exercise in intellectual objectification; the point of illuminating this theme of 'other-regard' is to help us identify its relation to everyday life, that we might practise it. These concerns thereby imply a missiology too.

Horrell suggests that corporate solidarity – the importance of 'many becoming one body' – is crucial for Paul. His rhetoric of 'brothers' (or 'sisters') operates so as to press the ethical demand, by opposing division and constructing 'a new unity through the reversal of conventional hierarchies, and the establishment of mutual and equal other-regard'.[34] Horrell acknowledges that, for Paul, there are limits to this equality and transcendence of differences, including with regards to gender politics and Paul's presentation of himself as authoritative leader. Solidarity in Christ does not necessarily equate to transformation of all social relationships. Nonetheless, 'corporate solidarity, based on a vision of incorporation into Christ, many becoming one, is a basic metanorm in Pauline ethics'.[35] As Horrell explains, 'the basis for solidarity, for the construction of community ... is found in Paul's Christology: as believers make the story of Christ their own, participating in his death and new life, so they leave behind the old world, and become members of

---

[32]   Ibid., p. 111.
[33]   David G. Horrell, *Solidarity and Difference: A Contemporary Reading of Paul's Ethics* (London, 2005), pp. 5–6, 177, 241–2, 274.
[34]   Ibid., pp. 129–30.
[35]   Ibid., p. 131.

one body, in Christ.'[36] Thus, whilst such corporate solidarity has 'impulses towards egalitarianism', and is not closed to its surrounding culture, but can even draw on the ethical norms of the culture, it is nevertheless concerned with constructing a distinctive, alternative community which gives any 'other' norms new meaning within the Christian story, by virtue of their appropriation by the Christian story.[37] In other words, Horrell alludes to the tradition's ability to sustain 'difference', both within itself, in terms of the varied brothers and sisters who are defined by their solidarity in Christ, and beyond itself, in terms of the cultures with which it is necessarily engaged.

He suggests that 'other-regard' is the second metanorm in Paul's ethics which enables Christian sisters and brothers to affirm the difference of each 'other'.[38] It is a generous and accepting ethic, since it does not seek sameness or the 'erasure of difference', but its centrality is such that all Christians are called to conform to it. For example, regarding the debate in the Corinthian Church as to whether Christians should eat food offered to idols, Horrell notes Paul's ultimate concern: 'Do not seek your own advantage, but that of others' (1 Corinthians 10:24). The point is that neither side of the ethical debate should use their morality as a weapon against the other; rather, each should seek the common good.[39] It is evident, too, that this 'other-regarding' ethic is deeply christological: for Christ's giving of himself for the (weaker) other evokes in us a readiness to sacrifice our own advantage in the interests of the other.[40] So the shape and substance of these ethics is determined by Paul's Christology, his understanding of God's saving acts in Christ, in which believers are called to participate through our 'imitating Christ's self-giving and God's gracious welcome, dying to sin and living anew in the Spirit'.[41] It is particularly in the self-giving death of Christ that Paul identifies 'the determinative paradigm of other-regard'.[42]

So, to bring Wink and Horrell together, it is because of Christ's radical regard for 'the other', not least in his dying to the powers, in solidarity especially with 'the least', 'the last', or 'the lost', that we are urged to conform to such a pattern, in solidarity with each other. It is because we cannot imitate Christ, or embody the myth of the Human Being, on our own, that we seek to build a community 'in Christ', embodying such solidarity with one another that we are thereby encouraged to expose the 'Domination System' and heal each other of its dehumanizing effects. It is important to stress, though, as with Wink's analysis of the Human Being's servanthood, that the call for 'other-regard' is not about 'abasement per se, but redistribution with a view to the establishment of equality', or as Horrell also

---

[36]　Ibid., p. 132.

[37]　Ibid., pp. 274–5.

[38]　Ibid.

[39]　Ibid., pp. 176–7, 180–81.

[40]　Ibid., p. 181.

[41]　Ibid., p. 278.

[42]　Ibid., p. 279.

puts it: 'self-sacrifice is commendable *in situations where human relations are distorted*, and that the aim of such action is to restore or create a form of equitable solidarity within which such self-sacrifice will no longer be required'.[43]

Of course, there is a christological distinction between Horrell's analysis of these concerns in Paul's theology and Wink's analysis of similar ethics in the Gospels. Although Paul believes we can participate in Christ's acts, suggesting Christ is indeed relational, his focus is nevertheless the relation between God and Christ, whereas Wink argues that Jesus not only embodies the myth of *the Human Being* but believes other humans can embody it too.[44] (The cross is also more pivotal for Paul than Wink means it to be.) On the basis of Horrell's analysis, however, it is certainly arguable that Paul's theology contains more traces of Jesus 'the Shaken One' than we may normally see. After all, he indicates that God's acts of solidarity and other-regard 'in Christ' call for our solidarity and other-regard 'in Christ', and that such solidarity and other-regard are not only about the church's internal life but our interaction with others in the world. He sees other-regard as 'primarily a community-focused virtue, practised in relation to "one another", that is, towards one's (weaker) siblings, other members of the Christian movement',[45] but because Paul exhorts the movement to be concerned about the reaction of outsiders and to do good to all, Horrell suggests this other-regard is broader.[46] While there is a sense in which Paul idealizes the ecclesial community, over-emphasizing its moral standing in contrast to the world, he does not argue for isolationism, rather for positive interaction with others, and urges Christians to do good to all.[47] For example, Paul's first letter to the Thessalonians (5:15) exhorts, 'repay no one evil for evil, but always strive to do good to one another and to all', and Horrell identifies 'to one another and to all' as a recurring moral responsibility. Interestingly, Paul believes such goodness will indeed be seen by others as goodness, implying an underlying if not universal connection between insiders and outsiders; so there is an ongoing and creative tension between the community's identity and those who are different, or between an ecclesial solidarity of the different (the distinctive but varied 'insiders') and an other-regard or concern for those 'outside'. It is as though Paul's Christ, perhaps not explicitly shaken by otherness but at least attentive to the needs of 'others', effectively shakes us to the extent that, even in our building a distinctive community, we remain sensitive to the other.

---

[43]   Ibid., pp. 243, 245 (his italics).

[44]   Wink, *Human Being*, pp. 257–60.

[45]   Horrell, *Solidarity and Difference*, p. 245.

[46]   Ibid., pp. 257–69. Regarding concern for the reaction of outsiders, see, for example: 1 Thessalonians 4:11–12 ('aspire to live quietly ... so that you may behave properly towards outsiders'), 1 Corinthians 10:32 ('Give no offence to Jews or to Greeks ...').

[47]   Ibid., pp. 276–7.

Justice in the Jewish Tradition: Jesus and Anti-Domination

Stassen's observations about biblical justice are relevant here. After all, both Wink's concern for our mutual liberation and healing and Horrell's emphasis on other-regard resonate at least implicitly with the quest for justice.[48] Stassen, writing in the same activist tradition as Wink, identifies Jesus' attack on the Temple system as critical to his mission. (This is confirmed by others.[49]) He argues that Jesus was attacking the cover-up of four kinds of injustice: the exclusion of outcasts, the deprivation of the powerless, the domination by the political/priestly/economic powers, and the violence of bloodshed. It constitutes an attack on idolatry, unfaithfulness to God's ways, too. Stassen also gives us a useful definition of justice, in Hebrew terms, out of which Jesus operated as a distinctly prophetic Jewish figure: it is that kind of justice – God's justice, as distinct from human justice – which 'delivers the powerless from their oppression and bondage and into covenant community … in the way that YHWH hears the cries of the weak and acts to deliver them and bring them into covenant community'.[50]

Consequently, Stassen identifies a four-fold justice practised by Jesus: non-violence; confronting the wealthy; confronting those who dominate others; and including the outcast.[51] It is in the jubilee tradition, which declares that injustice is temporary (as debts are to be cancelled periodically) and affirms the dignity of all (not of creditors over and against debtors). Fiorenza, too, suggests Jesus reinvigorates the prophetic jubilee traditions within Judaism, both to emphasize that he not only shaped a tradition but was himself shaped *by* a tradition and to clarify that his religious movement did not replace Judaism but was emancipatory Judaism of the prophetic kind.[52] It is no surprise, then, that Stassen sees Jewish Michael Walzer's theory of justice as correlating closely with the Jewish Jesus' approach.[53]

---

[48] Glen Stassen, 'The Kind of Justice Jesus Cares About', in Ray Gingerich and Ted Grimsrud (eds), *Transforming the Powers: Peace, Justice and the Domination System* (Minneapolis, MN, 2006), pp. 161–75.

[49] For example: N.T. Wright, *Jesus and the Victory of God* (Minneapolis, MN, 1996), pp. 61, 335, and E.P. Sanders, *Jesus and Judaism* (Philadelphia, PA, 1985), chapter 1.

[50] This is also a citation from Glen Stassen, *Just Peacemaking: Transforming Initiatives for Justice and Peace* (Louisville, KY, 1992), p. 71.

[51] Stassen argues that John Howard Yoder, in *The Politics of Jesus* (Grand Rapids, MI, 1994) and *Body Politics: Five Practices of the Christian Community before the Watching World* (Scottdale, PA, 1997), confirms these dimensions, respectively: non-violence, jubilee, servanthood authority and the alternative community/ the fullness of Christ.

[52] See Fiorenza, *Jesus – Miriam's Child*, pp. 4, 28–31, 50–57, 88–96, and *Jesus and the Politics of Interpretation*, p. 21. She problematizes the mainstream/malestream presumption that christology is all about Jesus, by urging us to rediscover the community of 'others' around him, whether explicitly present or apparently absent.

[53] Stassen cites Michael Walzer, *Spheres of Justice: A Defense of Pluralism and Equality* (Cambridge, MA, 1984).

(This illustrates that a theory of justice cannot be founded on an abstract universality, as supposed by Enlightenment rationality, but must be rooted in a particular tradition: which is why Hick's framework has its own Kantian particularity, universalizing a particular reduction of Jesus' personhood and ethics.)

Pertinently, Stassen identifies the theme of 'anti-domination' as central for Walzer, a political theorist and critic of Western imperialism, so his justice 'builds barriers against domination', as Stassen and I argue Jesus does. To elaborate on this correlation, Stassen explains how the three 'rights' which Walzer affirms do not arise from Enlightenment commitments but from the particular tradition of Judaism. It is relevant, too, that Walzer's model is also dialogical, not reducing traditions to a 'thin' lowest common denominator, arguably unlike Hick, but engaging 'thick' traditions in deep conversation so as to challenge and enrich each other. (This form of postmodern turn, more 'critical postmodern' than 'counter-modern', resists the modern construction of universal rationality, but nevertheless avoids wallowing in an insular rediscovery of the particular, as it insists on the need for open and critical engagement with plurality.[54]) The three rights are thus: 1) the right to community, akin to Jesus' commitment to inclusiveness and restoration; 2) the right to liberty (from domination), akin to Jesus' opposition to domination and Paul's 'rule' that everyone has gifts to bring and a part to play in participative community; and 3) the right to life, including a commitment to 'violence reduction' (if not total non-violence) and to develop people's 'life-calling', correlating with Jesus' emphasis on justice for the poor.

In other words, as in Wink, but unlike in Newbigin, it is not that Jesus wholly determines the content of justice, though he certainly gives it a distinctive shape. That his role is genuinely distinctive means, unlike with Hick, that he does not simply reflect a more general and universal justice, but he is not wholly responsible for bringing to fruition the new humanity or new world. (As Wink notes, Jesus is hardly 'modest', since he understands himself as being pivotal to 'ushering the Reign of God into the world', but the Human Being is a 'catalyst for personal and social transformation', and is bigger than the individual Jesus.[55]) So we can speak of Jesus' embodying 'the myth of the Human Being', but not with finality, since the *basileia* vision remains unfinished and 'others' are actively involved. He comes from and reinvigorates a particular tradition of justice; he does this in community with others, being shaped by others, and in solidarity with those othered or marginalized by dominant forms of community. He awakens in us a related concern for each other's mutual liberation and healing – or our mutual humanization. The embodiment of the myth of the Human Being (or in Fiorenza's terms, the embodiment of Divine Wisdom) is thus more than a matter of an

---

[54]   Stassen, 'The Kind of Justice', p. 174, and Glen Stassen, 'Michael Walzer's Situated Justice', *Journal of Religious Ethics* (Autumn 1994): pp. 375–99, where he argues that Walzer's model is not merely grounded in particular narratives but is concertedly 'transcultural'.

[55]   Wink, *Human Being*, p. 22.

idealized, individual Jesus; it is a social reality, defined by the other-regard of its particular Judaeo-Christian heritage and practice, but with a vision of universal scope – to shake us into ever greater solidarity, not simply 'with' others, but as a solidarity 'of' others.

Signs of the Shaken One: Being Human with Each Other

Wink does not give us a systematic picture of Jesus as the Shaken One; that is not his language or goal. Rather, his achievement is to establish, biblically, the relationality of Jesus by way of his focus on Jesus' embodiment of the myth of the Human Being. We should note that this implies a more sophisticated view of myth, or metaphor, than Hick utilizes, regarding this vision of Jesus. For Wink allows for both the 'is' and the 'is not', the truth and the untruth, some historicity and an appropriate degree of projection, in our coming to be that which we see. That is, the language of Jesus' embodiment of 'the myth of the Human Being' both relates to a historical reality, by which people and relationships are changed, and allows for an element of untruth, recognizing that the embodiment and transformation was not final; the challenges and tasks continue. Therefore, although Wink's vision is not explicitly of the Shaken One, it is an appropriate elaboration or extrapolation of his work to suggest that his vision of Jesus embodies such humanity in and through relation with various kinds of 'other'; but it is my framework, building upon the insights of Hodgson, Shanks and Žižek, which makes this relationality more explicit. As I suggested in Chapter 1, Jesus demonstrates such shakenness in his attentiveness to the otherness of the other, and he effects or enables our shakenness, prompting us to engage deeply with others' otherness as well, in pursuit of an ever greater solidarity of others.

Still drawing on some biblical examples, I will expand briefly now on Wink's myth with regards to the three kinds of 'other' – the other within the tradition, the other in plural other traditions and beyond the particular, and the invisible other, seeking liberation. These are concerned with the respective issues of identity, difference and solidarity. This is therefore a specific reading of Jesus, which aims to identify further biblical traces of his shakenness.

Jesus and the Other Within

Although the theological approach of James Alison comes from a different perspective, which draws specifically on René Girard's work, his exposition of the story in John 9 of Jesus and the man born blind illustrates Jesus' attentiveness to 'the other within'.[56] It is as though Jesus is debating with other teachers the very identity of his tradition. For the man's blindness prevents him from participating

---

[56] James Alison, *The Joy of Being Wrong: Original Sin through Easter Eyes* (New York, 1998), pp. 119–25. I suspect it would be worthwhile to bring my approach into more

fully in the cultic life of Israel; he is an 'other' whose place within the community is defined by his disability – in its physical and spiritual terms. Jesus, however, heals him and so enables him to participate in the community. He does this using clay (*adamah*) and spittle, as though to fulfil the original creation of humankind. The man is sent to a pool outside of the city, which alludes to the cross outside the city, and to the Church's use of baptism as the means of entry into its life, as though this act is a sign of and participation in Jesus' life, death and resurrection. Still having not 'seen' Jesus, since his sight was not restored until he bathed, the man grows in his consciousness of Jesus' identity, but at the point of his realization the Pharisees drive him out, having become increasingly agitated through their interrogation of these events. On finding the man again, Jesus declares, 'I came into this world for judgment, so that those who do not see may see, and those who do see may become blind' (John 9:39).

As Alison suggests, this story illuminates Jesus' recasting of the tradition. Firstly, judgment is subverted from within, as Jesus the crucified one – one expelled in the extreme – claims the authority to judge those who think they 'see'; so the man born blind, who is also expelled because of Jesus' actions, shares in his judgment. The judges become the judged; the judged become the judges. Secondly, perceptions of sin are transformed: where once it was identified with the defect in the blind man, so as to justify his exclusion, Jesus redefines it as that which uses any so-called defect as the basis for another's exclusion. Sin is the 'mechanism of expulsion', including the Pharisees' violent driving out of the man born blind. It 'is not what excludes in the person of the excluded one, but the dynamic act of excluding in the person of the excluders'. Again, this revolution is related to Jesus' life, death and resurrection, since it is his expulsion which reveals to us that the System is blind to its sin. For Alison, there are also signals of the original, deep-seated blindness and violence within humanity, which Jesus is addressing through his acts of recreation and healing. It is his death and resurrection which enable us to 'see' what is happening: it is the victim of the System, not its guardian, who has the right to discern or judge and forgive or heal.

These things may be expressed more explicitly in the terms of Wink's myth, or my reading of it. There is a complex of idolatrous values which constitute the 'Domination System'; even religious traditions are partly powers of domination, to the extent that they 'blind' us to our objectification of each other, justifying our idealization of certain particulars and our demonization and exclusion of others. Jesus, however, by virtue of his embodiment of the myth of the Human Being, reconfigures his particular tradition, so as to draw out the prophetic emancipatory stream, identifying the victim of the System as the measure of judgment. Thus, those 'others' within the tradition whose status is deemed questionable, and who are effectively pushed to the margins, are 'seen' through the lens of Jesus and his *basileia* vision as active participants in the tradition. While Alison is like Newbigin

---

systematic dialogue with Alison's innovative theology, but it is not the agenda of this book to engage in that demanding enterprise.

to the extent that they both 'see' the cross-turned-resurrection as the revelatory event through which our vision of things undergoes a revolution, nevertheless Alison's reconfiguration of the tradition more explicitly blends the personal and the theopolitical, just as Wink allows us to see Jesus' tradition in terms of his critique and transformation of *religious* 'powers of domination'. Essentially, the tradition is a living tradition, one in which the relation between the apparent centre (the dominant) and the margins (the others) remains subject to ongoing revolution, as the other within is named and valued. The tradition's 'shadow side' must be constantly unearthed, so not to disown the violence it does to others within.

Although John's Gospel points more clearly to how Jesus shakes those whom he encounters, and the tradition itself, than to his own *being shaken*, I believe his shaking of others is related to his own being shaken. After all, in each critical engagement with Jewish 'others' (both the dominant and the marginalized), Jesus is shaken in the sense that human differences and social relations confront him and prompt him to express and embody increasingly the breadth and depth of 'the myth of the Human Being' and the *basileia* vision. For some observers, it may seem that it was all within him from the beginning, and that each encounter simply leads him to reveal it more fully, but that would stretch his relation with others to breaking-point, idealizing him and viewing others only as recipients of his truth. Instead, I am arguing that there is interdependence between Jesus and others – the prophetic tradition shapes him, for instance – so those whom he encounters also open him to a different aspect of (the myth of) Being Human, and it is embodied in those social interactions. Thus the tradition is reconfigured not by Jesus' acting alone, but by way of a shaking experience between him and others. His otherness is clear, since he confronts the dominant grip on the tradition's identity, but his rootedness in the wider tradition is also clear, in solidarity with those who preceded him and who continue to shape him. He is the heir of the prophetic tradition, identifying with its critique of the religio-social System, so acts as the basis for a new solidarity of others, 'from the outside in'. Since the Church sees itself as his heir, being the Body of Christ, it must be self-critical and committed to rediscovering others within its community.

Jesus and the Other Beyond

It is clear, though, that Jesus is not only engaging with Jewish others, whether dominant or marginalized, but with Gentiles too. The political reading of Mark's Gospel offered by Ched Myers draws insightful attention to the challenge of racial reconciliation. In particular, the metaphorical actions of the 'perilous crossings' across the Galilean sea illustrate Jesus' role in this regard.[57] For Jesus exhorts his disciples, 'Let us go across to the other side' (Mark 4:35), as though he is deeply sensitive to the ingrained nature of the divisions between Jew and Gentile and feels compelled to address them. One side of the lake was Jewish, the other Gentile, so

---

[57] Myers, pp. 194–7.

it is no wonder that such exhortation might lead to a 'storm'. To make the passage towards integration, the disciples need to be challenged but also encouraged. They need help to see that reality need not be so dangerously divided; even 'peace' can be found in their courageous willingness to make the crossing between 'us' and 'them'. As Wink suggests, Jesus' frustration with them, which is expressed in his question, 'Have you still no faith?', might not be about their lack of faith *in him*, but their lack of faith *in themselves*.[58] It is a sign that these fishermen, people used to the lake and its storms, have instead learned to project all their ideals, hopes and strengths on to Jesus, whereas he locates such strengths in the social relationships between one and another, between him and them and us. The powers have trained us to believe that we lack power, or to obey those whose power is more overt, whereas Jesus retrains us in the art of engagement, to utilize our power both to confront and transgress our own finalities, barriers or fears and to reach out in hope towards 'the other'.

That such engagement illustrates Jesus' own shakenness, not only his ability to shake others, is demonstrated by the story of his encounter with the Syro-Phoenician woman (Mark 7:24–30). As Myers indicates, this is an encounter between Jesus, one of the Jewish 'us', and a Gentile woman, one of 'them', which initially dramatizes the ethnic, cultural and sociopolitical tension between Jews and others.[59] She is transgressing the rules of engagement, by approaching him and even driving the encounter, whereas he is living within the norms of experience, by apparently attempting to close down the conversation. That she should not only believe in his power but argue for its exercise for her daughter's sake, and that he should concede to her argument, is a sign of his being both shamed and shaken by her! A foreign woman persuades a Jewish prophet to use his power for this other's advantage, and he allows himself to be persuaded, embodying the equalizing power of the gospel: for he becomes 'least', being shamed by this other beyond, 'so too Judaism will have to suffer the indignity of redefining its group boundaries (collective honour) in order to realize that gentiles are now welcomed as equals'. Jesus may instruct his disciples to 'go across to the other side', but it is this unnamed woman who brings home to Jesus the implications of such a crossing. He is shaken by her argument and changes accordingly. Together, they embody the myth of the Human Being more fully, and God's *basileia* comes closer.

Jesus and the Invisible Other

Of course, the Syro-Phoenician daughter is also, in a sense, an 'invisible other', a person not seen by the Jewish tradition, officially, nor even quite 'present' in the encounter between Jesus and her mother. Like many characters in Jesus' embodiment of the myth of the Human Being, she is unnamed, unseen and only mentioned briefly. As such, this observation is not a criticism; it is of the nature of

---

[58] Wink, *Human Being*, p. 135.
[59] Myers, pp. 203–5.

our social relations that we do not name, see or personally encounter every person with whom we are somehow connected. Nevertheless, change occurs; there is a transformation when the Human Being impacts upon and is embodied by us. Thus, as we see time and again in the Gospel narrative, Jesus' 'presence' and sensitivity to the social transformation of God's humanity brings to light those who appear to be 'absent' or invisible.

There is the woman who has bled for many years, who is invisible within the crowd, but who draws out power from Jesus (Mark 5:24–34). Her condition defines her as unclean, and the disciples discourage him from identifying her, but Jesus stops to bring her to light, to make her an example not of dirtiness but of faithfulness. As Myers notes also, this woman interrupts and takes priority over Jesus' mission to heal the daughter of Jairus, a man of social and religious standing.[60] Whereas others would no doubt continue to see her as unworthy of such an interruption, Jesus instead deems *her* the 'daughter'; from 'the bottom of the honour scale' she is restored not only physically but socially and in the sight of the crowd. The invisible other is seen and valued. The fact that it cost Jesus some power suggests he was shaken by it: her intrusion into the narrative of Jairus' daughter represents the shaking of Jesus, which is a cause for celebration. For, together, he and she embody the myth of the Human Being more fully, and God's *basileia* comes closer. He is prompted, by her, to express more publicly the social and political nature of the Human Being's solidarity; to the extent that he is even socially shamed by dancing to her tune, showing that this is a solidarity *of* others, of Jesus' and this woman's mutual transformation. The 'Domination System' is shaken, too, since this healing encounter embodies a new reality: the vision of God's *basileia* where the last become the first and the first become the last.

Similarly, the Gerasene demoniac (5:1–21)[61] is encountered when Jesus and his community dare to cross to 'the other side'; he is an invisible other consciously restricted to this 'outside' location amongst the tombs. He is so othered, sociopolitically, that he can no longer be restrained by his chains; for he is Legion, the name for a division of Roman soldiers. In fact, as Myers demonstrates, the narrative is littered with military imagery – the term for the 'herd' of pigs often referred to military recruits; Jesus' dismissal of the pigs is a military dismissal, and the pigs' charge suggests troops rushing into battle. After all, Gerasa was infamous for a brutal Roman suppression of the Jewish Revolt, which Mark knew his readers would recognize. Is the demon therefore a representation of Roman military power, and is the predicament of this man a painful sign of the violent consequences of military occupation? For Myers, Jesus' act of exorcism represents political repudiation of such violence; the 'other' figure of this man, objectified and excluded, is healed of his social dislocation and even entrusted with a task, to tell others the good news that liberation has come. Thus, in confrontation with the powers, including the people's fearful refusal to engage them personally,

[60] Ibid., pp. 200–203.
[61] Ibid., pp. 190–94.

Jesus and this man together embody the myth of the Human Being more fully, and God's *basileia* comes closer. The political implications of the Shaken One become clearer.

Conclusion

We have been identifying traces of Jesus 'the Shaken One' in the biblical witness. Our discussion of the scholarship of Dunn and Theissen illustrates the diversity of christological imagery in the New Testament, which encourages resistance to the dominant tendency to read the gospel primarily through the lens of ontological incarnation. The sheer fact of development and difference within the Church's early witness problematizes not only Newbigin's implicit vision of a united narrative but also Hick's particular attempt to re-read the tradition mythologically. The problem is that Newbigin's emphasis on biblical unity and Hick's concern to parody that which he seeks to revise cause them both to overlook 'other' visions. Their views of Jesus are too partial, not engaging with his shakenness, whether with regards to Jewish others, Gentile others, or those othered sociopolitically. As Theissen suggests, and Wink develops, 'myth' is more complex than Hick's understanding: for there is both a sense of Jesus' historicization of the myth of God's future reign and a sense of Jesus' history being appropriately mythicized. In Wink's terms, the point is that some projection on to Jesus is inevitable and reasonable, because 'the myth of the Human Being' is about becoming what we see: Jesus becomes what he sees in God's humanity, and sees and liberates in us the power to become what we see in him and each other.

As the interpreters of the biblical witness employed here indicate clearly, christology is not about an isolated Jesus, but a community of interpretation and embodiment. The particular tradition, as attested to in scripture, can be seen in terms of Jesus' dependency on the prophetic heritage, which shapes his openness to the other within (transformed from judged to judge), the other beyond (those 'on the other side' with whom peace must be made) and the invisible other (victims of violence and exclusion). Such sensitivities are signs of his emancipatory Jewishness and of his embodiment of 'the myth of the Human Being', with others, religiously, socially and politically. Also, these sensitivities suggest Jesus himself undergoes shakenness: each encounter prompts further embodiment of the Human Being, mutually, as he becomes more human in and through relations with others, so acts as the catalyst for our building an ever greater solidarity of others. The individual Jesus is thus not idealized, since he is part of the matrix of other-regard and solidarity, being open to and shaped by others, engaging critically with the powers of domination so as to liberate others, and enabling his co-workers to continue the work.

These traces of the Shaken One are the basis for further engagement with the three issues, taken in turns over the next three chapters. Firstly, in what ways does the Shaken One shape our vision of the particular tradition's identity and otherness? Secondly, in what ways does the Shaken One shape our understanding of and dialogue with the otherness of different traditions? Thirdly, in what ways does the Shaken One shape our solidarity, our commitment to the mutual liberation of each other?

Chapter 5

The Shaken One and the Other Within

The Shaken One and the Particular Tradition

This chapter is concerned with the nature and identity of the Christian tradition, the distinctiveness and otherness of its particularity. In what ways does a vision of Jesus in terms of 'the Shaken One' properly resist his objectification and shape his corporate Body? For I am arguing it is appropriate to problematize the dichotomy between 'Jesus' as object and 'I' as subject or interpreter, since such a dichotomy underpins our idealization of him, denying his 'shadow side', or indeed our tradition's shadow side. The point is that, by supposing there is the definitive, or final, Jesus, in absolute contrast to our partial glimpses of him, we are divorcing him from his social relationalities and thus dehumanizing him. Any such notion of an objectified Jesus, in history, in our knowledge or in our practice, will tend towards sectarianism, even imperialism, being disinclined to attend to the otherness within the tradition.

By contrast, following Shanks's concept of Third-Person theology with its 'flair for tradition', as epitomized by the Holy Spirit's exposure of that which we dishonestly 'disown', a vision of 'the Shaken One' enables us *both* to affirm the distinctiveness or otherness *of* the tradition – that is, its untranslatable otherness – *and* to attend to its intersubjective diversity, the otherness within itself. It is possible, in other words, to display 'sanctity' to the Christian tradition, seeing it as a meta-narrative which makes scandalously universal claims, even as we recognize that it instinctively problematizes its own sectarianism. It is of the very essence of the Christian tradition that it is self-critical, raising questions about the exactness of the relation between its particulars and its universal scope – in other words, we ought to be wary of correlating *this* tradition with *the* meaning of everything. The Jewish Jesus was shaped in a particular context, with a prophetic sensibility to the particular tradition's concern for universal human well-being, and the Christian tradition interprets his vision and practice through a varied array of culturally-sensitive lenses. Since I see his 'other-regard' as being integral to this complex of lenses and practices, it is right that we should attend to others within the tradition who see his personhood and meaning in different ways.

Having identified traces of such shakenness in the biblical witness, we therefore turn to these further areas regarding the Christian tradition: our understanding of history, our claims to knowledge, our reflective practice, and the meaning of the Trinity. In each quest we shall identify the presence of the Shaken One.

The Shaken One and Christian History: A Mediating Myth

The fundamental problem for Hick and Newbigin is that, whilst they both speak to contemporary questions of culture and religious plurality, there is a sense in which they assume such relevance automatically transcends their formative contexts. They are, after all, both rooted in modernist discourse and dichotomies, polarizing reality and its appearance and oversimplifying the similarity or contrast between the gospel and Western modernity. That is, whilst Hick allows Kantian modernism to obscure the distinctiveness of the gospel, Newbigin sees the gospel and modernism in stark opposition. They would both be better to see the ongoing kinship and rivalry between such meta-narratives, rooted in the gospel's vision of the worth and relationality of every individual.

Fuelling such contrasts, neither Hick nor Newbigin properly attends to the otherness within the tradition, or to the danger of sectarianism, because of their implicit impatience with historical truth. Hick's vision of the historical Jesus is reductionist, because ultimately it is not his concern to engage deeply in the historical debates; he instead is driven by an epistemology which prioritizes personal experience of the religiously ambiguous universe. Newbigin, too, is not really concerned with historical debate, because he is committed to a vision of the historical Jesus which has essentially been revealed, as witnessed to in scripture. Both thus prioritize their personal experiences and preserve them from the rigours of historical questing as such.

Regarding Newbigin, there is thus a fundamental paradox, or dual discourse. Whilst he purports to value the historicity of the gospel's key events, his revelational positivism actually means that his faith (or faith experience) determines what should be deemed historical. That is, particular details are put beyond question. In fact, he takes for granted from the 'inside' the unity of the biblical narrative and its congruence with the revelation of God's presence in history, the particular elected history revealing to us the clues by which the whole of history is to be understood and measured. This is possible because, although we do not know the whole of history, so we must continue to be open to the insights of secular historians and the experiences of people of other faith traditions, we nevertheless can be confident that confessing Jesus as Lord *will* be shown at the consummation of history to be *the* true commitment. Necessarily, arguments from revelation cannot be tested by human rationality, but the real problem here is that, while Newbigin claims to value historical events, it is not apparent that he takes historical inquiry seriously.

As Shanks suggests, it can be problematic to take certain historical particulars for granted, because Christian claims were developed under persecution, or the threat or fear of it, so were potentially distorted by the community's human urge for survival rather than demonstrating 'truth-as-Honesty' as such.[1] The point is that the experience of being shaken (by the gospel) is likely to be moulded by the fear

---

[1]   Andrew Shanks, *Faith in Honesty: The Essential Nature of Theology* (Aldershot, 2005), p. 3.

of death. Rather than enabling disciples to participate in the risk of openness, such fear might ideologically urge individuals and communities towards the premature closure of 'truth-as-correctness'. That is, the prospect of persecution makes Christians define themselves over and against the other, emphasizing the boundaries and enforcing orthodoxies so as to maintain the (righteous) distinctiveness of the tradition. However, the distinctiveness maintained may not be the gospel's spirit of shakenness, but its management or diminution. For Shanks, the initial Jesus-movement was 'a radical contrast society ... strictly for pure Honesty's sake, but without the strategic defences', whereas the post-Jesus Church hastily developed the strategies to 'camouflage' the scandalous risk and hospitality of the gospel by instead conforming to society's codes; and in such terms, its martyrs died more in thrall to 'sacred ideology' (that which was prematurely determined as 'the truth') than to Honesty as such.[2] Care should therefore be taken when seeking to find security in the historical claims of the early Church and its fiduciary framework, since things may not be as they seem.

Hick, of course, professes to know that things may not be as they seem, but he too shows relatively little interest in historical inquiry, despite being an empiricist. For him, personal experience – demonstrating the Kantian turn to the subject – trumps the value of corporate, historical tradition; or in other words, *his* faith-experience is as determinative of his understanding of history as Newbigin's faith-experience is as determinative of *his* understanding of history. For Hick, the key facts are therefore people's experiences of them, not the events in themselves. For the historical Jesus is revealed to show how we too may 'incarnate' the divine presence and purposes without making exclusive claims to religious truth.[3] While Newbigin oversimplifies the tradition, according to his limited vision of its central 'historical' verities (which, for Peel, are defined by the 'Augustinian-Calvinist-Barthian wing of Reformed theology'[4]), Hick oversimplifies and parodies the tradition, so to knock down some of its unacceptable claims. As we shall note again in the next section, Hick seeks to establish that the tradition claims to mean 'this' but not 'that', as though truth and its interpretation can be fairly neatly distinguished, whereas his own argument could be better served by attending to and respecting the genuine plurality of historical claims.

Their suppression of historical debate is evident particularly in their failure to attend to biblical plurality. Newbigin focuses on the narrative unity, at the cost of its complexity, and Hick focuses on those texts which problematize deification,

---

2   Ibid., pp. 154–6. (See also Andrew Shanks, *God and Modernity: A New and Better Way to Do Theology* (London, 2000), pp. 110–11.)

3   See Stephen Davis, 'Critiques', in Stephen T. Davis (ed.), *Encountering Jesus: A Debate on Christology* (Atlanta, GA, 1988), p. 23.

4   See David R. Peel, 'The Theological Legacy of Lesslie Newbigin', in Anna M. Robbins (ed.), *Ecumenical and Eclectic: The Unity of the Church in the Contemporary World – Essays in Honour of Alan P.F. Sell* (Milton Keynes, 2007), p. 146.

as though to prove metaphorical incarnation, to the neglect of other elements.[5] They overlook the interplay between what Theissen identifies as the mythicization of history and the historicization of myth. In Wink's terms, 'history' is itself our modern 'myth', citing a conversation with Hal Childs who sees 'the myth of history' as constituting 'a significant dimension of our ontology today'; so the point of historical research is to become 'more conscious' of this myth.[6] For Wink, historical research is thus about the past and the present being in constant self-critical dialogue, resisting the oxymoronic 'objective view' (all 'views' being subjective) but without falling into 'pure subjectivity'.[7] Similarly, Crossan asserts that all we have are historical 'reconstructions' of Jesus, not 'the' historical Jesus, but that they are sufficient.[8] As Wink suggests, there is a degree of appropriateness in our projecting of our ideals on to our reconstructed images of Jesus, or God, as they act like mirrors in which we see ourselves and grow into our vision.[9] This is preferable to any sharp identification of Jesus as a separated individual, which would suppress the relational truth that he not only shaped a community but was (and is) himself shaped by community/ies, as Fiorenza argues.[10] This also lies behind Pattison's concern with uncovering the 'shadow side' of Jesus, which includes his violent metaphors and dualistic vision, so as to redress the widespread one-sidedness of the idealized Saviour and reaffirm how Jesus' human-roundedness gives insight into the shadow side incarnate in the *Body* of Christ.[11]

Of course, my understanding of history will also be shaped, in part, by my faith and experience, but the point is that the Shaken One prompts us not to oversimplify the historicity of Jesus, as though he is 'this' but not 'that', or as though 'this' Christian tradition but not 'that' one captures his personality. Rather, if we believe he is fully human, it is vital that we attend to the socially constituted nature of his humanity, then and now, by resisting any temptation to close down the conversation about his historical identity. Instead we must engage with the range of historical insights, not so as to accept them all equally, but recognizing that revelation is mediated culturally and intersubjectively. For historical inquiry is rightly never-ending.

---

[5]   See Davis, 'Critiques', p. 25.

[6]   Walter Wink, *The Human Being: Jesus and the Enigma of the Son of the Man* (Minneapolis, MN, 2002), pp. 12–13.

[7]   Ibid., pp. 7–8.

[8]   John Dominic Crossan, 'Jesus and the Kingdom: Itinerants and Householders in Earliest Christianity', in Marcus Borg (ed.), *Jesus at 2000* (Oxford, 1997), p. 51.

[9]   Wink, *Human Being*, pp. 34, 38, 129–30, 145–7, 258 ('anthropic revelation').

[10]   Elisabeth Schüssler Fiorenza, *Jesus – Miriam's Child, Sophia's Prophet: Critical Issues in Feminist Christology* (London, 1995), pp. 50–57, 88–96; Elisabeth Schüssler Fiorenza, *Jesus and the Politics of Interpretation* (London, 2000), p. 21.

[11]   Stephen Pattison, 'The Shadow Side of Jesus', *Studies in Christian Ethics*, 8/2 (1995): pp. 54–67. (The notion of a person's 'shadow side' comes from Jung vis-à-vis one's journey of 'individuation', integrating one's different 'sides'.)

Ustorf is illuminating in this regard. Although he shares Newbigin's primarily missiological concern, he is far more positive about the capacity of dialogue to enrich Christian faith. He believes the question of Jesus' role as 'mediator' is especially pertinent in Western cultures today, and argues that Jesus is most able to operate as such if his similarity to other humans is emphasized, rather than making us dependent on him as the idealized other.[12] Ustorf develops Heisig's concept of 'the disestablished Christ' and argues that what matters for us is the way a more rounded appreciation of Jesus enables us to grow into greater human maturity, integrating our light and shadow sides. This helps in de-idealizing Jesus so that the onus for making ethical decisions is on us.[13] For Ustorf, as we shall see further in relation to religious plurality and multiple liberations, this points us to the need for engagement with other traditions and overcoming any anxieties we may have. This allows a crucial affirming in 'the other' of that which enables us to grow in human maturity, such that different liberative emphases may cross-fertilize for the reconciliation of all things. Wink, too, is concerned that Christian faith should not disempower us, which an idealized Jesus might inadvertently cause. Rather, he believes, things are true if they expose the 'Domination System', that complex of forces which feed our objectification and dehumanization of one another, and help us become more fully human.[14]

In other words, as Wink sees it, what matters in terms of the truth of the historical Jesus is the way in which he leads us, and gives us the strategies, to engage and transform the powers of domination which harm our shared humanity. Like Hick, Wink is putting his criterion above 'Jesus' as such, and it is apparently beyond question, in much the same way as Newbigin's norm – the belief that God is historically revealed in Jesus Christ as the measure of all things – is also beyond question. Whilst Hick prioritizes ('natural') reason over revelation, Newbigin conversely prioritizes revelation over reason, such that they both oversimplify the ambiguities of history in-between. However, Wink's approach is different, since it demands ongoing reflexivity: for the history and myth of Jesus is never complete, as the claims to revelation and reason interact psychologically and politically, engendering both self-criticism and assertion in the field of history. Of course, Hick and Newbigin each suggest they are open to ongoing reflexivity: Hick argues that his framework is built from the ground upwards, and Newbigin insists that no Christian's christology is final, only Christ himself. However, Hick's reductionist vision of Jesus risks being ahistorical, since its reflexivity is limited by the presumption of commonality between various responses to the Real: as we shall argue further, the differences are only superficial, thus engagement with the distinctive Jesus is historically restricted. As for Newbigin, the notion of a person's

---

[12] Werner Ustorf, 'The Emerging Christ of Post-Christian Europe', in Thomas F. Foust, George R. Hunsberger, J. Andrew Kirk, Werner Ustorf (eds), *A Scandalous Prophet: The Way of Mission after Newbigin* (Grand Rapids, MI, 2002), pp. 134–8.

[13] Ibid., pp. 138–44.

[14] Wink, *Human Being*, pp. 37, 15.

being 'final' is historically problematic, because of the sociality of human life. Wink's focus instead on 'the myth of the Human Being', on Jesus' engaging us in the process of embodying God's humanity with each other, immediately draws our attention to historical reflexivity. For such a myth does not deny the significance of historical context/s but invites us into ongoing conversations regarding such details. It is thus a mediating myth, in which Jesus' being the Shaken One is integral, shaking us out of premature answers concerning his and our historical embodiments of God's humanity.

Essentially, while Hick and Newbigin select particular strands of Christian history with which to dominate or marginalize 'others', Wink's historicized myth and mythicized history sets out to resist the very domination of others, consciously attending to the politics of history and engendering the Christian quest for a solidarity of others. This is both a particular feature of Christian history and a vision with scope beyond Christians, to offer the practice of 'solidarity of others' as a model for the benefit of the world.[15]

The Shaken One and Christian Knowing: An Anti-Domination Discourse

The question of history is obviously related to the question of knowing, and as we have already seen, both Hick and Newbigin exercise 'dual discourses' in their epistemologies. I suggest these rely on modernist dichotomies and distort the relational integrity of Christian faith. By contrast, the epistemology related to the Shaken One is reflexive and wary of dichotomies.

Newbigin's dual discourse consists, as we noted in Chapter 3, of relativizing the claims to knowledge made by the plethora of culturally conditioned traditions (a 'from below' epistemology), except insofar as the gospel is called into question (a 'from above' epistemology). This avoidance of post-Enlightenment critiques indicates that his epistemology is subordinate to the constitutive nature of christology; the finality of Christ necessarily supersedes all other claims. While that is an epistemological claim in itself, it effectively means that faith holds sway over the discipline of epistemology. Thus we see how, as Hunsberger notes, the doctrine of election drives Newbigin's explanation of the Christian narrative and its missiology; how the chosenness of Jesus incorporates related claims *vis-à-vis* Israel, Gentiles and the Church.[16] This is how he addresses the scandal of particularity, relating the tradition's particularities to God's universal plan; the chosen particulars imparting God's universal message of salvation, not exclusively possessing its benefits but generously displaying and sharing its bounty.

---

[15]   See Anselm Min, *The Solidarity of Others in a Divided World: A Postmodern Theology after Postmodernism* (New York and London, 2004), pp. 151–2, 193–4.

[16]   George R. Hunsberger, *Bearing the Witness of the Spirit: Lesslie Newbigin's Theology of Cultural Plurality* (Grand Rapids, MI and Cambridge, 1998), pp. 95–6.

While Newbigin makes some attempts to relate this particularity to religious plurality, such that the tradition must resist self-righteousness and be humbly open to what it may learn *about the gospel* from the others beyond it, the dominant force is nevertheless the way in which the finality of Christ's chosenness constitutes the particular tradition's revelation of universal meaning. As we see with regards to Hick too, such a dual discourse is utterly dependent on modernist dichotomies; even as it purports to criticize dichotomies, it fails to appropriate the way in which the saving resources of the Christian tradition/s are concerned with 'reciprocity and holism'.[17] If *the* tradition, or an aspect of it, becomes congruent with *universal* meaning, there is little room for 'others' to voice an alternative perspective or experience.

Hick, meanwhile, is explicit about his epistemological dichotomy: the Kantian scheme differentiating between that which is experienced (the phenomenal) and that as it truly is (the noumenal). He knows it drives his revision of the ontological incarnation tradition, in the light of religious plurality, as each human experience is relativized by the inaccessible truth of the noumenon. That is, while we each are entitled to own our personal experience of, and descriptive language for, the transcendent reality, we ought to recognize its partiality. This is, however, another dual discourse – or, in the light of Shanks's criticisms, two dual discourses: the former explicitly between reality which cannot be experienced and reality which can, and Hick's more confused conflation of religious experience and language.

In relation to the former, how can we speak of reality which cannot be experienced? How do we know it exists at all? Following Kant's transcendental conditions of knowledge, for Hick this is explained in terms of inference: we can 'know' some things without having to experience them. Thus he is no solipsist: there *is* a reality outside of human conception; and, as Cheetham shows, Hick is indeed committed to theistic realism: God *is* real.[18] However, Hick makes significant claims about the transcendent reality, particularly in terms of what it cannot be, which presupposes there is a reliable connection between what we know and what we do not know. He is basically hypothesizing on the basis of what people have experienced of the different phenomena and on the basis of his own understanding of the logic of his scheme.[19] In effect, for Hick, the dichotomy between the noumenal and the phenomena must be true – there truly must be something beyond all religious claims – in order to resist the absolutist tendencies

---

[17]   Peter C. Hodgson, *Winds of the Spirit: A Constructive Christian Theology* (London, 1994), p. 157.

[18]   David Cheetham, *John Hick: A Critical Introduction and Reflection* (Aldershot, 2003), pp. 16–17. Sinkinson questions this theism, perhaps unfairly: Christopher Sinkinson, *The Universe of Faiths: A Critical Study of John Hick's Religious Pluralism* (Carlisle, 2001), pp. 55, 73, 77, 81, 84, 124.

[19]   See John Hick, *An Interpretation of Religion: Human Responses to the Transcendent*, 2nd edn (Basingstoke, 2004), pp. xix–xxii; and Christopher Insole, 'Why John Hick Cannot, and Should Not, Stay Out of the Jam Pot', *Religious Studies*, 36/1 (March 2000): p. 32; and William L. Rowe, 'Religious Pluralism', *Religious Studies*, 35/2 (June 1999): pp. 143–50.

of each claim; but the fact that inductive dialogue can uncover commonality between different traditions suggests the dichotomy must also collapse – there is a meaningful connection between experiences and that which supposedly is beyond experience. In other words, like Newbigin's epistemology, Hick's also has its own convenient 'from below' and 'from above' dimensions. While Newbigin's dualism allows him to confirm the finality of Christ, Hick's dualism allows him to confirm the validity of different traditions' claims (as long as they are liberal enough to tolerate each other).

In respect of Hick's second dual discourse, as noted in Chapter 2, Shanks argues that he conflates the problem of religious experience (we cannot experience everything directly) and the problem of religious language (the True God transcends our concepts), so to justify reductionism *vis-à-vis* the referent of 'Trinity' and so forth.[20] In other words, for Shanks, Hick takes a shortcut, conflating and confusing experience and language, levelling the playing-field according to a predetermined schema and constructing an Esperantoist approach to 'religion', to avoid the hazards and ambiguities of true openness; whereas Shanks argues that Wilfred Cantwell Smith keeps the channels of communication truly open, allowing for real mediation between genuinely different but related religious traditions.[21] Hick disagrees with this criticism, insisting he does value the differences between traditions;[22] but his problem is that, epistemologically speaking, he subsumes them within a grander dichotomy (between phenomena and the noumenon), effectively presuming their relation to each other, or objectifying their relativity. That is, his schema, with its 'highest common denominator', purports to 'know' how the traditions are located in relation to each other, in the sense that their superficial differences hide their fundamentally common ethic.

Hick does not mean this to represent a new Esperanto-style language, as in a new super-religion; rather it is an abstraction equivalent to a linguist's model describing how different languages relate. For Sinkinson, however, it is a new religion in itself, not unlike deism; or rather, it is old, like Kant's universal ethical religion.[23] So yes, although he may well accept that there are differences between religious traditions, his concern is not with allowing them to converse, but presumes an abstraction 'above' religion as such. Thus he conflates language and experience, and diminishes the awkward particularity of the Christian tradition.

It is true that the dual discourse epistemologies of both Hick and Newbigin are critical of dichotomies. Newbigin attacks the polarization of public and private, object and subject, fact and value; and Hick resists the dichotomies between faith and knowledge, and philosophy and theology,[24] and reaffirms the validity

---

[20]   Shanks, *God and Modernity*, pp. 44–7.

[21]   Ibid., pp. 47ff.

[22]   In personal conversation with John Hick, 14 November 2005.

[23]   Sinkinson, *Universe of Faiths*, pp. 93, 120, 132, 144.

[24]   See Eleanor Jackson, 'Reviews', *British and Irish Association for Mission Studies*, 22/6 (March 2004): pp. 6–7.

of personal experience too easily lost within a corporate tradition's objectifying force. Even so, they perpetuate certain dichotomies. Newbigin turns Western culture into an 'object' of criticism, effectively demonizing it, rather than attending to the complex, symbiotic and incomplete relationship between the Christian meta-narrative and (Western) modernity.[25] Hick, on the other hand, polarizes the literal and the metaphorical, the corporate historical tradition and individual human experience, faith as 'given' and faith as 'interpreted', truth and interpretation, and Ptolemaic (christocentric) and Copernican (Real-centred) models of religious diversity.

As the example of language, discussed in Chapter 2, illustrates, Hick would do well to appreciate the interpenetration of literal and metaphorical models, their interdependence and inseparability. So with our knowledge: it interpenetrates our grasp and ignorance of history, such that we must continually dialogue with each other and allow for both the 'is' and the 'is not'. In fact, both Hick and Newbigin would do well generally to appreciate postmodern complications regarding the tradition's 'knowledge': Hick ought not simply to rework the tradition in terms of Kantian universal religion, and Newbigin ought not simply to presume christocentric finality. For Christian identity consists of plural saving resources which are not fixed or settled in history or in our knowledge, but remain open, even in tension with each other, but necessarily related. It is a living tradition in which the Shaken One is present and active. Hick and Newbigin handle this tradition as though it can be reduced to a kind of truth-as-correctness – whether to be revised or affirmed, whether in 'liberal' or 'traditionalist' terms, respectively; but the Shaken One instead nurtures anti-ideological truth-as-Honesty, openness to the otherness of the other, both within and beyond.[26]

In other words, the Shaken One encourages ongoing openness to each other, each element of and perspective on the historical tradition and its relationships. This does not mean it refuses to make claims to knowledge, but that it engenders awareness of the bias and practices which shape such claims. As biblical scholars like Theissen, Wink, Crossan and Fiorenza illustrate, to 'know' the history of Jesus is to engage with the linguistic sign systems of the cultural context, the psychology and politics of human projection and reconstruction, and the relationality between Jesus, as the focus of this quest, and those around him. Wink insists that 'the myth of the Human Being' is embodied not by Jesus solely, but in the matrix of his relationships, then and now. For Fiorenza, the dominant study of Jesus proves to be the non-study of those around him, so is easily complicit with forces of domination.[27] The problem, as she sees it, is that the usually narrow focus on the identity of Jesus, as though to 'fix' the varied and ambiguous metaphors of Christ 'into a single, definite discourse of meaning', effectively ignores the rhetorics of

---

[25]   See Bert Hoedemaker, 'Rival Conceptions of Global Christianity: Mission and Modernity, Then and Now', in Foust et al. (eds), *A Scandalous Prophet*, pp. 13–22.

[26]   Shanks, *God and Modernity*, pp. 5–8, and *Faith in Honesty*, pp. 1–6.

[27]   Fiorenza, *Jesus and the Politics of Interpretation*, pp. 2–4.

such narratives.[28] For each reconstruction involves 'memory' and the selection of historical and theological strands: so Fiorenza argues that it is better for us to own our agenda, specifically not so as to claim the objective correctness of the consequent christology, but to determine whether the rhetorics and structures of domination are being supported or challenged.[29]

The point is that there is no 'god's-eye-view' outside the complex of human power relations, and that we are all involved in the processes of 'othering', in terms of both our demonizing and our idealizing of 'the other', whether the poor and oppressed or the identity of Jesus.[30] In simple terms, we are shaped by our relationships; they contribute to our vision of each other, such that we see both Jesus and the poor in general in idealistic terms; whereas ongoing historical and faithful engagement with the 'original impulse'[31] of Jesus in community shakes us out of such perspectives and directs us towards mutual transformation.

Claims to knowledge are indicators and shapers of identity. For Fiorenza, this means that we should turn from a concern with the 'historical' Jesus to a concern for the movement of divine Wisdom of which he was a part and which shaped him decisively. It is a movement defined by its transformation of dominant, and dominating, social relations, which therefore interrupts and challenges elitist, anti-Jewish, colonialist, racist, anti-feminist structures.[32] This is strikingly similar to the criteria at the heart of Wink's 'myth of the Human Being': the identification of truth with that which brings about subversion of the 'Domination System' and our interrelated embodiments of God's humanity. As we explore further in the following section, the Shaken One thus encourages us to attend to 'the interconnections of knowledge and power',[33] which inform our understanding and selection of history. Essentially, the Shaken One demonstrates that our knowledge of the Christian tradition must continually reinterrogate the questions of history and epistemology, because our position is always political: so we must decide, again and again, who we are for. It is a matter of enabling those 'others' whose experiences are ignored or belittled to contribute to what we 'know'. As such, our particular tradition is committed to subverting domination and manifesting its scandalously universal vision of an ever greater solidarity of others.

The Shaken One and Christian Praxis: A Self-Critical Tradition

I should elaborate briefly on my implicit accusation that neither Hick nor Newbigin properly engages with the diversity of Christian perspectives and practice. It is

---

[28]   Ibid., pp. 5–6, 15–16.
[29]   Ibid., pp. 6–7, 11.
[30]   Ibid., pp. 22–3.
[31]   Wink, *Human Being*, p. 15.
[32]   Fiorenza, *Jesus and the Politics of Interpretation*, pp. 21, 12–14.
[33]   Ibid., p. 14.

a problem of 'praxis' – the relation between the tradition's self-reflection and discernment and its practice in each context. While they both intend to appreciate the range of Christian praxis, their schemas prevent them from fulfilling such intentions.

Newbigin, on the one hand, believed in and pioneered the development of local theology and leadership in India. He denounced totalitarian tendencies in the world and wanted the Church globally to allow its diverse expressions mutually to correct each other. Thus Hunsberger discerns a 'theology of cultural plurality', a commitment to the perspectival and the essentially relational character of truth. Christians should love each other, learn from each other, work together and, in the process, build up both a fuller understanding of Christ and a fuller manifestation of the Body of Christ, as a sign of the gospel of reconciliation. Yet, on the other hand, Newbigin's approach warns that contextualizations can replace the finality of Christ with their own finality; he even showed signs of being 'against' culture, believing fundamentally that there is a radical discontinuity between Christ and everything else, such as to question the 'gift' of cultural diversity. He basically maintained particular doctrinal readings of the central 'clue' that is Christ, so arguably manifested a Christian brand of imperialism. That is, by taking for granted the evangelical verities, he pre-empts the ecumenical conversation and delimits legitimate reflection on Christian history and practice. Being confident that 'In the name of Jesus' will be vindicated as the starting-point and the finishing-point of all historical reflection and practice, he implicitly subjects Christian diversity to the expectation that all Christians should accept Christ's finality in those terms. Thus it is debatable whether he honestly engages the heterodoxy of diverse Christianities, even as he commits himself to ecumenical unity.

As for Hick, on the one hand, his Kantian epistemology ensures that all claims are seen as partial phenomena, each a valid experience of reality but none an absolute grasp of it. Thus he affirms the perspectival nature of truth, evident in the way distinct cultural contexts give rise to different religious traditions. Also the questions raised by his metaphorical christology indicate that he is keen for the Church to reflect critically on the ethical implications of its claims. In that sense Hick is appreciative of Christian heterodoxy, not least because he wants his alternative reading and its critique of the dominant perspective legitimized. Yet, on the other hand, though he denies and does not intend this, Hick's 'Enlightenment' epistemology is simultaneously imperialistic, because he systematizes a grand scheme designed to place all (major) religious traditions in a framework of relations (untainted by their historical-cultural contexts); going to abstraction in order to universalize his common norm – the movement from self- to Real-centredness and thus the generation of saintliness.[34] The problem is that, even as he seeks to affirm the distinctiveness of each tradition and its contribution to the

---

[34] Again, Hick's material 'saintliness', the transformation from self-centredness to Real-centredness, is not the same as Shanks' formal 'sanctity' (faithfulness to one's tradition/culture).

understanding of the whole, he essentially reduces them all to a specific dynamic: the individual's move from selfishness to saintliness. This not only imposes on the framework a shape significantly informed by his own experience of Christian faith, but imposes that very Western framework on to our grasp of religious others, without truly requiring them to engage one another, simply to validate or tolerate each other. As Milbank argues, the very notion of dialogue between different others itself presupposes the modern, liberal assumption that commonality is there to be found, in fact imperialistically reconstructing itself in the other.[35] We return to this in Chapter 7.

In short, neither Hick nor Newbigin properly grasps the significance of context for the internal nature of Christian faith and its relatedness to perspective, place and politics. Any oversimplification of Christian faith as 'a religion', separated from cultural relations and understood in 'these' terms but not 'those', runs the risk of objectifying it and imposing it imperialistically. Even though Newbigin's 'theology of cultural plurality' is said to enable different parts of the global Church to converse with each other, I believe his engagement with Christian diversity is rather limited by the particular form of his attachment to evangelical 'orthodoxy'; so too with Hick, who parodies orthodoxy in order to revise it,[36] and fails to address the multiple nature of the Christian tradition/s. So even as they both believe wholeheartedly that they value the perspectival, their respective limitations of 'the tradition' do not bode well for their handling of plural other traditions.

Here it is worth returning to the critical tradition of Wink, specifically the work of Nancey Murphy who speaks to the question of the tradition's practice and politics. She is particularly concerned with epistemology, how the social practices by which we pursue truth are themselves 'fallen' but redeemable. She values MacIntyre's approach: that traditions are socially embodied in the lives of individuals and communities; that narratives are constructed to tell the story of how a tradition's authority is challenged by a crisis; and that a tradition is superior to others if it can overcome a crisis without losing its identity.[37] She notes that MacIntyre rejects both the absolutism of the Enlightenment's belief in 'traditionless reason' and the relativism of all claims, because, even as a claim is tradition-laden, each tradition is nevertheless able to assert itself if it can overcome crises. The trick is to affirm particularity without denying plurality.

In contrast to the Enlightenment's tradition of epistemology, as Murphy outlines, MacIntyre identifies two other traditions – the Genealogists, following on from Nietzsche, who insist that all claims and moralities must be unmasked to expose

---

[35]   See John Milbank, 'The End of Dialogue', in Gavin D'Costa (ed.), *Christian Uniqueness Reconsidered: The Myth of a Pluralistic Theology of Religions* (Maryknoll, NY, 1990), pp. 174–91.

[36]   See pp. 39, 43, 45, 73, 92, 119.

[37]   Nancey Murphy, 'Traditions, Practices and the Powers', in Ray Gingerich and Ted Grimsrud (eds), *Transforming the Powers: Justice, Peace and the Domination System* (Minneapolis, MN, 2006), p. 86.

the vested interests behind them; and MacIntyre's own revival of the Aristotelian/ Thomist tradition, by which intellectual traditions are passed on as social practices via teachers.[38] For Murphy, MacIntyre is relatively optimistic about our capacity to realize what is good through our social practices, following a more Catholic line, while Reformers/ Protestants tend to follow the line of Nietzsche and Foucault, believing that social practices distort human knowledge and that this distortion deludes us all – including MacIntyre.[39] Murphy argues that we should accept the Genealogists' point that social practices distort knowledge because of 'the will to power', but believes a more nuanced account of social practices is possible. For her, the social practices not only *can* be corrupted and are *likely* to be, but *need not be* if only we can tame the will to power.[40]

Murphy identifies the Radical Reformers (namely, Anabaptists) with this more nuanced approach to epistemology. She notes how such churches have developed a 'Christian epistemic practice'; that is, discernment of truth involves engagement with scripture (the tradition) *in the whole community*. This ameliorates the risks of 'the distorting influences of the will to power', especially because of the commitment to listen to 'the least', and deliberately to favour teaching which flies in the face of the will to survive – this is itself represented by Anabaptist commitment to pacifism, 'revolutionary subordination' (wilful servanthood), free-church polity (refusing to align with the power of the state), and simple living (minimizing the need for power to defend one's privileges).[41] In short, it is a community 'that does not need to rely on the usual sorts of worldly power to survive and flourish', and in Wink's terms, such a community allows 'the Holy Spirit [rather than the will to power] to function as the interiority of the gathered community'.[42] (Wink's reference to the Holy Spirit further suggests, for me, that it is God who resources our mutual humanization as a solidarity of others.)

The will-to-power, conversely, in the terms of my argument, consists of those exercises of 'kyriarchal' powers which objectify and dehumanize 'the others', thus working against other-regard and solidarity. Rather than being facilitated – or 'shaken' – by God's presence to embody the practices of other-regard, solidarity and justice, such will-to-power generates various distortions of religious and political relations. We shall discuss these further in Chapter 6, but in essence, as

---

[38]   Ibid., pp. 87–8.

[39]   Ibid., p. 89.

[40]   Ibid., pp. 89, 91; she uses James Wm. McClendon Jr, *Ethics: Systematic Theology*, vol. 1 (Nashville, TN, 1986; rev. edn 2002) who develops Wink's thought to speak of 'powerful practices'.

[41]   Murphy, 'Traditions, Practices and the Powers', pp. 91–3. See John B. Cobb Jr, 'Christ beyond Creative Transformation', in Davis (ed.), *Encountering Jesus*, pp. 153: the more one has to lose, the more skewed one's grasp of truth; and Ian McFarland, *Listening to the Least: Doing Theology from the Outside In* (Cleveland, OH, 1998), pp. 5–7, 28, 36, 38–9, 65.

[42]   Murphy, 'Traditions, Practices and the Powers', pp. 91, 93.

I see it, the will-to-power, which is indicative of the impatient quest for truth-as-correctness rather than truth-as-Honesty, leads to entrenchment (represented by religious exclusivism), assimilation (represented by inclusivism) or indifference (represented by 'superficial' forms of religious pluralism).[43] Thus, instead, using Ricoeur's term, Murphy insists a 'hermeneutic of suspicion' is in order,[44] and that it must apply to the Radicals' own beliefs, to ensure they are not the product of self-interest; but she commends their social practice so long as the voices of outsiders and those participating in rival (other) traditions are heard as well. Murphy affirms MacIntyre's recommendations, for he urges traditions to become familiar with the language and crises of other traditions and to allow one's tradition to be subject to critiques from rival perspectives. Most of all, this demands humility. However, for Murphy, 'mere' humility is not enough; active self-criticism directed towards curbing self-interest and the will-to-power is called for.[45] My point is, the practice of the tradition is integral to our identity, and the Shaken One urges our practice to be self-critical, so to curb the will-to-power and build an inclusive community.

In essence, whilst both Hick and Newbigin attempt to value the diversity of Christian practice, they are less patient with it, less self-critical, and less attentive to the practical and political consequences of their interpretations than they intend to be. Of course, Hick focuses on the imperialism of Christian history which he clearly associates with the tradition of ontological incarnation, so exercises a form of self-criticism with regards to the praxis of the particular tradition; but he stops short of self-criticism with regards to his reinterpretation of the tradition. As we explore specifically in Chapter 7, his Westernized liberal tradition has its own imperialism, which Hick refuses to see. Newbigin, too, is inclined to criticize imperialism and religious praxes which distort human interdependence, but is not inclined to associate such praxes with his own approach to the tradition. Rather, it is the tradition of the Shaken One who draws our attention to our historical 'disowning' of the damage done by sectarian Christian praxis. Specifically, it is Jesus' critique of the Temple tradition and the purity codes, with their exclusiveness and dehumanization of many 'others', which reflects this prophetic, emancipatory tradition's capacity for self-criticism, and Fiorenza in particular illuminates the way in which this Jewish discourse should feed Christian self-criticism.

The particularity of our tradition, if attentive to Jesus' being the Shaken One, is thus concerned with the diversity of Judaeo-Christian praxis, parts of which are more liberative than others. It is not about idealizing 'this' strand over and against 'the other', since the very essence of the tradition of the Shaken One is

---

[43]   This common typology is considered in Chapter 6, but I mean it broadly in these senses: Christian exclusivists believe only Christians are saved; inclusivists that Christ's saving effects are operative in other traditions; and pluralists that each religion is effective in its own terms.

[44]   Paul Ricoeur, *Freud and Philosophy: An Essay on Interpretation* (New Haven, CT, 1970), p. 27.

[45]   Murphy, 'Traditions, Practices and the Powers', pp. 93–4.

its concern to resist 'kyriarchy', the lordship by some over others; but it does make a distinctive and positive contribution to our reading of the Christian tradition. For it highlights the way in which every grasp of the tradition remains susceptible to those social practices and ideologies which can cause us to objectify and dehumanize each other and it nurtures such strategic other-regard that we can corporately resist those powers of domination. Its particular emphasis, in terms of the interconnection between reflexive history, intersubjective knowledge and the praxis of the social Jesus, envisions and energizes a Body of Christ committed to working for an ever greater solidarity of others.

The Shaken One and Trinity

Normative not Exhaustive

This book is primarily a constructive *christology*, by way of its identification of Jesus Christ as the Shaken One. However, while I do not attempt to offer a comprehensive vision of the Trinity, it is right to note that not even a christology which affirms Jesus' sociality can exhaust the Shaken One. Jesus' being the Shaken One begs questions regarding his relation not only to other humans but to the very being of God. Though this section and the next are brief relative to the scale of the issues they explore, they are an attempt to engage with the trinitarian tradition, particularly the way in which it illustrates the plurality and otherness within Christian identity. They are also a bridge between this chapter and the next, since they point us towards Christian engagement with external plurality: for the Trinity itself is integral to our understanding of and dialogue with the other beyond.

As for Hick, his Kantian schema essentially renders trinitarian debate and doctrine irrelevant, because the language of the Trinity becomes simply culturally conditioned metaphor which expresses our partial experience of and response to the one transcendent reality. He has no particular concern to engage with trinitarian discourse, even though its plurality could relate to his approach. Once again, the impoverished vision of metaphorical language with which he works, together with his emphasis on personal experience rather than the corporate tradition, debilitates against serious appreciation of 'Trinity' *vis-à-vis* the particularity of Christian identity.

Newbigin, on the other hand, is committed to the ontological truth of the Trinity, though his vision of the Spirit is largely about bringing all things to their true end under Christ. In other words, Christ is the measure of the Trinity, since it was the Father's gift of Christ to the world which effected the objective change in the course of things, making it possible for us to relate to God as originally intended, and it is for the Spirit simply to help us bear witness to this reconciling event and reality. He retains a degree of openness, however, by warning against Christians' prejudging of others' capacity to teach us truths about God and by declining to presume the eternal destiny of others. Nevertheless, he remains confident that his vision of Christ as the final clue to the meaning of all history will indeed be confirmed to be the final clue, since it is given to us as such through revelation; it is only our interpretations of it which are partial. This self-assurance about the reliability of evangelical faith need not be an indication of any modernism, nor counter-modernism, but simply an indication of his more traditional Christian faith! It is, for him, of the very nature of Christian faith that Christ alone determines the contours of faith.

I do not dispute that Jesus Christ is determinative for Christian faith, but simply suggest these two things – one with regards to his humanity, and the other with regards to his relation to God. On the one hand, as we have been exploring, to envision Christ's identity is to be sensitive to his sociality and the interrelated questions of history, knowledge and praxis, which resist the objectification and idealization of any dominant reconstruction. By virtue of his engagement with others within the tradition, beyond it and relatively invisible to it, Jesus the Shaken One is inseparable from other humans. In particular, his vision and practice, in relationship with others, enables our mutual healing and liberation from the dehumanizing powers of domination. This is inherently a self-critical tradition, engendering resistance to all traditions of objectification, including those in which we participate. On the other hand, as I argue now, further engagement with the trinitarian tradition can both problematize and clarify the centrality of Jesus Christ. His identity and centrality is problematized because the Trinity, in its various interpretations, shows us that Jesus does not exhaust the Shaken One. His identity and centrality is clarified because the Trinity shows us that relationality is integral to embodying the Shaken One. So we turn to some specific arguments about the trinitarian tradition to elaborate these assertions.

Of course, as Schmidt-Leukel notes, it does not automatically prove very much for Newbigin to claim his theology is trinitarian.[46] There is, after all, a plurality of trinitarian theologies, such that it is justifiable to criticize Newbigin's position. For instance, viewed in one way, Lampe's 'God as Spirit' theology is perhaps at one end of a trinitarian range, as its 'spirit christology' identifies Jesus as a human powerfully inspired by God as omnipresent Spirit, such that 'inspiration' and 'incarnation' equate.[47] Some may see this as rendering the human achievement equivalent to the divine initiative and denying the Trinity's mutual in-dwelling of God the Father, Son and Spirit. Nevertheless, it is arguable that spirit christologies are authentic to (though inevitably selective with) the biblical witness and speak to a very basic notion of trinity: for God simply *is* Spirit, transcendent, immanent, and mediating. The later Hick, of course, accepts this summary, adopting an 'inspiration christology' himself, but the Christian tradition's breadth and depth goes much further. For Greene, however, Schmidt-Leukel is suggesting that,

---

[46]   See Perry Schmidt-Leukel, 'Mission and Trinitarian Theology', in Foust et al. (eds), *A Scandalous Prophet*, p. 57.

[47]   Geoffrey W.H. Lampe, *God as Spirit: The Bampton Lectures 1976* (Oxford, 1977), pp. 11–12.

since trinitarian doctrine emerged over time, it is self-evidently *only* true in a metaphorical not ontological sense.[48] In that light, Greene sees Schmidt-Leukel's pluralistic perspective as so fatally dividing God's immanent being from God as economic trinity that he ought not to call his pluralistic theology 'trinitarian' at all. For Greene, like Rahner, the immanent and the economic Trinity *are one*, such that the division of theological approaches into exclusivist, inclusivist and pluralist is utterly false *because of God's trinitarian nature*.[49] As Newbigin argues, trinitarian theology allows for truths in all three approaches, while rejecting elements of each as well.[50] (We return to Newbigin's handling of religious diversity in Chapter 6.)

From a different perspective, Heather Ward criticizes Schmidt-Leukel's claim that the Trinity is a human construct, a (mere) metaphor devised to give expression to the Christian's grasp of the God whom others grasp differently. For Ward, this denies 'otherness' itself, as though 'diversity' is 'simply another style' contrived by us; whereas the point of the Trinity is to answer people's concern with the incarnation's handling of Jesus' likeness to us and his otherness.[51] In other words, as metaphor the Trinity *can* be taken genuinely to mean what it says, while also being incomplete, just as with the incarnation, such that they 'point us in the right direction' while hinting at the otherness of God who gathers all diversity together.[52] This brings to mind Kenneson, discussed in Chapter 3, who speaks of the Trinity as a model of community by which humankind can learn to handle difference/s non-violently and as mutual gifting.[53] It is not clear whether for him it remains simply a particularly useful model or the very nature of God. So, too, with Young, who argues that trinitarian doctrine impresses on us the oneness of God, the need for humility in the light of this 'uncontainable' God, and a proper balance between immanence and transcendence, which leads her to advocate 'practical relativism' due to our relative ignorance.[54] But is the doctrine pragmatic, or is it about how God *is*?

Essentially these issues show that trinitarian and christological debates are inseparable, and that by their very nature they speak to religious plurality. In fact, a focus on trinity is conducive to a certain kind of openness, concerned with holding

---

[48] Colin J.D. Greene, 'Trinitarian Tradition and the Cultural Collapse of Late Modernity', in Foust et al. (eds), *A Scandalous Prophet*, p. 67, referring to Schmidt-Leukel, 'Mission and Trinitarian Theology', pp. 62–3.

[49] Greene, 'Trinitarian Tradition'.

[50] Newbigin, *Pluralist Society*, p. 182.

[51] Heather Ward, 'The Use and Misuse of "Metaphor" in Christian Theology', in Foust et al. (eds), *A Scandalous Prophet*, p. 74.

[52] Ibid., pp. 74–5. On metaphor, see Sallie McFague, *Metaphorical Theology: Models of God in Religious Language* (Philadelphia, PA, 1982). Barth's solution is that God sends *some* words *to* us; we must trust them. I find this problematic.

[53] Philip D. Kenneson, 'Trinitarian Missiology: Mission as Face-to-Face Encounter', in Foust et al. (eds), *A Scandalous Prophet*, p. 81.

[54] Frances Young, 'The Uncontainable God: Pre-Christendom Doctrine of Trinity', in Foust et al. (eds), *A Scandalous Prophet*, pp. 85–90.

things in unresolved tension, so as to foster a largely orthodox faith resistant
to any exclusive closed-mindedness. Whether this is adequate for handling the
complexity of people's religious experiences and claims, and for nurturing a
solidarity of others in the face of the objectifications and universal pretenders of
the 'Domination System', I withhold judgment for now; but the point is that, as the
following examples show, Hick and Newbigin have a limited appreciation of the
breadth of the Christian tradition/s.

Take D'Costa and Dupuis, both Roman Catholics, who offer, respectively,
'Christocentric Trinitarianism' (a name also given to Newbigin's approach)
and the 'Trinitarian Christology' of 'inclusive pluralism'. As D'Costa argues,
pluralists are right to raise questions about relativity, the mystery of God, justice
and imperialism, but wrong to lead us to plural*ism*, because God's trinitarian
nature can itself resolve the problem of balancing historical particularity and
God's universal saving activity.[55] How? Because the God revealed everywhere is
the triune God revealed in Jesus Christ, who extends beyond Christianity because
of the Holy Spirit. Also, because of the Trinity, both Christomonism, which
exclusively identifies God with Jesus, and pluralist universalism or theocentricism,
which diminishes the identification of God with Jesus, are avoided.[56] As Dupuis
maintains, Jesus does not exhaust God; nor does the transcendent Logos exhaust
God; nor does the Spirit exhaust God.[57] In D'Costa's terms, Jesus is 'wholly
God, but never the whole of God', and Christ is 'normative' but not exhaustive,
which means that Christians have more to learn about God in Christ through
God's revelation in other (inter-related) histories.[58] Even though there are tensions
which result from this, not least because D'Costa still ties the *extent* of the Spirit's
freedom to Christ's *content*, Knitter notes that D'Costa sees these as inevitable for
Christians.[59] Dupuis develops this relatedness. Firstly, because Christ is 'imbued
with … intra-Trinitarian relationships' as a hermeneutical key for handling
revelation in all times and places, he names it an 'integral christology'. Secondly,
he emphasizes Jesus' human-relatedness to other religious traditions and human
cultures – by virtue of a human being a 'becoming' and a social being. As Rahner
put it, each human tradition can thus contain 'supernatural, grace-filled elements',
by virtue of our connectedness with each other and God.[60]

---

[55]   Gavin D'Costa, 'Christ, the Trinity and Religious Plurality', in Gavin D'Costa
(ed.), *Christian Uniqueness Reconsidered: The Myth of a Pluralistic Theology of Religions*
(Maryknoll, NY, 1990), pp. 16–17.

[56]   Ibid., pp. 17–18.

[57]   Jacques Dupuis, 'Trinitarian Christology as a Model for a Theology of Religious
Pluralism', in T. Dayanandan Francis and Israel Selvanayagam (eds), *Many Voices in Christian
Mission: Essays in honour of J.E. Lesslie Newbigin* (Madras, 1994), pp. 87, 88, 91, 92.

[58]   D'Costa, 'Christ, the Trinity and Religious Plurality', pp. 18–19.

[59]   Paul F. Knitter, *Introducing Theologies of Religions* (Maryknoll, NY, 2002), p. 89.

[60]   See Dupuis, 'Trinitarian Christology', pp. 87–9, 93. For Barth, 'religions' are *not*
God-given; for Rahner, nature *in general* bears grace; but for Dupuis, God wills the diversity

To an extent, D'Costa's and Dupuis's approaches are very similar: both the Son (the Word, the Logos) and the Spirit are deemed active in traditions other than Christianity, because of God's universal saving activity, while the Christian tradition continues to have its own historical particularity. For D'Costa this entails the normativity of Christ, which involves the normativity of crucified self-giving love in both praxis and dialogue. This requires attentiveness to God through one's neighbour, attentiveness to narratives of oppression (hearing the oppressed), attentiveness to others' holiness (and their criticisms of us), and attentiveness to the ongoing process of indigenization (resisting imperialism by embedding Christian faith in each culture).[61]

D'Costa and Dupuis do, however, differ – namely with regards to the role of the Church in terms of trinitarian thinking. D'Costa notes that Roman Catholic Conciliar teaching still affirms that the Church 'is necessary for salvation' (*Lumen Gentium*, 14).[62] What, then, of the Spirit's presence and activity beyond the Church? D'Costa suggests:

> The main route for reconciling these tensions lies within the Conciliar teaching that whenever God is present, this is the presence of the triune God; and it is the triune God who is the foundation of the church. Hence ... the Holy Spirit's presence within other religions is both intrinsically trinitarian and ecclesiological.[63]

In D'Costa's analysis, Dupuis's affirmation of the relation between Christ and the Spirit does not extend to the Church and the kingdom. D'Costa writes: 'While Dupuis's position is extremely nuanced, it still falls short of retaining this delicate Conciliar balance by removing some of the terms of the relations (church), rather than by fruitfully engaging with them as necessary parameters.'[64] However, they agree on the necessity of the constitutive uniqueness of Jesus. For D'Costa, the 'person' of Jesus, the life of God and the 'imitation of Christ' by his disciples (as the Church) are bound together.[65] So for Dupuis: while he is clear Logos-christology needs Spirit-christology, since the economy of the Spirit 'knows no bounds', and that God's saving will (not the Son) is absolute, nevertheless, the

---

of *traditions* themselves. But (as for Newbigin, too) how do 'intra-Trinitarian relationships' permit certain kinds of relationships with other traditions, but not other kinds?

[61] D'Costa, 'Christ, the Trinity and Religious Plurality', pp. 20–26.

[62] Gavin D'Costa, *The Meeting of Religions and the Trinity* (Edinburgh, 2000), p. 110.

[63] Ibid.

[64] Ibid., citing Jacques Dupuis, *Toward a Christian Theology of Religious Pluralism* (Maryknoll, NY, 1997), pp. 330–57. (Also see D'Costa, *Meeting of the Religions*, p. 113: 'the Spirit is shorn of its relationship to Christ or the church'; thus D'Costa is a critic of 'inclusivism', arguing instead for a specifically *trinitarian* handling of religious plurality, pp. 22–3.)

[65] D'Costa, *Meeting of Religions*, pp. 119–20.

'punctual event' of Jesus Christ depends on his being 'constitutively unique'.[66] For 'in his incarnate [and ultimately crucified and risen] Son God has contracted "once for all" an irreversible bond of union with the human race'.[67]

So, on the one hand, the Logos enlightens and the Spirit inspires people other than Christians – such that diversity exists *in principle* because of 'the one but manifold plan of God for humankind', rooted itself in God's triune being;[68] and this means, for D'Costa, that Christians *need* the Spirit's judgment *as revealed through other traditions* so to keep us faithful to the ever-more-fully translated Christ.[69] On the other hand, this must be grounded fundamentally in Jesus' uniqueness. As Dupuis puts it, this uniqueness *is* 'constitutive' (he really *is* the way by which salvation is effected) though 'relational', since his historical particularity does not exhaust God's saving will. So for Dupuis, different traditions live with 'complementarity' – they enrich each other mutually, interacting dynamically – and head towards some kind of 'convergence', defined as 'inclusive pluralism'.[70] As Knitter describes it, Dupuis says the others exist as a matter of principle (God *wills* them), and the Spirit can act *differently from* but not in contradiction to Christ.[71] It is not clear that for Newbigin other traditions exist by God's will, though he argues that they help to hold the Church under the Spirit's judgment.

These discussions confirm that Jesus' relationality is critical not only to our vision of his humanity but to the Christian vision of God. In my terms, Jesus embodies God's humanity in and through relationship with others; that is, the Shaken One is a social reality and God is in the social matrix. D'Costa and Dupuis thus imply that the Shaken One should be understood christologically and in trinitarian terms, but suggest this is possible only because of his constitutive uniqueness. I offer an alternative vision.

---

[66]   Dupuis, 'Trinitarian Christology', pp. 85, 90.

[67]   Ibid., p. 93.

[68]   Ibid., pp. 96–7.

[69]   D'Costa, 'Christ, the Trinity and Religious Plurality', pp. 22–3. As Knitter explains, D'Costa's point equates with saying to newly-weds that their marriage will be all the better because of their relationships with other friends (and *vice versa*!): the existence of other religious traditions is vital to Christian faithfulness: see Knitter, *Introducing Theologies*, p. 88.

[70]   Dupuis, 'Trinitarian Christology', pp. 96–7. For Knitter, this 'qualitative' not 'quantitative' uniqueness of Jesus (citing Jacques Dupuis, '"The Truth Will Make You Free": The Theology of Religious Pluralism Revisited', *Louvain Studies*, 24 (1999): p. 382) is 'a fullness of focus, of intensity, rather than one of detail and totality' (Knitter, *Introducing Theologies*, p. 92).

[71]   Knitter, *Introducing Theologies*, pp. 90–91.

'Movement of Manifold Change'

Panikkar's approach offers a different way forward. Knitter, for instance, who places D'Costa and Dupuis within his 'fulfilment' (inclusivist) models of theologies of religions, defines Panikkar's as a 'mutuality' model (one kind of pluralism). He explains how Panikkar sees the Divine Mystery as being both one *and many* – for the one peak would collapse without the many paths; diversity will always keep the upper hand over unity – so he 'gently chides' Hick for an over-emphasis on commonality and seeks to affirm instead that religious traditions cannot always be translated into each other's terms.[72] In fact, as Knitter notes, Panikkar is wary of theologies which purport to frame all traditions within one scheme.[73] As Williams indicates in his exploration of Panikkar's thought, a path between Christian exclusivism and liberal pluralism is again being enacted. It identifies and affirms in other traditions that which is analogous to Christianity's 'own goal of common work for the kingdom in the Body of Christ',[74] the 'christic universal vision' being, for Panikkar, the *Christian*'s vision, while his 'genuinely interactive pluralism' affirms that differences do matter.[75] In other words, as Williams explains, Panikkar is speaking of the Christian faith in terms of its vision – he has 'confidence' in humankind's general future 'as capable of displaying what is shown in Christ'; that is, being Christian is more about 'distinctive witness to the possibility of human community' than 'preoccupation with self-identity'; and it is the Trinity which ensures this avoids inward-looking self-description or mere 'toleration'.[76]

This looks more productive for my argument. Christ is both the human Jesus and 'the shape of the future potential of all human beings', a distinct form of community defined by shared relatedness to Christ and liberty to be God's children; and 'spirit' is the working out of this form 'in a diversity as wide as the diversity of the human race', the 'movement of manifold change, the endless variety of imitations of Christ.'[77] So it has its historical reference-point but perhaps more as a springboard than a benchmark. For Panikkar, interfaith cooperation flows from this – as mutual nurture and challenge, involving neither the triumph of one theory

---

[72] Ibid., pp. 128–9.

[73] Ibid., p. 129.

[74] Rowan Williams, 'Trinity and Pluralism', in D'Costa (ed.), *Christian Uniqueness Reconsidered*, p. 10, citing Bishop Laksham Wickremesinghe, while recognizing that Panikkar himself emphasizes that other traditions have other goals. See also Raimundo Panikkar, 'The Jordan, the Tiber, and the Ganges: Three Kairological Moments of Christic Self-Consciousness', in John Hick and Paul F. Knitter (eds), *The Myth of Christian Uniqueness* (London, 1987), pp. 89–116.

[75] Williams, 'Trinity and Pluralism', pp. 4, 5, 9.

[76] Ibid., pp. 5–6.

[77] Ibid., pp. 7–8.

over another nor the relativism which fails to be critical of 'what limits or crushes humanity'.[78] That is, a concern with domination and dehumanization is central.

Such a concern means that Panikkar's witness to a 'christic fact' resembles the approach of both Hodgson and Wink. D'Costa and Dupuis (like Newbigin) insist the Church is under the judgment of the Spirit as revealed in other traditions, so affirm that interfaith interdependence has a critical dimension, and D'Costa is explicit about a liberative praxis (grounded in the relatedness of christocentricism, theocentricism and pneumatology);[79] whereas Panikkar, Hodgson and Wink crucially prioritize mutual human flourishing over its plausibly christological foundations.[80] Thus Panikkar's pluralism is not limitless, as it entails criticism of homogenizing tendencies (universal pretenders); his 'incarnation' is 'the centre of [the] network of relations in which a new humanity is to be created' rather than the expression of privilege and exclusivity; and his Church is a focus for common hope, not claiming 'the totality of meaning'.[81]

The main point of this diversion into Panikkar's thought is to see the diverse possibilities of the trinitarian tradition/s. As Williams shows, Panikkar obviously does not say everything, since the relation between logos and spirit is ongoing; so he suggests Panikkar's approach might benefit more (to paraphrase him) from Lash's trinity as the 'grammar' of 'discipleship' by which we avoid freezing in any given position and prevent Christian empire. In fact, for Williams, it is the Trinity which is the precondition for our making our distinctive contribution to human community, avoiding both the totalizing empire of a grand theory and uncritical relativism, constituting instead a 'redeemed sociality' which genuinely heals.[82] Here, Williams implies the need for the Trinity's constitutive reality, reflecting his Barthian influences, just as Hollenweger argues that a '*Pentecostal* Missiology' must essentially address the (constitutive) relation between God's 'modes of being' (Barth's term) in order to handle the God who transcends us all (the Father), who gives life in all cultures (the Spirit) while having been manifested in Jesus (the Son).[83] While Newbigin was ahead of his time in recognizing the rise

---

[78]   Ibid., pp. 8–9.

[79]   D'Costa, 'Christ, the Trinity and Religious Plurality', p. 21.

[80]   Pannenberg, though, unlike Barth/Newbigin, suggests the many particularities will be *more* fulfilled in Christ, because of the trinitarian nature of identity; for mutuality entails more than dialogue, but 'I am who I am in relation to others'. See, for example, *Jesus – God and Man* (London, 1968), pp. 383–90.

[81]   Rowan Williams, 'Trinity and Pluralism', pp. 9, 11. Panikkar is considered further in Chapter 6.

[82]   Ibid., pp. 12–14. Schwöbel criticizes Panikkar for postulating a history of religions that few 'would recognize as their own', because of such emphasis on incommensurability: see Christoph Schwöbel, 'Particularity, Universality, and the Religions', in D'Costa (ed.), *Christian Uniqueness Reconsidered*, p. 32.

[83]   Walter J. Hollenweger, 'Towards a Pentecostal Missiology', in Dayanandan Francis and Selvanayagam (eds), *Many Voices*, p. 74. Amos Young, *Beyond the Impasse: Toward a*

of Pentecostalism and drawing it into ecumenical bodies,[84] his Spirit appears to remain determined by the Son. I suggest this reflects the Barthian bias for Second-Person theology, as Shanks calls it.[85] For Newbigin is primarily concerned, as Barth was, with identifying a Christ strong enough to subvert any dominating and manipulative 'gang', which aims to defy the gospel's reconciling power – namely the distortion of reality by Western modernity. A fuller outworking of trinitarian theology, instead, such as that suggested by Shanks, advocates resistance to the three related dishonesties together. So what is needed is First-Person theology's resistance to any herd-mentality, to nurture openness to the other beyond; Second-Person theology's resistance to any gang-mentality, to counteract any power of domination; and Third-Person theology's resistance to whitewashing tradition, to foster openness to the other within.

The point is that both Hick and Newbigin oversimplify the trinitarian tradition, so as to argue from a position of premature simplicity. In Shanks's terms, they close off the possibilities of other forms of theology simply on the grounds that others do not share their preoccupations. For Hick, the issue is how to overcome the herd-mentality of a given tradition, even as his modernist presuppositions themselves foster a particular herd – that of liberal pluralists. As Griffiths puts it, from a postliberal perspective, Hick is so attached to 'functionalist' views of the doctrinal tradition, that he exercises at least as much self-assurance and epistemic certainty as the exclusivists he criticizes.[86] For Newbigin, the issue is how the finality of Christ is *the* – one and only – way to address the homogenization of the world in the thralls of Western, secular and fragmentary values (a gang-mentality), even as his Western discourse unavoidably shapes the finality (and dichotomies) he believes in. Instead, genuine trinitarian openness to the preoccupations of other theologies, rooted in Third-Person theology's question of a tradition's self-awareness, might benefit them both. This could be advanced in terms of the theology of Dupuis, emphasizing mutuality as preferable to homogenization, since God *wills* diversity, without turning to imperialism or relativism, though I will suggest a different approach.[87] Nonetheless, what this survey of trinitarian issues suggests is that a constructive christology begs a constructive pneumatology and trinitarian theology. For example, God as Spirit continually energizes the *Body* of Christ, while also judging its closed-mindedness

---

Pneumatological Theology of Religions (Carlisle, 2003) develops such an approach.

[84]   Hollenweger, 'Towards a Pentecostal Missiology', p. 59.

[85]   See Chapter 1, pp. 24.

[86]   Paul J. Griffiths, 'The Uniqueness of Christian Doctrine Defended', in D'Costa (ed.), *Christian Uniqueness Reconsidered*, pp. 159–61. However well-intentioned Hick's revisionism may be, he totally overlooks how religious doctrines constitute community rules, defining boundaries, being shaped by and forming spiritual experience, functioning as teaching instruments and having 'cognitive content' which is 'expressive of salvifically significant truths' (pp. 162–7).

[87]   See 'deep pluralism', pp. 131,133, 138–42.

and sectarian behaviour, in the light of the vision of God's *basileia* to which the Body is oriented. In that way, the mutuality of Christ and Spirit, in community/ ies, and rooted in the being of God, reflects and enables the growing solidarity of others – and our mutual humanization.

In essence, the particularity of the Jesus-tradition, which is rooted in the prophetic Jewish tradition, energizes criticism of every power or tradition of domination, including those infecting its own praxis. Jesus, though, does not exhaust the embodiment of the Shaken One, but is integral to it, enabling us both to be open to other aspects of the Christian tradition, not least the array of trinitarian traditions as they foster in us a commitment to other-regard and solidarity, and, as we explore next, to engage with other traditions. The particularity of Jesus' shakenness shapes this tradition distinctively, not least in terms of its degree of self-criticism marked by its persistently reflexive approach to history, knowledge and power relations, being directed to expose and transform each dominating and dehumanizing force which impedes its pursuit of the solidarity of others.

Chapter 6
The Shaken One and the Other Beyond

The Shaken One and Other Traditions

This chapter is concerned with the nature of the relationship between the particular (person, community and vision of Jesus) and other particular traditions. As we have seen, it would be disingenuous to deny that the Christian tradition does indeed make universal claims, that is, the tradition has a radical otherness which should be affirmed. However, the question is: how should this otherness be affirmed in the light of other traditions which themselves also make universal claims and consist of distinct relations between particularity and universality? We should not generalize about these others, so as to dehumanize their constituents, but should attend to their genuine otherness, even as we also recognize that the traditions are not entirely separate from each other but are in fact interrelated.

In other words, this chapter seeks to examine how 'the scandal of particularity' – the problematic notion of a tradition's universal claims, or its radical otherness – is to be understood in the light of 'the scandal of plurality' – the fact that no tradition exists in a vacuum. While this could be read as a discussion of 'theologies of religions', since it briefly surveys several, the issues are directed by my particular vision of the Shaken One. The contours of *this* theology of religion are defined partly by their relation to the christologies of Hick and Newbigin and the vision constructed through engagement with them. We have seen that Hick's attempt to take religious diversity seriously certainly does 'transgress' the finalities or otherness of the Christian tradition. However, this relies on a particular reading, even a caricature, of the Christian tradition, and a particular finality of his own: his Kantian modernism which, even as it purports to appreciate difference, is effectively superficial in its reading of difference.[1] His reductionist christology need not properly engage with the dissonant others, because he has already discovered that the dissonance is not really so significant. Newbigin, on the other hand, openly declares his vision of finality, as being defined by the Christ-event, while also seeking to affirm that 'others' can illuminate 'our' gospel. That is, 'they' are valid to the extent that they serve the purpose to which 'we' are

---

[1]   See John V. Apczynski, 'John Hick's Theocentrism: Revolutionary or Implicitly Exclusivist?', *Modern Theologians*, 8/1 (January 1992): pp. 39–50. In particular, pp. 47–9, he identifies Hick's method as relying on 'the particular conception of reason as espoused by modern liberal culture', which requires 'a universal subject'. He sees this epistemological commitment as 'rather parochial', since it belittles the 'substantive truth claims of traditions' while 'circumventing' real dialogue.

committed, because Christ's finality is so absolutely unshakeable. There is a sense, then, in which both Hick and Newbigin oversimplify the relation between Christ and the other, and between 'us' and 'them', whether by belittling or absolutizing the differences, arguably by way of an impatient pursuit of truth-as-correctness instead of the more reflexive quest for truth-as-Honesty.

The point is: both Hick and Newbigin fail to attend to plurality *as genuine plurality*. Hick's pluralism, while defined as a first-order discourse in terms of its modernist meta-narrative, is informed also by a second-order description of relativism: there is a sense of indifference to genuine difference, the underlying commonality being deemed more significant and defined merely in terms of the traditions' shared movement from self-centredness to Real-centredness, an ethic with little bite. Newbigin, on the other hand, is illustrative of counter-modernism, by way of his reaction against Western modernity and reassertion of earlier narrative certainties, with insufficient regard for the otherness and relatedness of each tradition. Instead, a theology of religion focused on the Shaken One is concertedly pluralistic, in the sense that we are prompted to be open to others and the relation of each to 'us', so as to build a solidarity of others – not an easy harmony, but an uncomfortable vision of never-ending reflexivity and mutual liberation. It is a dialogical theology.

First, then, we consider the nature of dialogical theology, in the light of Hodgson and also David Lochhead. Then I contrast it with exclusivist and inclusivist theologies. Thirdly, as I argue that the Shaken One requires dialogical theology to be genuinely pluralistic, I use Griffin's terms to distinguish two categories of pluralistic theology: 'superficial' pluralism is more focused on the underlying commonalities, whereas 'deep' pluralism is committed to attending respectfully to the differences. Fourthly, with Cobb as the basis, I outline a potential shape for a 'shaken' theology of religions: dialogical, deeply pluralistic, and transformative. It consists of the praxis of 'critical humility'. The aim is to establish that christology cannot be done in isolation from dialogue and how a dialogical approach to christology necessitates deep openness to the otherness of the other. It is not about establishing the absolute relativity of all truths, since this dialogical theology is shaped by Jesus' distinctive, prophetic commitment to resist the 'Domination System', especially for the sake of those regarded as 'the last' or 'the least'. Like Hick, I do want to take seriously the religiously ambiguous nature of the universe, but without impatiently generalizing or idealizing the nature of pluralism.

The Shaken One and Dialogical Theology: Resisting Ideological Closure

It is partly in the light of Hodgson's recommendations for christology that I offer a vision of Christ which strives to be attentive to religious plurality. He makes this recommendation in the light of three quests he identifies in the postmodern context.[2] The first two are the emancipatory and the ecological, which I understand to be deeply interrelated with each other because of my essentially humanitarian view of ecological care. That is, since environmental damage has starker effects on poorer communities and it flows from our denial of humanity's ecological connectedness, the concern for environmental sustainability and the concern for mutual liberation are inseparable.[3] This liberative concern is more explicitly considered in Chapter 7. The third quest identified by Hodgson is dialogical; it is a postmodern quest not because plurality itself is new, but the depth of our awareness of it and determination to engage it is relatively new.

Hodgson argues that the dialogical quest relates to the other two, because, while it arises 'out of respect for differences', even so, it 'is always pressing toward wholeness and mutual transformation', as is the ecological quest; and although it relates to 'conceptual or logical rationality', it 'is always pressing toward discursive or communicative practices that have freedom as their telos', as in the case of the emancipatory quest.[4] In my terms, dialogue is about engaging identities with regards to their differences, but also the quest for solidarity; it is about understanding the other, but also about praxis and transformation in solidarity with each other. So, as we shall see, dialogical theology comes from being shaken but also engenders deeper shakenness. Specifically, the tradition of the Jewish Jesus in community shakes Gentiles but is also shaken by them; the Jewish Jesus shakes Christian presuppositions, but is also shaken through our ongoing christological reflections and reconstructions, so as to expose any previously unseen idealizations or dehumanizing tendencies and affirm that which enables us to heal each other of the damage done by the 'Domination System'. So, for Hodgson, citing Habermas, the point of 'communicative action', or dialogue, is that 'differences are never dissolved', communication remains incomplete, every project unfinished. This is about privileging the dialogical moment of postmodern rationality over the deconstructive, which sees only the differences, never the 'positive possibilities' of 'meaningful speech about God's presence and action in the world'.[5] Thus Hodgson concurs with Cobb that dialogue is the only alternative to both essentialism, which assumes a common essence in all religious traditions, and relativism, which rules out all normative critiques of norms on the basis of the context-dependence of every tradition.[6]

Hodgson notes that Hick's editorship of *The Myth of Christian Uniqueness* gathered together a particular kind of pluralists, in which Ogden identified a common error: they were largely shaped by practical or 'external' grounds (the

---

[2]   Peter C. Hodgson, *Winds of the Spirit: A Constructive Christian Theology* (London, 1994), pp. 66, 67–85, 86–98, 99–114.

[3]   See, for instance, Mary C. Grey, *Sacred Longings: Ecofeminist Theology and Globalization* (London, 2003).

[4]   Hodgson, *Winds of the Sprit*, p. 99.

[5]   Ibid., p. 100.

[6]   Ibid., pp. 100–101, 304.

fact of plurality, the question of cultural relativity, growing awareness of Western imperialism and collaboration *vis-à-vis* the problems of justice and environmental degradation), without valid theological grounds.[7] So Hodgson wonders whether something *within* the Christian tradition can engender a theology of pluralism.[8] What theologically can nurture a Christian pluralism? D'Costa's *Christian Uniqueness Reconsidered* pooled various criticisms of these attempts to be pluralistic, but Cobb's contribution differed again (as we see below), believing that the broad approach of *The Myth of Christian Uniqueness* is not genuinely pluralistic; that Hick et al. are wrong to see a common essence; and that a 'relatively objective norm' for judging the traditions is instead their capacity 'to be transformed by openness to other traditions, to expand and enrich their own understandings of reality while being faithful to their own heritage'.[9]

We are thus concerned with dialogical theology which can both display 'sanctity' to the particular tradition, affirming its identity of otherness, and practise 'transgression' of its boundaries, through genuine openness to others' otherness. For Hodgson, it is about affirming 'both the plurality and the solidarity' of the traditions, though he recognizes that theologians such as DiNoia, Milbank and Surin do not think it possible.[10] In *Christian Uniqueness Reconsidered*, between them, they argue that:[11] 1) the discourses of dialogue and pluralism are a Western form of domination obscuring the truth of real differences; 2) religions are unique cultural-linguistic-social systems not to be integrated into hybrids; 3) the propositional force of doctrines is essential as the only basis for debating religious truths[12]; 4) the 'praxis solution' of collaboration around practical goals presupposes particular Western values (justice, equality, freedom); 5) the manifestations of Western hegemony (as embodied in multinational corporations and the free market

---

[7]   Ibid., p. 105; citing also Schubert M. Ogden, 'Problems in the Case for a Pluralistic Theology of Religion', *The Journal of Religion*, 68 (October 1988): pp. 493–507; Ogden, *Is There Only One True Religion or Are There Many?* (Dallas, TX, 1992).

[8]   Hodgson, *Winds of the Sprit*, p. 105.

[9]   Ibid., pp. 105–6; John B. Cobb Jr, 'Beyond "Pluralism"', in Gavin D'Costa (ed.), *Christian Uniqueness Reconsidered: The Myth of a Pluralistic Theology of Religions* (Maryknoll, NY, 1990), pp. 81–92. While Cobb's criterion appears to be as formal as Hick's standard of 'transforming self-centredness to Real-centredness', so it should be the subject of similar critiques, it does not, however, objectify 'others': see below, pp. 139-42, and Chapter 8.

[10]   Hodgson, *Winds of the Sprit*, p. 304.

[11]   Ibid., pp. 304–5; J.A. DiNoia, 'Pluralist Theology of Religions: Pluralistic or Non-Pluralistic?', in D'Costa (ed.), *Christian Uniqueness Reconsidered*, pp. 119–34; John Milbank, 'The End of Dialogue', in D'Costa (ed.), *Christian Uniqueness Reconsidered*, pp. 174–91; Kenneth Surin, 'A "Politics of Speech": Religious Pluralism in the Age of the McDonald's Hamburger, in D'Costa (ed.), *Christian Uniqueness Reconsidered*, pp. 192–212. See also Chapter 7.

[12]   See Paul Griffiths, 'The Uniqueness of Christian Doctrine Defended', in D'Costa (ed.), *Christian Uniqueness Reconsidered*, pp. 157–73.

ideology) obstruct the conditions for any supposedly 'global' theology; 6) since the ideal goal of conversation is conversion, it must be subject to a hermeneutic of suspicion; and 7) in general the project homogenizes differences, systematically overlooking the asymmetries of power, so disallows real otherness.

In response, Hodgson asserts that, while the excesses of dialogue must be subjected to deconstruction, these criticisms caricature pluralist theologies, as though they are unaware of the dangers of *naïveté*, optimism, essentialism, power imbalances and homogenization.[13] As we shall see, pluralism is, after all, a very varied family of theologies, some of which engage the pitfalls more than others. He also retorts that 'being western' does not automatically invalidate a perspective: dialogical/pluralist theologies 'represent a western contribution to human self-understanding and well-being'; and he notes that Asia's pluralism predates Europe's. He suggests the critics do not offer a constructive alternative, whereas dialogue converts conflicts away from violence while refusing to wallow in 'indecipherable particularities' and engages proactively with 'the realities of dominance and hegemony'. For Hodgson, the appropriate kind of pluralism is thus grounded in God's 'radical relativity', the many traditions reflecting God's 'manifoldedness', arguing for dialogue between the different on the basis that it

> presupposes a new model of truth, whose criterion is not that of exclusion but rather that of the ability to relate to other expressions of truth and to grow through these relationships. Truth-through-relationship enables us to affirm that each religion has a particular grasp of divine truth, and that religions relate to each other in terms not of contradictions but of dialogical tensions and creative polarities. Truth is by nature dialectical: Every discovery and insight must be balanced by its opposite, every statement is both true and not true. Each religion needs what the others can give.[14]

This process clearly reflects Hodgson's Hegelian sensibilities, which I explain briefly in Chapter 8. It is also reminiscent of postmodern resistance to false dichotomies – between truth and interpretation, subject and object, individual and community – and it relates well with Ricoeur's model of metaphor, by which something 'more' comes to light than could otherwise be known. So for Hodgson, this kind of theology has two tasks, one critical, 'exposing idolatries' (whether in our language or in any dominating social practice), and the other constructive, to draw out 'convergent truths', the Spirit being involved in both: for we all need freeing from our idolatries, our cravings for 'security and certainty', and need our capacity for 'open-endedness' and 'constructive imagination' to be nurtured.[15] He says that without 'revelatory moments' of this *in history*, history would be an endless sequence of 'the will to power'; so there is a need to 'identify a paradigmatic gestalt

---

[13] Hodgson, *Winds of the Spirit*, pp. 305–6.
[14] Ibid., p. 307.
[15] Ibid., pp. 106–8, 309.

of God's presence in history', which Christians associate with Jesus of Nazareth and is worked out *throughout* history, through dialogue with others.[16] In my terms, the Shaken One exposes our ideologies, by problematizing our correlations between the particular tradition and universal truth, since such correlations oversimplify the tradition's history, language and interrelatedness; and the Shaken One draws us into solidarity with each other, that we might see both commonality (not least, common humanity) and affirm genuine difference.

Lochhead's distinction between theology and ideology is also useful in this regard.[17] He believes that Cobb, to whom we return below, offers a way of being faithful to the tradition while being open to others,[18] grounded in a theology of dialogue. Most others, by contrast, tend to be captive to one of four ideologies. An ideology of 'isolation' treats others as self-deceiving, out of touch with reality, not really worthy of engagement. An ideology of 'hostility' justifies those views of others which see them as hostile to one's message, fuelling suspicion and tension. An ideology of 'competition' treats others as in need of the fulfilment which only one's tradition offers, understanding itself as being compelled to sell its message in the marketplace of ideas. And an ideology of 'partnership', different from the other three, presumes common ground where it may not exist, projecting one's norms on to others even for the most peaceable of intentions.

For Lochhead, the point is that dialogue is not merely about sharing in conversation; it entails openness and vulnerability to one another, so flows from God's invitation to us as demonstrated by the self-emptying, openness and vulnerability of Christ.[19] Therefore it must not be justified by the results it seeks, because God's love towards us is not a 'neurotic' or needy love, but is about dialogue *as such*, and any *a priori* presumptions about the other with whom we dialogue would thus compromise the dialogue. That is the risk: to dialogue because we must, even though we may be used in the process, or even if the good of it is impeded by our or their 'ideological' captivity.[20] Lochhead grounds this in the I–Thou relationship commended by Buber, whose primary concern, pertinent to our quest, was to defy objectification by which one presumes to possess or categorize the other. Instead, it is only in *the relation* or the 'between' of dialogue that truth is really encountered,[21] which concurs with Hodgson's emphasis on the relational nature of Truth. Lochhead suggests this should be definitive for the entire way in which the Church does mission: dialoguing with the world (including its religious traditions), *because of* our faithfulness to the God revealed in Christ

---

[16]   Ibid., p. 314.

[17]   David Lochhead, *The Dialogical Imperative: A Christian Reflection on Interfaith Encounter* (Maryknoll, NY, 1988), pp. 3–4, 5–26, 92–7.

[18]   Ibid., pp. 92–3.

[19]   Ibid., pp. 80–81.

[20]   Ibid., p. 81.

[21]   Ibid., pp. 48–53; Martin Buber, *I and Thou* (New York, 1958), pp. 7–8, 75, 80; Martin Buber, *Between Man and Man* (London, 1947), pp. 23–4.

as self-emptying. So our witnessing and proclaiming, which is essentially about storytelling, is a mission of invitation to dialogue.[22]

Lochhead thus deems Hick to assume mistakenly that christology must be reformed as a precondition for effective dialogue, as though a constitutive christology necessarily excludes non-Christians from God's providence. Instead, Hick should understand that when 'exclusivists' deem others to be outside God's providence, they are captive to an *ideology* of isolation or hostility, to which their theologies lend themselves.[23] By contrast, as Lochhead outlines, Barth attacks all 'religion'.[24] For it always consists of limitations or provincialism – or objectifications – so there is no basis for Christian 'triumphalism'. We all stand under judgment and in need of criticism. While Barth affirms that God's sovereignty is revealed in the Christ-event, to which the Christian tradition attests, there remains a distinction between the events and the religion: thus we must not claim any premature closure. Unlike Barth, in this regard, Newbigin more explicitly draws the conclusion that 'others' are primarily validated to the extent that they serve the purpose of the gospel. Nonetheless, Lochhead's point is not to congratulate Barthians while criticizing followers of Hick or Newbigin, but to alert us to the ideological captivity of any theological or religious provincialism. We cannot presume to know the other prior to dialogue, but must enter dialogue vulnerably and openly. What, then, of those Christian traditions which appear to prejudge the outcome of dialogue? In what way are they shaken?

The Shaken One or the Only One: Scandalizing Each Other

Here I briefly survey the issues with regards to those theologies of religion which are essentially exclusivist or inclusivist, which both allow for shakenness only to a certain extent, because they fundamentally maintain that Christ alone is the source of salvation. In short, I seek to show how the Shaken One scandalizes such theologies by way of its radical openness to the other no less than such theologies scandalize the Shaken One!

Christ and No Other: Exclusivist Theologies

There are several terms used in relation to these theologies. At their most extreme Fackre speaks of 'imperial singularity',[25] which totally correlates the particularity of God's acts in Christ with God's universal mission, so as to exclude any possibility of any other particulars' contributing salvifically to the whole. A 'softer' version is

---

[22] Lochhead, *Dialogical Imperative*, pp. 82–7.

[23] Ibid., pp. 90–91.

[24] Ibid., pp. 34–9.

[25] Gabriel Fackre, 'The Scandal of Particularity and Universality', *Mid-Stream*, 22/1 (1983): p. 42.

represented by Barth (and Newbigin), which Fackre calls 'centrifugal singularity', by which the Christ-event is 'definitive and determinative', the effects radiating outwards, such that we ought not to second-guess the limits of its impact. For it is not we but God who is sovereign; so it is Christ, not the Christian's interpretation of him, who is final. Knitter talks of 'replacement' models, in the sense that the exclusive Christian tradition replaces and supersedes all others; it is the only effective particularity; though he identifies both 'total' and 'partial' replacements, the latter allowing for 'revelation' in other traditions even as Christ alone does the saving.[26] Christology within such theologies is clearly constitutive: we need him not only for our salvation but for us to know the fullness of salvation; or, for Pannenberg, Christ is the eschatological clue to the whole, without whom we could not know that God is God of the future.[27]

As Knitter affirms, these theologies teach: 1) the centrality of scripture, which must be taken seriously; 2) the reality of evil, which needs a response more objective than our ideologically-laden delusions and practices; 3) the possibility at least that Jesus is the only way; and 4) an appropriate wariness about 'religion' itself, as it can be distorting, even 'demonic'. On the other hand, as Knitter notes, the Bible is pluriform and our interpretations of it are themselves ideologically-laden – and we must remember that other traditions make some similarly scandalous claims to exclusivity.[28] Fackre's proposed 'universal particularity' is an attempt to hold these things in tension: to affirm that revelation can be effected beyond Christ but that salvation is exclusive to the Christ-event; to emphasize both the continuity of this event with others and its genuine newness; acknowledging that it 'will grate harshly with the ears of modernity', but such is the nature of Christ.[29]

As for Newbigin, he asserts the 'unique truth of the revelation in Jesus Christ', though allows for the possibility of salvation for non-Christians; he 'refuses to limit the saving grace of God to members of the Christian Church', but denies that other traditions might be 'vehicles of salvation'; and acknowledges that God can work in all people, but maintains that God's acts in Christ are unique and decisive.[30] For him, inclusivism and pluralism arise as theological traditions out of an understandable concern for unity, rather than a concern for truth, and suggests that, in truth, some paths may not lead to the same summit but may indeed lead

---

[26]   Paul F. Knitter, *Introducing Theologies of Religions* (Maryknoll, NY, 2002), pp. 19–60. Knitter also distinguishes between 'pessimistic' partial replacement theologies, which deny that non-Christians can be saved, and 'optimistic' partial replacement theologies, which are intentionally more ambiguous with various 'qualifications' afforded by God's universal saving will: pp. 45–7.

[27]   Ibid., pp. 36–40; Wolfhart Pannenberg, *Basic Questions in Theology*, vol. 2 (London, 1971), pp. 107–14.

[28]   Knitter, *Introducing Theologies*, pp. 50–60.

[29]   Fackre, pp. 44–7.

[30]   Lesslie Newbigin, *The Gospel in a Pluralist Society* (London, 1989), pp. 182–3.

'over the precipice'.[31] Schmidt-Leukel thus describes Newbigin as an 'undecided exclusivist' – there is only one way, but others may be saved.[32] However, Greene rightly points out that Newbigin should be understood missiologically; that his theology should not be read in terms of responses to religious plurality, but as a response to God's self-revelation in Christ; and that it will inevitably appear scandalous through the lenses of individualism and subjectivism.[33]

For Lochhead, however, such theologies demonstrate 'monological' discourse, pre-empting the question of religious plurality by asserting that the vital events are already located within the witness of our tradition.[34] They cannot envisage being shaken by other traditions beyond; it is only the radical otherness as revealed in the particular Christ-event which truly shakes our worldviews. The resistance of these theologies to questioning may suggest ideological powers are at work: by surrendering to the divine mystery of their scandalous particularity, they refuse to engage with otherness, possibly being fearful of and scandalized by the prospect of shakenness. For what if their apparent entrenchment is shown to be ideological? What would happen to the power they have over their adherents and the generalized, objectified vision of others which they engender? Might they be confronted with the interrelatedness not only of theology and ideology, but the interrelatedness of one tradition and another?

Christ in the Other: Inclusivist Theologies

Knitter speaks of this category of theologies in terms of 'fulfilment': that is, there may be both truth and grace, both something revelatory and even something salvific, in the other tradition, perhaps due to the Spirit's presence and activity, but it is Christ who fulfils such traces of God's providence.[35] Thus the traditions are good (even if they each have the capacity for the demonic), and it is right to engage in dialogue on this basis, expecting mutual enrichment – though it basically involves reading 'their' tradition in 'our' terms; 'they' are included, or assimilated, within 'our' language-game.

Fackre thus identifies Rahner's theology as 'centripetal singularity', as it affirms continuity between others and the Christian tradition, but maintains that they come to their fulfilment in Christ.[36] For Rahner, the Church is the 'vanguard and socially constituted explicit expression of what the Christian hopes is present as a hidden

---

[31]   Ibid., p. 183.

[32]   Perry Schmidt-Leukel, 'Mission and Trinitarian Theology', in Foust et al. (eds), *A Scandalous Prophet*, pp. 59–60.

[33]   Colin J.D. Greene, 'Trinitarian Tradition and the Cultural Collapse of Late Modernity', in Foust et al. (eds), *A Scandalous Prophet*, pp. 65–6.

[34]   Lochhead, *Dialogical Imperative*, p. 82f.

[35]   Knitter, *Introducing Theologies*, pp. 100–103.

[36]   Fackre, p. 41.

reality even outside the visible Church'.[37] In this context he speaks of 'anonymous Christians', those whose commitments are effectively Christian without an explicit confession, by virtue of Christ's impact beyond Christianity. Roman Catholicism has not officially gone as far as Rahner, but does affirm the good in other traditions by way of the Spirit of truth.[38] As we have seen, both Dupuis and D'Costa also affirm the role of the Spirit, arguing that God wills this plural state of affairs. In Dupuis's case, for example, although Jesus is constitutively unique, the Christ-event is also 'relational', such that Christians must remain open to what others may teach us of the Divine Mystery, for any culmination in Christ will not occur until the end of history.[39]

The approaches of D'Costa and Dupuis have political dimensions and implications, but Knitter alludes to the particularly liberative demands of interreligious dialogue as espoused in Asian contexts. Jesus is understood not simply to draw Christians into dialogue but as the servant of the poor.[40] The common concern for liberation draws people of different traditions into deeper dialogue with each other. The criterion for mutuality is the extent to which God's *basileia* is furthered: that is, the Christian tradition determines the benchmark, but the point is not to absorb others within the Christian framework, as though to belittle the genuine distinctions, rather to include others in shared, Christlike action, affirming what is liberative in each.[41]

This is the context for M.M. Thomas whose 'Christ-centredness' emphasizes that, just as Jesus collapses the division between Jew and Gentile, so he also collapses the division between believer and unbeliever, being for the whole world.[42] While *The Myth of Christian Uniqueness* relativizes and relegates the position of Jesus, Thomas argues that Jesus is a positive 'universal'. With Christ as the criterion, the task is to distinguish between the light and the dark sides of all traditions, so adopting elements of exclusivism, inclusivism and pluralism: for example, he excludes 'docetic spiritualities' because of their 'crusading' tendencies and is both self-critical and critical of others, including of the pluralism which fails to condemn evils. It is crucially a matter of praxis rather than doctrine, focused on three levels of 'koinonia-in-Christ',[43] which resonate with Hodgson's three

---

[37]   Knitter, *Introducing Theologies*, p. 74, citing Karl Rahner, 'Christianity and the Non-Christian Religions', in *Theological Investigations*, vol. 5 (Baltimore, MD, 1966), p. 133.

[38]   *Redemptor Hominis* (1979), pp. 3, 31–2.

[39]   See Knitter, *Introducing Theologies*, pp. 92–3.

[40]   Ibid., pp. 96–8.

[41]   Ibid.; Gaudencia B. Rosales and C.G. Arévalo (eds), *For All the Peoples of Asia: Federation of Asian Bishops' Conferences Documents from 1970 to 1991*, vol. 1 (Maryknoll, NY, 1992), pp. 315, 300.

[42]   M.M. Thomas, 'A Christ-Centred Humanist Approach to Other Religions in the Indian Pluralistic Context', in D'Costa (ed.), *Christian Uniqueness Reconsidered*, pp. 49–62.

[43]   Ibid., p. 61. (Note the Greek word *koinonia* may equate to 'fellowship', 'communion', 'partnership', even perhaps 'solidarity'.)

christological criteria: 1) the eucharistic community, a unity of diverse peoples professing the *person* of Jesus as Messiah (that is, there must be appropriation of the breadth of the tradition); 2) a larger *koinonia* of dialogue with diverse traditions reflecting the ultimacy of the *pattern* of suffering servanthood as exemplified by the crucified Jesus (that is, there must be engagement with other traditions); and 3) a still larger *koinonia* of involvement in the sociopolitical struggle for new societies and a world community based on a secular anthropology *informed* by the agape cross (that is, there must be commitment to liberation and justice).

However, the Asian contexts and M.M. Thomas illustrate that 'others' are essentially being seen through a Christian lens, validating them basically to the extent that they confirm the Christian vision. Although Thomas, like Newbigin, is clear that self-criticism should be part of this engagement, the Shaken One might suggest a more nuanced process, certainly willing to expose any dehumanizing tendencies in the others but also more open to hear them on their own terms. For the particularity of the Christian language and vision does not exhaust the language and vision of the divine; there are other languages and visions which may yet scandalize our tradition.

Christ Sees the Other: Comparative and Postliberal Theologies

Comparative and postliberal theologies are two implicitly inclusivist approaches which are more explicit about the fact that Christians must be true to our language-game while acknowledging that we inevitably 'see' the other through our own conditioning lenses.

For comparativists, in brief, to the extent that we live within a particular skin, so always see others from within our perspective, we are all 'inclusivists'.[44] The Bible, after all, claims universal vision, so we '"read" the non-Christian within the Christian horizon'.[45] The point, though, of comparative theology is to study sacred texts alongside each other, recognizing the genuine novelty and diversity, that each is a classic cultural text, and that we can learn much about ourselves from such dialogue.[46] It is not about reforming one's vision in the light of others' perspectives, however, but learning to see oneself with others' eyes, being both loyal to Christ and vulnerable to the other. Our realization that we see them within our vision includes the realization that they see us within theirs:[47] this does not point to common ground, but to the scandal of plurality. For comparativists, however,

---

[44]   Knitter, *Introducing Theologies*, p. 217.

[45]   Francis X. Clooney, SJ., 'Reading the World in Christ: From Comparison to Inclusivism', in D'Costa (ed.), *Christian Uniqueness Reconsidered*, pp. 67–8; Knitter, *Introducing Theologies*, p. 213: for the Christian, it is simply impossible to contemplate anything 'outside' of the biblical view.

[46]   Clooney, 'Reading the World', p. 69; David Tracy, *The Analogical Imagination* (New York, 1981), p. 68.

[47]   Knitter, *Introducing Theologies*, p. 219.

there remains the presumption that we will not be shaken by such scandalous plurality: we can go so far but no further.

So it is with postliberal theologies, too. Their achievement is to identify the power of language in shaping tradition and practice. Language does not merely capture that which we already know, as conservatives might suggest, since language conditions our knowledge. Nor does it merely express our prior experience, as though it can be straightforwardly changed when our experience changes.[48] Rather, language shapes our thoughts, convictions and experiences, so identity is not formed individually but by communally developed language. As for dialogue, there is radical 'incommensurability' between different discourses; one cannot be easily translated into another's terms; not even 'God' or 'Love' have the same meaning or status in the various language-games, because each tradition's linguistic system has its own comprehensive rules and purpose. However, while language certainly colours how we construct identities, postliberal perspectives overstate the problem; for dialogue can be fruitful and we need not be imprisoned by our language.[49]

In fact, it is questionable that all adherents of a tradition recognize their discourse as being wholly comprehensive. As social beings, we live with hints of several discourses; for no tradition has such stark boundaries. If each tradition is really so locked into its own language-game, are we not resigned to fideism – the inability to explain our faith in any terms at all other than our own?[50] Of course, as with comparative theology, it is right to be wary of any claim to understand the other, since we see and read them from within conditioned experiences and practices; but dialogical theology, as encouraged by the Shaken One, scandalizes the finalities and presuppositions of our vision and reading more than this. The process of learning to see the other not in generalized terms but more concretely can genuinely lead to new understanding and new possibilities for action.

The Shaken One and Pluralistic Theology: Attending to Difference

I turn to pluralism, believing that truth-as-Honesty (that is, being open to transcendence, rather than captive to ideology) demands our being shaken to such an extent that our theology is genuinely pluralistic: not a solidarity of shaken Christians, or shaken liberals, but a solidarity of the different but related; a solidarity of Being Human together; a solidarity of mutual humanization. In christological terms, I am arguing, 'the myth of the Human Being' demands that we see Jesus

---

[48]   Ibid., pp. 178–80; George Lindbeck, *The Nature of Doctrine: Religion and Theology in a Postliberal Age* (London, 1984).

[49]   Knitter, *Introducing Theologies*, pp. 183–5.

[50]   Ibid., pp. 220–26; Werner Ustorf, 'The Emerging Christ of Post-Christian Europe', in Foust et al. (eds), *A Scandalous Prophet*, pp. 132–5: for example, for a European Christian, Christianity cannot be all-embracing.

embodying it in and through relationship with others, which includes engagement with and openness to those interrelated traditions and communities which raise questions different from those raised by the Judaeo-Christian community of Jesus. In other words, if Jesus Christ is 'the Shaken One' he (and his Body) must be shaken by religious others, while also shaking them.

It is essential first to explain, as Griffin outlines,[51] that there are two broad families of religious pluralism, the first of which – 'superficial pluralism' – is insufficiently shaken. Only 'deep pluralism' offers the possibility of a christology genuinely attentive to the demands of shakenness and generating a transformative solidarity of others. The two families, however, have certain things in common, which Griffin describes as 'general pluralism'.[52] Essentially they reject absolutism and embrace truth in others. Although some forms of inclusivism claim to embrace truth in others, the fact that they presume or project a Christian answer to others' questions indicates that their openness to others' truth is less than that of pluralism.

The Pluralistic Shift: Ontologically Different

For Griffin, pluralism consists of four main shifts in worldview, compared with exclusivism and inclusivism: they are sociological, theological, ethical and ontological. Sociologically, the fact that our knowledge of other traditions has grown so much, especially in a post-colonial world, acts as a challenge to any claims to Christianity's unique uniqueness. Theologically, any doctrine of Christian absolutism or finality arguably conflicts with divine love: so for Ogden, divine love trumps any constitutive christology; for Toynbee, the Judaeo-Christian God of love exceeds any Judaeo-Christian tribal deity; Gilkey asks whether divine love would 'choose' us because of our particular external religion; Huston Smith argues that 'the deity cannot play favourites'; and Knitter (using Rahner) sees God's universal salvific will as implying that other traditions might not only have revelation but be 'ways of salvation'.[53] For Hick, the point is that theodicy demands universal salvation; for it would not be infinite love were it to exclude most people. Although Griffin notes that Hick's later focus on the Real, which lacks

---

[51]   David Ray Griffin (ed.), *Deep Religious Pluralism* (Louisville, KY, 2005), pp. 3–4.

[52]   Ibid., pp. 5–15.

[53]   Ibid., p. 10: Ogden, 'Problems in the Case', p. 495; Ogden, *Is There Only One?*, p. 92; Arnold Toynbee, 'What Should Be the Christian Approach to the Contemporary Non-Christian Faiths?', in Owen C. Thomas (ed.), *Attitudes toward Other Religions: Some Christian Interpretations* (London, 1969), p. 161; Langdon Gilkey, 'Plurality and Its Theological Implications', in John Hick and Paul Knitter (eds), *The Myth of Christian Uniqueness* (London, 1988), p. 39; David R. Griffin and Huston Smith, *Primordial Truth and Postmodern Theology* (Albany, NY, 1989), p. 41; Paul F. Knitter, *No Other Name? A Critical Survey of Christian Attitudes toward the World Religions* (Maryknoll, NY, 1986), pp. 125, 116–17, 140.

positive attributes such as love, undermines his appeal to theodicy, nevertheless this 'theological' shift does represent Hick's general approach. In particular, Hick illustrates the 'ethical' concern, as we saw in Chapter 2, because he associates Christian absolutism with ethical issues such as anti-Semitism and imperialism, and he suggests religion can only heal if its absolutism is dismantled. Or Knitter suggests we cannot truly 'love' the other while trying to convert them to 'our' way; and for Suchocki, to live the reign of God is not to imperialize one religion but to create a new community of genuine diversity in friendship. So for Heim, the moral impulse is the pluralist's primary impulse.[54]

We have seen, however, Newbigin's responses to each of these three concerns: our sociological knowledge of the others cannot shake the ultimate authority of the plausibility structure founded on the Christ-event; our theological concerns are signs of modernity's dislike of God's election of particularity for the good of the whole; and our ethical sensibilities, though laudable, can only be fulfilled by the crucified and risen Saviour: for God's choice of the cross shows that God does not dominate but liberates, humbling the imperialism of both Christian and non-Christian alike. While I do not think Newbigin's responses necessarily defuse those concerns, they do suggest that Griffin is right to view the fourth shift, the 'ontological', as being fundamental to general pluralism. He argues that exclusivism and inclusivism are rooted in ontological 'supernaturalism'. It maintains that certain divine/human events override our normal epistemic fallibility in such a way that the truth of these decisive events can be settled by an appeal to their intrinsic authority. Pluralism rejects this epistemic supernaturalism and authoritarianism, being rooted instead in 'naturalistic theism'. It means that God is not simply refraining from intervening; rather, God retains causal influence but cannot interrupt 'normal causal relations'.[55] While this is clearly informed by 'the scientific project', it is not an argument for mere materialism or sensationism, which accepts as real only what our senses perceive. Instead, it relates to 'the new physics', the ambiguity and relationality of the universe, the integral worldview's understanding that everything interpenetrates everything else, and Hodgson's

---

[54] Griffin, *Deep Religious Pluralism*, pp. 11–12: John Hick, *God Has Many Names* (London, 1980), p. 17; Hick, 'The Non-Absoluteness of Christianity', in Hick and Knitter (eds), *The Myth of Christian Uniqueness*, pp. 18–19; John Hick, *The Rainbow of Faiths* (London, 1995), p. 123; Paul F. Knitter, *Jesus and the Other Names: Christian Mission and Global Responsibility* (Maryknoll, NY, 1996), pp. 39–40; Marjorie Hewitt Suchocki, *Divinity and Diversity: A Christian Affirmation of Religious Pluralism* (Nashville, TN, 2003), pp. 80–81, 86; S. Mark Heim, *Salvations: Truth and Difference in Religion* (Maryknoll, NY, 1995), p. 72.

[55] Griffin, *Deep Religious Pluralism*, pp. 12–16: Edward Farley and Peter C. Hodgson, 'Scripture and Tradition', in Peter C. Hodgson and Robert H. King (eds), *Christian Theology: An Introduction to its Traditions and Tasks*, 2nd edn (Philadelphia, PA, 1985), pp. 61–87.

concept of the God-World-Spirit dynamic, or I-You-We relations.[56] That is, God and creation interpenetrate each other.

Therefore, the transcendent God does not enter 'into' history or initiate Christian faith in person.[57] Rather, pluralism breaks with exclusivist and inclusivist theologies by, firstly, problematizing belief in God's nature-negating initiative; secondly, insisting that God's presence throughout creation must be taken seriously (attending to the interrelatedness of faith traditions, culture, science and praxis); and thirdly, emphasizing that the art of interpretation is intrinsic to faith and, even more basically, to being human. It is thus inevitable and right that we should interpret plurality. (As a result, for Cobb, the metaphysical uniqueness of the incarnation is to be rejected.[58]) For plurality flows from God's ontological relations with the world. In Suchocki's terms, God calls into being and creation's responses are increasingly diverse, especially amongst humans who have the greatest freedom; so other religious traditions are to be valued because God has been involved in calling them, too. Of course, critics of 'general pluralism' see such naturalistic theism as not Christian, because it apparently accepts modern rationality and the scientific project uncritically; so as Heim notes, pluralists need to justify the universality of Enlightenment assumptions about God's relations with the world – which Griffin sees Cobb as achieving.[59]

What, though, of the general pluralists most criticized? As Griffin describes them, their pluralism is 'identist' rather than 'differential' or 'deep', in that they see the traditions as being oriented towards the same identity or object (though they give it different names) and basically promote a common end.[60] That is, they are identist both ontologically and soteriologically. Knitter understands this group as a 'mutuality' model, since it believes mutual relations between the traditions are as important as the tradition's particularity.[61] However, that involves the promotion of a version of 'mutuality' whereby commonality is emphasized to the cost of identity and otherness. Griffin's other term for this, 'superficial pluralism', is preferable, as it captures this approach's tendency to belittle the reality of differences.

[56]   Hodgson, *Winds of the Spirit*, pp. 44–8, 153–4, 157, 162–4.

[57]   Griffin, *Deep Religious Pluralism*, pp. 15–16; Hick, *Rainbow of Faiths*, pp. 53, 15, 23, 87, 126; Hick, *Problems of Religious Pluralism* (New York, 1985), pp. 34, 36; Hick, 'The Non-Absoluteness', in Hick and Knitter (eds), *The Myth of Christian Uniqueness*, p. 23; Ogden, 'Problems in the Case', pp. 498, 502.

[58]   John B. Cobb Jr, 'Dialogue', in Leonard Swidler, John B. Cobb Jr, Paul F. Knitter and Monika K. Hellwig, *Death or Dialogue? From the Age of Monologue to the Age of Dialogue* (London, 1990), p. 14.

[59]   Griffin, *Deep Religious Pluralism*, pp. 19–21: Suchocki, *Divinity and Diversity*, pp. 28–33; Suchocki, 'In Search of Justice: Religious Pluralism from a Feminist Perspective', in Hick and Knitter (eds), *The Myth of Christian Uniqueness*, pp. 154–5; Heim, *Salvations*, pp. 92–3, 123–4, 214.

[60]   Griffin, *Deep Religious Pluralism*, p. 24.

[61]   Knitter, *Introducing Theologies*, pp. 109–10.

After all, where doctrinal differences problematically obstruct the ethical obligation to dialogue, they are revised. As Knitter explains, such theologies overcome the differences in three ways: philosophically, mystically and ethically.

Superficial Pluralism: The Philosophical Bridge

Hick epitomizes this approach, by philosophizing about that which is beyond each culturally conditioned language-game or religious tradition, calling it 'the Real'. Each tradition is thus a particular response to that which cannot be directly experienced. All religious language should therefore be understood as mythological, essentially orienting us toward the Real, such that each tradition transforms our self-centredness into Real-centredness. In this way, even those differences between traditions which appear contradictory may be explained in terms of the inadequacy of language and the conditioned nature of our religious experience. This does not reduce the religious enterprise to relativism, since there remains an ethical measure and eschatological verification will ultimately reveal whether our beliefs and actions were appropriate.

It is for the orthodox interpretations of the tradition to justify themselves, in the light of this philosophical critique and the question of ethical outcomes. For Hick, the mythological reading of Christian faith indicates that, while Jesus was inspired by God's Spirit and exemplified human resistance to self-centredness, he was not ontologically the incarnation of God; he stands simply as one colour of the transcendent light refracted through the prism of human cultural experience.

For Griffin, Heim and others, this approach is not really a pluralistic theology. Firstly, Hick denies that different traditions have different ends, suggesting instead they are broadly orienting us toward the same goal.[62] This assumption of commonality, even if based on real glimpses of each other, shortcuts the never-ending demands of dialogue according to generalizations of the traditions' identities, presuming we know certain things about each other. As we shall see further in Chapter 7, this betrays considerable Western assumptions, though it also reflects the Hindu belief in the mere *appearance* of differences, or indeed the secular agnosticism which generalizes about religion: 'They are all the same really.' Ironically, the deeper Hick leads us into a tradition, the more he is leading us out of it, seeing it as a mere cipher pointing us to that which lies beyond. While Heim takes this issue as a basis for generalizing about the failure of pluralism, Griffin instead takes it as evidence of Hick's 'superficial' rather than 'deep' pluralism.[63]

Secondly, Hick does not only oversimplify the differences between religious ends, but belittles the differences in 'surface' practices and beliefs. His Kantian distinction judges the mere 'phenomena' to be relatively unimportant, whereas, in fact, a tradition's surface details are meant to be related to its deeper, distinct identity. This judgment impedes dialogue, since it suggests that doctrines must

---

[62]   Griffin, *Deep Religious Pluralism*, pp. 24–8; Heim, *Salvations*, pp. 102–3, 129.

[63]   Griffin, *Deep Religious Pluralism*, p. 29.

be revised as a precondition of dialogue, according to an apparently 'neutral universality', as Griffin sees it, which transcends all particularities and judges their status.[64] As we have seen, Hick refutes that he claims such a privileged vantage-point, insisting that his framework is constructed inductively; but, like Griffin and Heim, I see Hick's framework as a meta-theology, an attempt at a theology above all theologies, conditioned by its Kantian particularism.[65] By contrast, as we shall see, Cobb explicitly rejects the possibility of neutrality; it is vital to own one's commitment.

The third issue with Hick's philosophical bridge between the traditions' differences is its consequent rejection of Christian particularism. On the one hand, it is its very point, since it associates Christian particularism with unethical practices; but on the other hand, Hick could make his case more carefully so as to distinguish between those aspects of Christian identity which are honourably distinctive (humanizing) and those which are dangerously distinctive (dehumanizing). His attempt to purge the tradition of its shadow side is dishonest and innocent, in the sense that he is denying the interpenetration of reality and the inevitability of a tradition's unintended consequences. As Griffin sees it, his superficial pluralism effectively obscures the validity of Christian distinctiveness – not only with regards to christology, but the general narrative of Christian faith. While Cobb, too, revises elements of the tradition, including the metaphysics of incarnation, he insists that each tradition achieves something unique and that each is superior *vis-à-vis* its particular achievement.[66]

Hick's approach, as I have argued, is problematic because his christology is insufficiently attentive to the shaken nature of Jesus Christ. By reducing the distinctiveness of both Jesus and the Christian tradition to the extent that he is a cipher and it is a language-game which simply alludes to an underlying commonality, his shaking power and openness to further shakenness is denied.

Superficial Pluralism: The Mystical Bridge

The 'mystical' means of bridging the (superficial) divisions between different traditions is best represented by Panikkar, for whom the cosmotheandric Mystery is both one and many.[67] Having three parts, the human, the divine, and the world, constituted by dynamic relations, this Mystery would collapse without its many

---

[64] Ibid., p. 30; Heim, *Salvations*, pp. 4, 10, 30, 34.

[65] Griffin, *Deep Religious Pluralism*; Heim, *Salvations*, p. 105.

[66] Griffin, *Deep Religious Pluralism*, pp. 27, 31–3; Cobb, *Transforming Christianity*, pp. 62, 72, 86, 182.

[67] See Knitter, *Introducing Theologies*, pp. 125–30; Raimundo Panikkar, *The Cosmotheandric Experience: Emerging Religious Consciousness* (Maryknoll, NY, 1993), p. ix; Panikkar, *The Trinity and the Religious Experience of Man* (Maryknoll, NY, 1973), pp. 74–5; Panikkar, *The Unknown Christ of Hinduism* (Maryknoll, NY, 1981), p. 19; Panikkar, 'The Invisible Harmony: A Universal Theory of Religion or a Cosmic Confidence

paths. Unlike Hick, Panikkar gives priority to diversity, not commonality, but argues for more than merely peaceful co-existence; there must be 'mutual fecundation', enriching, perichoresis. Within his vision of a 'discordant' concord, Jesus constitutes 'Christophany',[68] the appearance of the same Christ, or 'authentically universal Christology', discernible in all traditions. Christ is the dynamic, unifying current binding the human and the cosmic with the divine, and as such is not exclusive to Jesus of Nazareth;[69] rather, Jesus 'would be one of the names of the cosmotheandric principle'.[70]

The problem, though, is that the priority Panikkar claims to give to diversity or 'discordance' does not equate with the particularity of 'perichoresis', since, in trinitarian terms, that entails the sharing of the same substance. Similarly, Panikkar's claim to a 'universal Christology' implies that the love between or mutual fecundation of the traditions is not as awkward as he suggests; for there is a unifying abstraction.

Superficial Pluralism: The Ethical Bridge

The 'ethical' means of bridging the (superficial) divisions between the different traditions is represented by the theologies of Knitter, Pieris, and arguably Moltmann. Its focus is not the incommensurability of religious beliefs or ends, but the need for dialogue on the basis of humanity's shared problems: poverty, violence, patriarchy, ecological degradation.[71] It can avoid relativism, so long as commitment to justice and peace is prioritized, especially as judged by those who suffer most. Rather than Hick's philosophical approach to Jesus as one inspiring response to the transcendent reality, or Panikkar's mystical concept of the universal Christ, there is a reliance here on what historical scholarship tells us (even diversely) about Jesus the liberator, whose commitment to God's *basileia* energizes this approach to dialogue and praxis.

The issue is not whether we are properly Church-centred, Jesus-centred, or even God-centred, in our relating with each other, but whether we are kingdom- or regno-centric, in our commitments to sociopolitical transformation. Jesus' uniqueness is not denied but focused on his particular contribution to God's reign,

---

in Reality?', in Swidler (ed.), *Toward a Universal Theology of Religions* (Maryknoll, NY, 1987), p. 145.

[68]   Knitter, *Introducing Theologies*, p. 131: see Panikkar, 'The Invisible Harmony', in Swidler (ed.), *Toward a Universal Theology*, p. 122.

[69]   Knitter, *Introducing Theologies*, pp. 131–3: Panikkar, *The Unknown Christ* (London, 1981), pp. 14, 27.

[70]   Knitter, *Introducing Theologies*, p. 133: Panikkar, *The Trinity*, pp. 53–4; *The Unknown Christ*, pp. 27, 48–9.

[71]   Knitter, *Introducing Theologies*, pp. 134–48: Jurgen Moltmann, 'Is "Pluralistic Theology" Useful for the Dialogue of World Religions?', in D'Costa (ed.), *Christian Uniqueness Reconsidered*, pp. 149–56.

especially, as Pieris sees it, because of his intensification of the Jewish prophets' message and unique establishment of God's covenant with the poor.[72] In Pieris's provocative terms, 'Outside God's covenant with the poor, there is no salvation.'[73] So, for him, the Incarnation as such is not surprising, since the whole world is already God's body; but the shock is God's act in Jesus of solidarity with the victims of oppression.[74]

Thus Christians' unique contribution to dialogue, while listening and learning from others, is to enable others to find what may not be so clear to them in their traditions: that to be one with the Ultimate is to be concerned for the victims of the world; anything less is 'unfaithful' to the uniqueness of Jesus. Such uniqueness, as Knitter understands Pieris, will not be the same as Christian imperialism heard through the doctrinal claims to Jesus as God's only Son; rather it will be genuinely good news discovered in dialogue with others and which has already led people of other traditions to reflect on their ethical obligations.[75] So commitment to the poor is illuminated through dialogue – without syncretizing the traditions.

As Knitter argues,[76] these philosophical, mystical and ethical forms of pluralism each allow for plural 'one-and-onlys' without collapsing into relativism, since each proposes a universal criteria against which all particularities are to be judged. By virtue of the ontological shift of general pluralism outlined by Griffin, these models also all involve 'sacramental' or 'representative' christologies, rather than the 'satisfaction' or 'constitutive' christologies of exclusivism and inclusivism, since general pluralism rejects the notion of an intervening event objectively changing the course of reality. It is, Knitter suggests, the contrast between Spirit-christology, permissible for pluralism, and Logos-christology, rejected by pluralism. In Haight's view, for example, a Spirit-christology, while connecting the universal spirit with the historical person of Jesus and accounting for the 'normativity of Jesus for humankind generally', nevertheless testifies to the Spirit's capacity to act with a certain independence of Jesus, its agenda even going beyond that of Jesus.[77] Although the trinitarianism of D'Costa affirms that Jesus does not exhaust God's activities, Knitter is right to suggest that D'Costa insists 'that the Spirit can only be the Spirit of Christ'.[78] The same is true of Newbigin. Hence the contrast between general or superficial pluralists, on the one hand, for whom the normativity of

---

[72] Knitter, *Introducing Theologies*, p. 146; Aloysius Pieris, *Fire and Water: Basic Issues in Asian Buddhism and Christianity* (Maryknoll, NY, 1996), pp. 150–51; and see Pieris, *God's Reign for God's Poor: A Return to the Jesus Formula* (Sri Lanka, 1998), chapter 4.

[73] Aloysius Pieris, 'Christ beyond Dogma: Doing Christology in the Context of the Religions and the Poor', *Louvain Studies*, 25 (2000): p. 220. See also Chapter 7, pp. 164.

[74] Knitter, *Introducing Theologies*, p. 147; Pieris, 'Christ beyond Dogma', p. 220.

[75] Knitter, *Introducing Theologies*, pp. 147–8.

[76] Ibid., pp. 152–5.

[77] Roger Haight, *Jesus the Symbol of God* (Maryknoll, NY, 1999), p. 156.

[78] Knitter, *Introducing Theologies*, p. 155.

'other representations of God' may match Christ's normativity, and D'Costa and Newbigin, on the other hand, for whom the triune God has no match.[79]

For Cobb, by contrast, as we shall see below, both sides are right and wrong: in its own terms, the triune God is unmatchable, but in others' terms it is equalled. Thus Knitter is wrong to locate Cobb here, as another example of the apparent 'mutuality', or comparability, between various representations. Whilst Cobb affirms that Christians have truly encountered God in Jesus, without suggesting that this means they have encountered God only in Jesus,[80] he is more radical than Knitter's misnamed 'mutuality' model, or superficial pluralism, since he insists that religious ends are genuinely different. More than that, as Knitter does recognize, we ought to be wary of presupposing common 'rules' by which all right-thinking people can reasonably reject the validity of religious exclusivism.[81] As we shall see, Cobb proposes a radical way to address the projection of one's rules on to all others, whether it is exclusivists' using them to demonize all others, inclusivists' using them to demonize those elements of the other which do not confirm one's own vision, or superficial pluralists' deeming their common rules to be broadly shared by the others.

In my terms, Jesus the Shaken One is deeply attentive to the otherness of others, being open not only to the superficial differences between them but the radical otherness, while retaining the distinctive capacity to shake both his own community's and that of others' compliance with dehumanizing powers of domination. That is, one's rules are indeed distinctive, as are others' rules; and it is Christ-like, therefore Christian, to be attentive to such distinctions. Cobb in particular demonstrates how this may be possible.

The Shaken One and Catholicity: A Vision of Deep Engagement

Before turning to Cobb, I note the approach of Heim. For Knitter, Heim does not represent a 'mutuality' approach to religious plurality, but an example of 'acceptance', because, in effect, Heim more radically accepts both the deep differences between the traditions and their divine source. It is incumbent upon us, therefore, to engage with God-given diversity and to view it as a reflection of the manyness of God.[82] However, this manyness is defined by Heim in terms of the Trinity, and although he acknowledges its particularity, he nevertheless sees its particularity as the one that can enable future integration of all different traditions. It is the distinctive nature of the manyness, which is intrinsic to Christian faith,

---

[79]   Ibid., p. 156; citing, for example, Haight, pp. 422, 39, 403.

[80]   Knitter, *Introducing Theologies*, p. 156.

[81]   Ibid., p. 159.

[82]   Ibid., pp. 192–5; Heim, *Salvations*, pp. 149, 215; S. Mark Heim, *The Depth of Riches: A Trinitarian Theology of Religious Ends* (Grand Rapids, MI, 2001), p. 175.

which enables us best of all to facilitate good relations amongst all others.[83] As he puts it, 'The decisive and universal significance of Christ is for Christians *both* the necessary ground for particularistic witness *and* the basis for recognizing in other religious traditions their own particularistic integrity.'[84] It is thus the very particularity of Christian faith, including of Jesus Christ, which enables us to engage constructively with the particularity of others.

So, for Heim, it is not a matter of seeking commonality – whether on Hick's philosophical grounds, Panikkar's mystical grounds, or Pieris's ethical grounds – but of different dialogue-partners each contributing a vision of 'penultimate religious fulfilment', and through dialogue between 'incorrigible differences' each will reveal new things to the other.[85] However, as hinted above, on the one hand Heim is suggesting there are different ends, different ultimates, and that each tradition may be fulfilled in its own distinctive terms, not according to some common vision between them; but on the other hand, he roots this hypothesis in the very particularity of the Trinity.[86] As Griffin suggests, Heim is unsure how to present his view, having over-identified pluralism with identist or superficial pluralists such that he disowns pluralism as such, so fails to have due regard for the 'deep' pluralism of Cobb.[87]

I discuss Cobb also in Chapter 7, but it is necessary to establish here how his distinctive approach speaks to my identification of Jesus as the Shaken One, especially because Cobb is engaging not only with the scandal of particularity (how a tradition's identity relates to universality) but with the scandal of plurality (how a tradition's identity engages with the plurality of other particular traditions). For whilst most theologians, including Hick and Newbigin, assume there is one ultimate or universal, Cobb proposes more clearly than Heim that there is more than one. He recognizes more radically than superficial pluralists that the differences between traditions run deep, suggesting these might be rooted not only in cultural differences but in the complex nature of reality itself. As Griffin demonstrates, Cobb's pluralism is also 'complementary', because he believes that dialogue can enable the traditions to discover that their doctrines and visions might not be, in fact, either contradictory and competing or illusory versions of what is actually common ground; rather they may be complementary, in the sense that each may add to the vision of the other.[88]

This vision relies, in part, on Whitehead's distinction between God and Creativity: the latter is the 'power of being' identified by Tillich which is embodied by God just as the world/cosmos embodies such creativity as well; that

---

[83] Knitter, *Introducing Theologies*, pp. 194–5, 200–201; Heim, *The Depth*, p. 167.

[84] Heim, *Salvations*, p. 226.

[85] Ibid., pp. 153–4, 165, 195–8, 205–8. (See also Knitter, *Introducing Theologies*, pp. 193–200.)

[86] Knitter, *Introducing Theologies*, pp. 196–7, 233–4; Heim, *The Depth*, pp. 179, 264.

[87] Griffin, *Deep Religious Pluralism*, pp. 21–4, 29–30, 33–6.

[88] Ibid., pp. 39–40.

is, the metaphysical principles embodied by the world as a result of creativity are chiefly exemplified by God.[89] (Tillich's Being Itself reminds us, too, that language in relation to the transcendent is also metaphorical: it speaks creatively.) The implication of this, as Griffin indicates, is that there is not one ultimate, but two, possibly three: God is the Ultimate Actuality, Creativity (or Emptiness) is the Ultimate Reality, and the cosmos/physical universe may be an ultimate on yet another level.[90] So, for Cobb, if metaphysics rather than theologies are revised, we can allow for the differences between traditions.[91] That is, if we reorientate our vision of metaphysical reality, to allow that different kinds of religious tradition are oriented towards different ultimates, we need not radically revise our theology as such. For example: whilst Hick assumes that we cannot grasp the nature of the object of our religious orientation, because our interpretive apparatus conceptualizes the single Real in different ways, Cobb identifies the difficulty as being to do with the presumption of this object's oneness. What if one tradition understands its object of orientation as 'personal', and another understands it as 'impersonal', not because of the limitations of our theological language or human experience, but because they are not actually oriented towards the same ultimate?

This controversial assertion – that God, Emptiness and the cosmos are distinct 'ultimates' – connects a Whiteheadian metaphysics with the appreciation that the God worshipped by theists *is not the same* as the Emptiness realized by Buddhists. Although Hick does not actually say that the experiences of theists and Buddhists are the same, he does claim that distinct traditions speak of different experiences *of the same noumenal reality*. Cobb refutes this.[92] Instead, individual traditions have penetrated different 'aspects' of reality and found different things (he means more than merely different 'angles' on reality or merely different parts of the same

---

[89]   Ibid., pp. 42–5: Griffin refers to A.N. Whitehead (orig. edn) and D.R. Griffin and D.W. Sherburne (eds), *Process and Reality: An Essay in Cosmology*, corrected edn (New York, 1978), pp. 96, 343. While this metaphysical distinction may be criticized for objectifying God, by way of its reliance on process philosophy, my point is to attend to deep complexity at the 'ultimate' level. Also, even as process theology presumes to delineate the nature of God's power, it affirms the 'unrestricted relativity' or deeply relational nature of God with creation (see Charles Hartshorne, *The Divine Relativity* (London, 1948), p. 11), so it too constitutes a social rationality which both feeds objectification and generates tools to resist it.

[90]   Griffin, *Deep Religious Pluralism*, pp. 47–50, 60; John B. Cobb Jr, *Transforming Christianity and the World: A Way beyond Absolutism and Relativism* (Maryknoll, NY, 1999), pp. 88, 184–5; Cobb, *Beyond Dialogue*, pp. 124–8.

[91]   Griffin, *Deep Religious Pluralism*, pp. 45–6; Cobb, *Transforming Christianity*, pp. 88–9.

[92]   Griffin, *Deep Religious Pluralism*, pp. 46–7; Cobb, *Beyond Dialogue*, pp. 43, 135, 74; Cobb, 'Dialogue', p. 6 (and Knitter, 'Interreligious Dialogue: What? Why? How?', p. 43), both in Swidler et al., *Death or Dialogue?*.

'elephant', but specifically a different 'principle, element, reality or ultimate'[93]). Thus Hutchinson's description of three kinds of religion correlates with the three ultimates – the theistic kind reflects the focus on God, the acosmic kind reflects the focus on Emptiness, and the cosmic kind is illustrated by primal traditions which regard the cosmos as sacred.[94] From this mapping, Cobb traces two kinds of dialogue: 'purification' is conversation between those oriented towards the same ultimate, and 'enrichment' is between those whose emphases differ. The principle of 'complementarity' plays a crucial role in both forms of dialogue: for the point is not to identify and occupy common ground but to move 'towards a more comprehensive vision in which the deepest insights of both sides are reconciled'.[95] Crucially, this differs from polytheism, because the three ultimates exist on different levels – God is Supreme Being, the world/cosmos consists of finite beings, and Being Itself (creativity, emptiness) is not a god and has no being *apart from its embodiments* in the divine and finite actualities.[96]

As to what this means for the theology of a particular tradition, Cobb is concerned to move beyond the 'parochialism' of a 'specifically Christian theology' but without relativizing what is Christian. Unlike Hick, he therefore does not aim to construct a 'universal theology' on the basis of some pretension to stand above all traditions (even though that is not Hick's intention either).[97] 'In the name of realism', he protests against such false neutrality, and 'in the name of Christian faith', he protests against the relativization of Christian commitments.[98] Specifically, he argues this on the basis of christology, suggesting it is 'Christocentrism' which 'impels us' towards 'catholicity';[99] that is, because Jesus/Christ is 'the centre of our history … [in whom] we find the everlasting Wisdom',[100] we are prompted to re-examine the 'circumference' of our story, which for most of our history has been

---

[93]   Griffin, *Deep Religious Pluralism*, p. 28 (n. 113); Cobb, 'Response II', in Swidler et al., *Death or Dialogue?*, pp. 100, 115–16. Concerning the parable of blind men each holding the same elephant, see John Hick, *God and the Universe of Faiths* (London, 1973), pp. 140–41, where he notes its parabolic limitations, reiterated in *Rainbow*, pp. 49–50.

[94]   Griffin, *Deep Religious Pluralism*, p. 49: John A. Hutchinson, *Paths of Faith* (New York, 1969); Cobb, *Transforming Christianity*, pp. 120–23, 136–7, 140, 185.

[95]   Griffin, *Deep Religious Pluralism*, pp. 47–8; Cobb, 'Dialogue', pp. 5–7, and 'Response I', p. 80, in Swidler et al., *Death or Dialogue?*; Cobb, *Transforming Christianity*, p. 74.

[96]   Griffin, *Deep Religious Pluralism*, pp. 49–50: 'Among the actualities, God is ultimate' and 'God is the being that includes all beings' – as the 'worldsoul', see Cobb, *Transforming Christianity*, p. 122. This departure from conventional Christian theology illustrates further the inadequacy of language regarding what is 'ultimate', but it is an attempt to account for the deep differences between (and within) traditions.

[97]   Cobb, *Transforming Christianity*, p. 79. (This essay appeared first in Swidler (ed.), *Toward a Universal Theology of Religion*, pp. 86–100.)

[98]   Ibid.

[99]   Ibid., p. 84.

[100]   Ibid., p. 79.

'too narrow', more narrow than the pervasive presence of Wisdom as embodied in Jesus.[101] This relies on the distinction, shared by Hodgson, between the historical person of Jesus and that which is embodied in him. It is also like Wink's distinction between Jesus and the Human Being: that is, Jesus does not embody alone what it is to be truly human, but in and through relationship with others. While this whole book is, in a sense, an argument about the relation between the person (and sociality) of Jesus and that greater reality which he (and his Body) particularly embodies, the point here is simply that it is the particular nature of Jesus Christ (and his Body) which impels us towards catholicity.[102] As the focus of the Christian's attention, it is of the essence of Jesus that he draws us beyond ourselves and our own tribe – that is, the Shaken One shakes us – in pursuit of a greater solidarity. Christian theology is thus not undermined by the apparent scandal of plurality; rather, the focus of our theological attention prompts and enables us to engage constructively with plurality.

So for Cobb, Christocentrism is preferable to (Hick's) 'universal theology of religion', since it does not pretend to be neutral; nor is it biased or arrogant. 'It would be arrogant to assert that the project of catholicity is one that all should pursue, and it would be biased to assert that the only way catholicity can be attained is by Christocentrism.'[103] Thus the 'centrality' of Jesus is such that 'our' history is only adequate to the extent that it is also the history 'of life on this planet'.[104] In other words, Christians ought not to claim for themselves the centrality of Jesus if they are not concerned, as a result of their focus on Jesus, with the whole of life. Jesus' vision is concertedly more 'catholic' than we are tempted to allow, engendering sensitivity to the interrelatedness and interpenetration of all things. However, this is not inclusivism, by which everyone's perspective is subsumed within the Christian narrative, because there is genuine openness between universal narratives, each being equally entitled to share their deeply different perspectives in mutually critical dialogue. The point of 'catholicity' is that nothing can fall 'outside' of the concerns of Christian faith: so peace, justice, personal wholeness, ecological health, racism, sexism, hunger and freedom are intrinsically addressed by christocentric catholicity, far more than a 'theology of religion' is likely to 'call forth' such connections.[105] Cobb argues, therefore, that it is right to identify ourselves with the particularity of our tradition, since a supposedly 'universal' vision is less capable of inspiring or energizing committed action; but it is intrinsic to the Christian vision that we are directed towards engagement with others, religiously and sociopolitically, in pursuit of mutual transformation and a more just world. Jesus the Shaken One effects such far-reaching vision and practice.

---

[101] Ibid., p. 80.

[102] Ibid., pp. 80–81. Hodgson, *Winds of the Spirit*, pp. 249, 254: Though his 'Christ-gestalt' is not confined to Jesus of Nazareth, it must be incarnate in concrete human figures.

[103] Cobb, *Transforming Christianity*, p. 84.

[104] Ibid., p. 85.

[105] Ibid.

Conclusion

As Knitter argues, to engage with the plurality of religious traditions is thus also to engage with *Christian* plurality. So he commends aspects of the various theologies of religions to facilitate fuller and more honest dialogue. The replacement (exclusivist) approach reminds us that the gospel of Jesus Christ is often 'tough love', upsetting what is taken for granted; the fulfilment (inclusivist) approach, that the gospel confirms and adds to what others have; the mutualist approach, that it works both ways – *we* may be bettered too – and the acceptance approach, that love for others requires us to attend to their otherness as such.[106] In other words, the Christian narrative demands that Christians be concerned with constructing a Body of Christ, a solidarity of others, consisting of very different members – exclusivists, inclusivists, superficial pluralists and deep pluralists. While Knitter is more 'mutualist', he does not explicitly recommend one model over the others, but that we should keep moving between them, to engage with the tensions between the universality of God's love and the particularity of the Christian tradition, between unity and genuine diversity, between the individual's and the community's gifts and needs.[107] He does, though, specifically commend 'action-oriented dialogue', recognizing that dialogical theology is not to be done divorced from the common problems we face whether as religionists, human beings or co-inhabitants of a damaged planet: we are to engage in 'ethical or globally responsible dialogue'.[108]

What flows from this, especially in light of Cobb's christocentric catholicity and my quest for openness to the otherness of the other, is that christology in a postmodern context ought also to foster genuine conversation with 'outsider images' (to use Bennett's term).[109] It is not only the Christian insider's concern – Hick dialoguing with Newbigin, Schleiermacher with Barth, or, say, Fiorenza with Panikkar – but concerns Jews, Muslims, Hindus and Buddhists, and in each tradition includes all from the most conservative-minded to the most progressive. The point is that truth is not going to be resolved before dialogue, and neither can we suspend theology prior to dialogue; rather the data of theology and the data of dialogue are 'two moments of a single undertaking'.[110] What this kind of openness also implies, as I develop in Chapters 7 and 8, is the need for *both* humility before the other *and* preparedness to be critical – otherwise dialogue cannot be honest or properly 'shaking'. It is a praxis of 'critical humility', or in Barnes's terms, 'critical generosity', rooted in the Christian tradition's theology of hospitality.[111] It is the

---

[106] Knitter, *Introducing Theologies*, pp. 238–42.

[107] Ibid., pp. 242–3.

[108] Ibid., pp. 245–6. See also Moltmann, 'Is "Pluralistic Theology" Useful', pp. 155–6.

[109] Clinton Bennett, *In Search of Jesus: Insider and Outsider Images* (London, 2001).

[110] Knitter, *Introducing Theologies*, p. 235; Stephen J. Duffy, 'A Theology of Religions and/or a Comparative Theology?', *Horizons*, 26 (1999): p. 106.

[111] Michael Barnes, *Theology and the Dialogue of Religions* (Cambridge, 2002), pp. 21, 23. Barnes's argument comes from a different place from mine, rooted in Roman

Judaeo-Christian practice of hospitality for the stranger, including the religious or theological stranger, which helps to create the space for dialogue amongst the different and for mutually respectful critical engagement. This includes both self-criticism (recognizing the 'shadow side' of Jesus and his/our tradition, those signs of sectarianism which have demonized certain 'others within'), and other-criticism (exposing dehumanization in the others' traditions). It is not, as we shall see further, an easy dialogue which naively engages in conversation with all kinds of partners without any sense of the responsibilities borne by such engagement; rather it is a demanding dialogue, which judges dehumanizing voices and has its own moral force because the vision and goal of an ever greater 'solidarity of others' is constituted by material criteria. In particular, the question is: are we being shaken out of our compliance with the 'Domination System' so as to liberate each other mutually and embody 'the myth of the Human Being' more fully? Jesus the Shaken One, in community, is the mark of such transformation.

As has been apparent, the 'openness' of this dialogical process begs questions about the rootedness of its material criteria, so we turn in the next chapter explicitly to the question of christology's commitment to liberation and justice.

Catholicism, and draws on different resources, notably Continental philosophy, so has not been a direct dialogue-partner for me; but its emphasis on creating space for 'others' to meet, expecting something new to emerge in such encounter, in a spirit of 'critical generosity', resonates greatly with my argument.

Chapter 7

The Shaken One and the Invisible Other

The Shaken One and the Universal Quest

This chapter is concerned with the nature of the relationship between the particularity of the Christian tradition and the universal quest regarding our common humanity. The question of our common humanity comes into sharp focus in light of those people and groups who are 'othered' sociopolitically or rendered relatively invisible, in Wink's terms, under the sway of the 'Domination System'. Of course, the notion of a universal quest regarding our common humanity is problematic. I have been arguing that the Christian tradition must beware of any ideological tendency to identify itself with the universality of God's will and acts, and I reject the idea that a universal 'theology of religion' could account for all religious experience and hope. Rather, we need dialogical theology in order to express and demonstrate the particularity of our Christian commitment without objectifying, whether by idealizing or demonizing, those who are other. However, our narrative is scandalously particular; it does make universal claims; and I have suggested these are related to the Judaeo-Christian prophetic tradition, an anti-domination discourse and a praxis concerned for the well-being of all.

This motif is exemplified by Jesus the Shaken One. I have argued that the embodiment in Jesus' relationships of 'the myth of the Human Being', and his *basileia* vision and practice in solidarity with others, is not a neutral quest for truth, but a quest critically aware of the distorting and dehumanizing effects of ideologies, cliques and powers of domination. In Shanks's terms, the 'free-spiritedness' of Jesus exposes the manipulative dishonesty of any 'Empire' and reverses the lies of such a 'Gang'; in particular, God's raising of Jesus to new life demonstrates that the bullies' grip on reality is problematized. Though the System, in Wink's terms, announced in Jesus' death that its authorized violence was the last word, his resurrection subverted such truth-as-correctness. Truth-as-Honesty, instead, demands further openness to the possibility of a new last word: this includes openness to the dignity of those deemed expendable by the System. Truth-as-Honesty therefore invites us to envision social transformation. For Jesus the Shaken One is not only shaking our Christian sectarianism, our attempts to disown aspects of our history and suppress others within the tradition. Nor is his shaking power limited to our engagement with other traditions, confronting us with their genuine, deep otherness and our complex relatedness with them. Jesus the Shaken One also confronts us with our otherness to those who suffer at the hands of bullies and cliques and from distorted social relations; the dichotomy between our individual, privatized faith and the explicitly public dimensions of faith is falsified, because we cannot hide from our relatedness to the invisible others.

The point is that this abuse of our sociality needs to be identified and rectified. As Žižek helps us to see, social relations are distorted when certain 'imaginary others', others like us, are able to manipulate the social fabric – the 'symbolic Other' – in which we are all embedded, such that it becomes the 'impossible Thing' with which we cannot compare. Unless we constantly regulate the symbolic Other, in recognition of the way it binds us together for better and for worse, we persistently run the risk of overlooking the damage done to certain social constituencies: the oppressed become invisible and those who are not oppressed become indifferent or desensitized to their predicament. The aim is to see and treat such people again as subjects not objects, active agents in their own liberation and humanization, much as Jesus was open to the persistence of the Syro-Phoenician woman and the courage of the woman who had been bleeding. Once those who appear 'absent' are identified as being 'present', we increasingly attend to their reality and potential, and solidarity grows.

However, we cannot hold in check those objectifying and dehumanizing aspects of our social fabric without the existence and exercise of related and humanizing aspects of our social fabric. The integral worldview enables us to see that the interpenetration of reality is both the cause of the problem and the basis of the solution: for injustices are rooted in our distorted social relations, but social relations also provide the regulatory mechanisms by which we may identify and enact ways of resisting such distortions. Religious traditions themselves are embodiments of these tensions: each contains objectifying and dehumanizing tendencies, in part fuelling our disregard for the invisible other, but each also contains elements concerned with the regulation of such injustices. Thus, firstly, we must recognize the 'shadow side' of our tradition, its susceptibility to 'kyriarchal' or dehumanizing attitudes and actions, including the unintended consequences of our tradition's good intentions. For example, the choice of Christ and his Body to heal or transform some predicaments is implicitly the non-choice of others, which sometimes generates negative outcomes. Secondly, we must emphasize those elements of our tradition which enable us to identify, regulate and transform such distortions of social relations. This means we need to draw attention to our tradition's capacity for self-criticism, that is, its resistance to its own idealization, and its other-critical dimension, that is, its readiness to confront injustice and dehumanization in wider social relations. On both counts, this involves a preferential option for those rendered relatively poor or powerless, or in McFarland's terms, it is the dynamic 'from the outside in', in solidarity with those on or beyond the margins.

This defines the universal quest of the Christian tradition: its concern to generate a solidarity of others inclusive of those treated by the 'Domination System' as 'the last' or 'the least'. It is a vision of human beings in mutuality with each other and thus a vision of social justice or *shalom*, peace and wholeness. It is necessary, however, to establish whether this vision is itself shaped by ideology, in particular to see if it is limited by its Western presuppositions. Are my own material criteria, which are designed to combat the ideological distortions of social relations, themselves manifestations of Western ideologies? Are the concepts of 'liberation', 'justice', 'humanization' and even 'solidarity' forged by Western rationalities, such that I am projecting my cultural conditioning on to others and creating another universal pretender? By presuming to hear and heed some voices more than others, am I perpetuating the distorting effects of Western imperialism? Is this proposal of a universal quest, directed towards our mutual liberation and humanization, as liberative and as universal as it aims to be?

With those questions in mind, I reconsider the approaches of Hick and Newbigin and their Western conditioning, before turning to some alternative proposals. I briefly explore the suggestions of Ruether and Suchocki, and find their Western norms also insufficiently shaken. The incisive critiques offered by Milbank and Surin, which I try to take seriously, pose particular problems for Western universalism. Nevertheless, I proceed to a more constructive argument, thanks to Ustorf, Min and Cobb, which points to the possibility of a Western basis for a universal liberative solidarity. For the Shaken One is not an esoteric, transcendent reality, but is necessarily *subject to* the time and place of culture, as openness to the other requires. The point is that the Shaken One does not act alone, or promote Western individualism, but attends deeply to human relationality. This entails such openness to the other that we are inspired to be deeply self-critical, so as to avoid any idealization of context. Consequently the universal quest is not captive to Western rationalism, individualism or imperialism, but prompts perpetual engagement with others; and the basis of the Western impetus honoured here has its roots in the Judaeo-Christian vision of the worth of all human beings.

The Shaken One and Western Conditioning: The Limits of Hick and Newbigin

In Chapters 2 and 3, I argued that neither Hick nor Newbigin is deeply shaken in this regard. While Hick's Jesus, like a generalized figure of saintliness, illustrates for us how to move from self-centredness to Real-centredness, he offers few resources to confront the powers of domination more squarely: the otherness between the Gang and its victims is not sufficiently engaged by a focus simply on selflessness. The problem is the Western/Kantian commitment to the universal subject, an idealized individual whose identity is not sufficiently understood to be constituted by gender, ethnicity and sociality. Meanwhile, Newbigin's absolute Christ purports to expose ideologies, to bear the weight of their deadly power and ultimately to demonstrate that they are beaten, but such a dichotomy between Jesus and all others wrenches him apart from our social practices and the *basileia* vision. In Sobrino's terms, as we saw in Chapter 3, to focus on the absoluteness of Christ is to overlook the non-absolutes of history and the demand for ongoing critical praxis. Only a Jesus deeply rooted in and shaped by social relations can embody 'the myth of the Human Being' and thus facilitate a greater solidarity of others and our mutual humanization.

It is as though both Hick and Newbigin resolve the dissonances of history relatively hastily, papering over the cracks of 'kyriarchy' with their ideological neatness – that is, with Hick's modernist universal and Newbigin's christological finality. Arguably such neatness is related to their Western conditioning. The tradition of Western modernity has been impatient and hypocritical with regards to its claim to be concerned with universal liberation – impatient, in the sense that it often overlooks the presence of some 'others', and hypocritical, in terms of its inconsistency. Its vision, though universal in scope, is inevitably impeded by its particular roots: its rationalism, its individualism, its imperialism. I will argue that a more nuanced account of the relation between the Christian tradition and the Western vision of universal liberation is possible: but what of the limitations of Hick's and Newbigin's theologies?

It is evident that Hick's reading of the ethical achievements of the various traditions is an oversimplification of their nuances and that this is related to his Western presuppositions. For him, once the individual's worth is affirmed, all traditions are simply culturally distinctive ways of nudging us from self-centredness to Real-centredness.[1] While this transformation has sociopolitical as well as personal or spiritual implications, he concludes that it is not really possible to grade the traditions, since they all generate such saintliness and simultaneously display contrary characteristics; but they share the belief in doing good to others and that it is evil to do harm.[2] This is indicative both of Western reductionism *vis-à-vis* the contours and impact of 'culture', and of Western impatience with the universal quest, being almost cavalier with the historical and doctrinal particularities of the traditions in cultural contexts.

While Hick's thesis is meant to root out any superiority-complex or imperialism in Christian faith and Western self-righteousness, it is his Western presuppositions which limit such self-criticism. For example, having acknowledged the Judaeo-Christian roots of the Western Enlightenment's concern with the worth of all people, Newbigin nevertheless concludes that, 'the new faith of the Enlightenment saw Christianity as merely one of the surviving traditions of which it had no further need ... it became a tolerated private opinion'.[3] Hick does not explicitly intend this, but it is the worldview within which he re-expresses the more limited achievement of Christian particularity. His ability to criticize his own narrative is impeded by its emphasis on the fundamental ambiguity of the universe: his concern to combat the unethical consequences of any superiority-complex is

---

[1]   John Hick, *An Interpretation of Religion: Human Responses to the Transcendent*, 2nd edn (Basingstoke, 2004), pp. 36–55.

[2]   Ibid., pp. 300–303, 307–14.

[3]   Lesslie Newbigin, 'Religion for the Marketplace', in Gavin D'Costa (ed.), *Christian Uniqueness Reconsidered: The Myth of a Pluralistic Theology of Religions* (Maryknoll, NY, 1990), p. 136.

impeded by his insistence that any claim is merely another response to the same Reality. The confusion as to whether his thesis is a first-order or second-order discourse – a universal prescription or merely a description of plurality – thereby blunts its teeth. He is not relativist, since saintliness has material content, but he cannot hold domination in check.

Hick argues, though, that this approach is bigger than Western modernity. He finds points of contact with the Hindu insight that all views are equally valid, because, as Wilfred Cantwell Smith sees it, all particular claims are 'idols' or human constructs, as though each partial vision is illusory if not delusional.[4] However, even if the subjectivity of our responses to an ambiguous universe is rooted in ancient Hindu traditions, it clearly also reflects Western modernity's privatization of religious faith. In that light, Newbigin argues that Hick's 'Real' can provide much less guidance for the existential, and public, life of a believer than the record of Jesus can and does. Newbigin also suggests that Hick's reduction of religion to the quest for salvation/liberation – as though to belittle the question of what is actually true – plays into the hands of evils such as Nazism, which need to be confronted with hard truths.[5] For Newbigin, theologies such as Hick's appear to put experience, or the question of action, before truth, or the demands of reflection, such that we can decide and determine personally what is true and right. It illustrates the focus of liberal imperialism on tolerance and non-discrimination, even as Hick is intolerant of conservative readings of the tradition and arguably discriminates in favour of Western rational presuppositions.

In contrast, Newbigin understands the Christian gospel alone to be the undoing of all imperialisms: even if the Christian religion itself falls short of this vision, it understands God's self-revelation in Christ to be absolutely subversive of all such imperialism. While for Newbigin God's act in Christ 'relativizes our particular formulations and programs',[6] he argues that Hick's approach 'belongs to the world of the supermarket where the customer is king'; that is, the individual chooses his or her truth.[7] Instead, Newbigin could argue that it is the world of the supermarket where the supermarket itself is king, because the universal pretender of global capitalism surely dwarfs the power of any idealized human subject, giving the lie to such a subject's autonomy. The question is how we might effect liberation from such imperialism. For Newbigin, while 'praxis' approaches remain 'locked into' Western understandings of justice and freedom, so their good intentions are impeded by their conditioning, he purports to know that only Jesus provides effective 'realization of a justice and a freedom which are truly God's gifts', and insists that only 'those who confess an absolute commitment to the crucified and risen Lord' can truly

---

[4]   Ibid., pp. 137–42, citing Wilfred Cantwell Smith, 'Idolatry: In Contemporary Perspective', in John Hick and Paul Knitter (eds), *The Myth of Christian Uniqueness* (London, 1988), pp. 55–6.

[5]   Newbigin, 'Religion for the Marketplace', pp. 142–5.

[6]   Ibid., pp. 145–6.

[7]   Ibid., p. 138.

resist the force of the market by living lives which demonstrate such an 'option for the poor'.[8]

Although it is right to question the ability of Hick's (superficial) pluralism to resist great evils, Newbigin's critique of Western modernity is insufficiently attuned to the inseparability of the Christian narrative and unfinished modernity. He should not criticize the universal rationality of one without addressing the same possibility in the other. Similarly, to absolutize and idealize Jesus and his cross while relativizing all other programmes in their light is to objectify both Jesus as the ideal 'other' and all others as though they are already known. By purporting to know how Jesus and the other others are related, they are dehumanized, as Pattison, Ustorf and Wink suggest;[9] and it fails to integrate Jesus' light and shadow sides, so diminishes full humanity in general. For Ustorf, Hick too depicts Jesus in a 'romantic, immaculate, superhuman' way, not really human as we are, so divorcing him from his Body's dark side.

The point is this: Hick is conditioned by his foundational dual discourse, the dichotomy between reality as it really is and reality as it is experienced, which restricts the capacity of his theology to engage critically with the realities of concrete injustices. While he personally involved himself in resisting fascism in Birmingham, his liberal imperialism could not fully inform such action; his experience simply led him to act. Newbigin, too, is conditioned by a foundational dual discourse, the dichotomy between subjective narratives and the absolute finality of Christ, which also restricts the capacity of his theology to engage critically with the realities of concrete injustices. Similarly, he would involve himself in debate and action, but relying on the fundamental assumption of an absolutized Jesus. Both foundations point to Western imperialism, with its presumption of a 'god's-eye-view' which knows the goal to which all are heading.

By contrast, as I will argue further below and in the final chapter, the Shaken One orientates us towards liberative action, in solidarity with each other, but the end cannot be presumed – either in terms of Real-centredness or christocentric finality. Of course, we must act as though our Christian practices of peace-making, social justice and compassion are indicative of the universal goal, but the demands of openness to the other mean it is incumbent on us to be open to others' understandings of such norms and their different norms, trusting that only such mutually critical dialogue and engagement can foster an ever greater solidarity of others. My understanding of the Shaken One clearly has a Western bias, by virtue of my social conditioning, but it includes the need for openness to

---

[8]   Ibid., pp. 146–7.

[9]   Stephen Pattison, 'The Shadow Side of Jesus', *Studies in Christian Ethics*, 8/2 (1995): pp. 56–8, 66; Werner Ustorf, 'The Emerging Christ of Post-Christian Europe', in Thomas F. Foust, George R. Hunsberger, J. Andrew Kirk, Werner Ustorf (eds), *A Scandalous Prophet: The Way of Mission after Newbigin* (Grand Rapids, MI, 2002), pp. 137–42; Walter Wink, *The Human Being: Jesus and the Enigma of the Son of the Man* (Minneapolis, MN, 2002), pp. 146–7, 132–3, 259.

ecumenical dialogue, that is, with other Christians, and to interreligious dialogue, but is especially directed 'from the outside in', that is, with a particular political concern for those rendered relatively invisible by the System.

The Shaken One and Western Universalism: The Limits of Ruether and Suchocki

With those criticisms of Hick and Newbigin in mind, it is worth considering briefly two alternative approaches from feminist perspectives. Although they too are arguably limited by Western universalism, they point towards constructive criteria.

Ruether offers what is arguably a critical development of Hick's approach. On the one hand, she knows that 'ethical universalism' (as though religious traditions share a common ethical essence) is a very Western phenomenon, suggesting that it results from the synthesis of two universalisms in Christianity: Jewish messianic universalism, the promise of one who enables *shalom* for all, and the Greco-Roman imperialist universalism, promising that *this* empire humanizes the whole world.[10] So, unlike Hick's attempt to place traditions in relation to the Real, her point is that no comprehensive synthesis of the traditions is possible; for it is right simply to accept one's particularity and to allow others to stand equally alongside. (It is not easy, of course, to explain what such equality entails.) On the other hand, she applies Christian language to all traditions, saying that 'each has *incarnated* its way of symbolizing life and its relationship to the higher powers in unique ways'.[11] She usefully states, though, that a tradition's ideals should not be compared with another's practices, but ideals should be compared with ideals, practices with practices.[12] This implicitly criticizes the apparent ease with which Newbigin's 'ideal' Jesus relativizes all other ideals and practices. He should be more careful to compare the ideals of the traditions with each other, allowing them to speak on their terms and not only as implied servants of the gospel.

However, Ruether's fundamental argument is that all traditions are 'sexist', and that the struggle for women's suffering under patriarchy should be seen as revelatory of God's presence, as a 'Third Testament', so she argues for dialogue between feminists in all traditions and beyond.[13] As we will find Milbank noting, this betrays her own Western captivity, because of her concern for and conception of dialogue.[14] The point, then, is that she is wary of universalism, but that her

---

[10]   Rosemary Radford Ruether, 'Feminism and Jewish-Christian Dialogue: Particularism and Universalism in the Search for Religious Truth', in Hick and Knitter (eds), *The Myth of Christian Uniqueness*, pp. 142, 138.

[11]   Ibid., p. 142 (my emphasis).

[12]   Ibid., p. 141.

[13]   Ibid., pp. 146–8.

[14]   John Milbank, 'The End of Dialogue', in D'Costa (ed.), *Christian Uniqueness Reconsidered*, p. 182.

language and presumption of a common cause amongst the victims of patriarchy suggest she has her own universalism.

Marjorie Hewitt Suchocki develops the parallel between sexism and religious absolutism, or between equality and pluralism, again trying to walk a path that is both alert to Western norms and committed to something distinct from relativism. She argues that liberation theology teaches the danger of one mode of humanity being normative for others.[15] (Milbank disputes this, since what the oppressed need is not so much a valued voice but concrete freedom from oppression.[16]) Her point, though, is that any normativeness should be just. She defines justice as that which creates well-being in the world community, 'well-being' itself existing at the level of the physical, the communal (the need for social recognition and dignity), and the personal in community (the need for opportunities that enable self-determination and development).[17] She accepts that one cannot step outside of judgment-making, but rejects absolutism on the basis that the aim is to shift from ideological judgments to judgment on the basis of the norm of justice – the proper test being 'the degree to which it knows no boundaries to well-being'.[18]

Of course, justice bears considerable ideological weight itself (and Suchocki endows her terms with an almost self-evident authority); but the interesting point she is making is that, in the same way as women are rightly not to be defined in relation to men as the norm, so other religious traditions should not be defined or judged by a Christian norm; instead, all are to be judged by justice. For, as I interpret Suchocki's point, just as women are either 'included' silently and invisibly within the norm, as though men's experience innately speaks for them, or women's experience is othered as the idealized sensitive other or belittled as the weak other, so this imperialistic inclusion or presumptuous othering occurs in relation to other religious traditions.[19] For instance, Hick, as I see it, defines 'the others' according to a kind of liberal exclusivism, which deems religious differences to be merely superficial, focusing instead on a common 'core'. While Western/ized liberals in various traditions can agree with him, few others would recognize his depiction of their faith. Or Newbigin reduces the others to that which they confirm in our own gospel. This illustrates Suchocki's point: that just as women's contribution to men is deemed secondary to men's contribution to women, so what other traditions can give to us cannot compare with what Christian faith can give to them: 'we alone can fulfil the other', it is implied. Just as men barely achieve self-awareness, so the presumption of Christian superiority dulls our self-criticism.[20]

---

[15]   Marjorie Hewitt Suchocki, 'In Search of Justice: Religious Pluralism from a Feminist Perspective', in Hick and Knitter (eds), *The Myth of Christian Uniqueness*, p. 149.

[16]   Milbank, 'The End of Dialogue', pp. 182–3.

[17]   Suchocki, 'In Search of Justice', pp. 149, 154.

[18]   Ibid., pp. 150, 155.

[19]   Ibid., pp. 150–51.

[20]   Ibid., pp. 152–4.

Yet Suchocki is careful to insist that this rejection of absolutism, this suspicion of one's normativeness defining another's, need not lead to relativism: for justice is about the concern for ever-increasing well-being. This may mean that being true to Christianity may not be the same as being just, because some 'Christianity' is not very just – in which case, though, it is not very good Christianity or religion.[21] Just as Wink offers the distinction between truth being determined by Jesus' actions (Newbigin's approach) and the truth of Jesus' actions being determined by their subversion of the 'Domination System', so Suchocki understands justice not as being defined by Jesus' actions but as that which Jesus aims to do.[22] In other words, the norm is not Jesus, but justice. I would suggest, alternatively, that the relation may be more dialectical: justice is discernible in the life of Jesus through his reconciling of his light and shadow sides, as the one whose relationships particularly embody 'the myth of the Human Being', in the sense that, in and through relationships with others, he embodies God's humanity.[23] The norm is not Jesus or Justice as such, but in seeking one we discover more about the other. Suchocki is right to note, therefore, that there will always be diversity, because each tradition views 'justice' and 'well-being' differently, and ill-being is sometimes defined as well-being for the sake of greater purposes (as in the case of suffering). So what matters are the ultimate visions of a perfect world offered by different traditions: for such visions should each engage critically but constructively with the others, and, in the process of dialogue, a fuller justice/well-being is thus created.[24]

While Suchocki is herself bound by the Western presuppositions concerning the language she uses, which condition her understanding of justice and her vision of mutual, global well-being, she nevertheless points us towards two constructive possibilities which resonate with the Shaken One. Firstly, through a dialogue between her and Wink we see that Jesus as the Shaken One is not an idealized measure of all others; rather it is the nature of the Shaken One to be constituted socially, in pursuit of an ever greater solidarity of others. In the same way as 'the myth of the Human Being' is concerned with more than Jesus, since he embodies it not alone but in his relationships, so he is the Shaken One *by virtue of his connectedness with others*. Unlike Fackre's Barthian 'centripetal singularity', by which Christ acts and the effects only radiate outwards, *and* unlike Fackre's 'centrifugal singularity', by which Christ's actions resonate with already-present dynamics, the Shaken One does both: he is discontinuous with others, by virtue of his shakenness and capacity to shake others, but also continuous with and dependent on others, because his personhood is shaped by others. Secondly, then, as Suchocki suggests, Christians are free to offer their universal vision, shaped by the particularity of Jesus Christ in community, but we should anticipate that others

---

21 Ibid., p. 155.
22 Ibid., p. 156; Wink, *Human Being*, p. 15.
23 Pattison, 'Shadow Side', pp. 56–8; Wink, *Human Being*, pp. 146–7.
24 Suchocki, 'In Search of Justice', pp. 157–60.

will share their visions of well-being too. As with Cobb, to whom we will return, the vision of universal liberative solidarity and humanization is not a singular trajectory, but entails mutually critical dialogue and shared action.

The Shaken One and Western Imperialism: The Insights of Milbank and Surin

At this point we must bring to bear the cautionary insights of Milbank and Surin. In particular, they criticize the pluralistic approach to liberation and justice, identifying significant problems with Western presuppositions. For Milbank, there is a stark paradox: that dialogue and pluralism are favoured as the categories by which encounter with other traditions is to proceed, just as the West optimistically subsumes the norms of other cultures by the promotion of *its* brand of liberation and justice. Ironically, Western pluralism tends to 'curb and confine' the honourable causes of socialism, feminism, anti-racism, 'because the discourse of pluralism exerts a rhetorical drag in a so-called liberal direction', favouring both the Western nation-state and the capitalist economy.[25] So, as Milbank sees it, the problem for the writers of *The Myth of Christian Uniqueness* is that even those such as Driver, who try to distance themselves from the universals of Hick, Smith and Samartha, do not quite succeed because of their attachment to Western 'substructures' undermining their claim to universal relevance.[26] For Milbank, the only way by which those honourable causes can be achieved with integrity is to acknowledge that they *are* tied to Western roots inseparable from a Judaeo-Christian position, respecting otherness and locality, yet seeking peace, justice and the reconciliation of all things. In effect, he argues, more consciously than Newbigin, that the West's benefits are because of its Judaeo-Christian sources (so affirms 'the Good' of the West[27]), but is incisively critical of such unconscious embeddedness – with a view to a separation between the two meta-narratives and, like Newbigin, a reassertion of Christian theology over secularity.[28] His argument runs thus:

First, there is no such genus as 'religion'. Any categorization as such is a construction by Christians, Westerners or people of other traditions educated in the West who cannot avoid or resist the force of Western discourses. In this light, 'dialogue' is the process by which Christians/Westerners/Westernized others perceive others' contributions as merely different angles on the same core truth; that is, dialogue is a Western construct which obscures the truth *of difference*, making

---

[25]   Milbank, 'The End of Dialogue', p. 175.

[26]   Ibid., pp. 174–6.

[27]   Ibid., pp. 186–8.

[28]   See, in particular, John Milbank, *Theology and Social Theory: Beyond Secular Reason* (Oxford, 1990), for example: pp. 1–3, 9–10, 380.

'them' into liberal, Western subjects, images of oneself.[29] This analysis is reflected also in Surin's identification of a development in the Christian West's approach to 'others' (taken from McGrane). That is, up until the sixteenth century, 'others' were demonized as pagan, then in the Enlightenment were seen as primitive or unenlightened (ignorant, erring, in need of the truth); in the nineteenth century the difference became one of time – as though to say, 'they will evolve, given time' – before subsequently defining otherness in terms of culture or anthropology as 'mere' difference.[30] So for Surin, Hick's 'democratic' pluralistic hypothesis claims each particularity to be mythological, a mere cultural expression of the Real beyond, relativizing difference; and as such it is *not* dialogical but is a 'monological pluralism' which 'sedately but ruthlessly domesticates and assimilates the other – *any* other – in the name of world ecumenism and the realization of a [in Hick's words] "limitlessly better possibility"'.[31]

For Milbank, what is happening here is that Hick et al. overlook the nature of religious traditions as 'social projects' as well as worldviews; little wonder, because such pluralism follows on from *The Myth of God Incarnate* where Christian uniqueness is associated essentially with Christocentrism, as though there is nothing to say about the uniqueness of the ecclesial social project.[32] This is demonstrated by the fact that, although the contributors to *The Myth of God Incarnate* 'water down' their christology, they effectively remain true to the unique force of the Church's 'deterritorializing process'. For what is remarkable about christology, and what is evident in the Gospels, according to Milbank, is that Christocentrism is not about the fetishization of particularity, as *The Myth of God Incarnate*'s contributors suggest, but that the individual Jesus' representation of perfect sonship is to be repeated in the discipleship community, the Church, which is a deterritorialized social project of universal scope.[33] (We have noted before Hick's Kantian 'turn to the subject' at the cost of relationality within the *basileia* community.) As Milbank puts it, 'the particularity of Jesus is insisted upon *only* to define a new framework of more than local relevance'.[34] This, then, is why traditions tend to be resistant to conversion: they already have universalizing tendencies or aspirations which are not to be readily dissolved through dialogue; whereas *The Myth of God Incarnate* constantly confuses elements of grammars of universality with mere 'cultic' particularity. To compound the problem, religio-

---

[29]   Ibid., pp. 176–7. See also Kenneth Surin, 'A "Politics of Speech": Religious Pluralism in the Age of the McDonald's Hamburger', in D'Costa (ed.), *Christian Uniqueness Reconsidered*, p. 203, concurring that 'Third World pluralists are from the Western-trained elites'.

[30]   Surin, 'A "Politics of Speech"', pp. 197–9, citing Bernard McGrane, *Beyond Anthropology: Society and the Other* (New York, 1989), pp. ix–x, 113–17.

[31]   Surin, 'A "Politics of Speech"', p. 200, citing Hick, *An Interpretation*, p. 380.

[32]   Milbank, 'The End of Dialogue', p. 179.

[33]   Ibid.

[34]   Ibid. (his emphasis).

political imperialism is associated with the global imposition of a local view (namely of the Christian West), even though it is a contradiction to celebrate the West's universalism, rationalism and humanism while rejecting its imperialism – as both sides of the coin are deterritorializations, and empires are more ambiguous than critiques of imperialism imply.[35] Thus Milbank debunks four assumptions of the pluralists: 'religion' is *not* a clear-cut category; dialogue *cannot* be assumed to give privileged access to truth; uniqueness consists of more than cultic attachments; and imperialism is more complex than the arrogance of a locality (even the West's).

Milbank goes on, however, to argue that the praxis solutions are so bound up with Western ideology, uncritically, that they are oblivious to their proselytizing discourse: for even Panikkar's comment on the religious 'turn' to the political betrays *The Myth*'s dominant assumption that religion is primarily 'private inspiration', as though it is not also, fundamentally, a genuinely social project.[36] So Knitter and others naively believe that the religious traditions can discover a common 'social justice' element latent within them – since, for Knitter (and Hick), they are soteriologically more similar than theologically. As Milbank comments, even if such commonality exists, by treating religion as mere private inspiration which discovers a hidden political consensus, how is such a consensus able to facilitate dialogue with regards to the traditions' differences? The problem with this insistent belief in *dialogue* is that it prioritizes the essentially liberal view that justice consists of giving everyone freedom of action and expression – reflected by Suchocki's misdescription of liberation theology as the resistance to one mode of humanity's normativeness for others. For what the oppressed seek is not 'dialogue', but the circumstances by which their oppression may be transformed.

It is, then, Milbank argues, a mistake for liberals (naming Ruether) to compare religious difference with race and gender, as though race, gender and faith are merely the 'innocuous cultural variants' we experience of a 'single human reality'.[37] The point is that any universal religion or any consensus concerning the nature of justice is no closer, especially as the traditions are social projects not merely cultural phenomena; but the Western/liberal 'toleration'/'dialogue' consensus asks us to treat religious practices as merely different 'rites' which can safely be engulfed by the dominance of secular norms, even as some of the religious practices directly challenge those norms. The consequence of this consensus is that, far from realizing the potential of causes like socialism, feminism, human rights, anti-racism, and ecologism, it obscures them.

As for Milbank's alternative to dialogue, which he calls 'mutual suspicion', he acknowledges that it does not pretend to mean anything but 'continuing the

---

[35]   Ibid., pp. 180–81.

[36]   Ibid., p. 182, on Panikkar, 'The Jordan, the Tiber and the Ganges: Three Kairological Moments of Christic Self-Consciousness', in Hick and Knitter (eds), *The Myth of Christian Uniqueness*, p. 101.

[37]   Milbank, 'The End of Dialogue', pp. 183–5.

work of conversion'.[38] This is the case, even though he expects also to 'receive Christ again' and again, because in the same spirit as Newbigin he is committed to the vision of the Judaeo-Christian narrative as the *only* project – the ecclesial social project – capable of securing harmony through difference and continuous conversation, rather than being bound by Socratic dialogue around supposedly neutral topics. While he knows that this narrative is distinctly Western, and that in some respects the West is 'the great modern poison', it is nevertheless 'the only available cure' too, because unlike in the East where as a matter of principle 'ethical' action is not affirmed as such, he argues, the West's sense of justice and the Good are the very means of its imperialism.[39] (In Newbigin's terms, 'when the Church affirms the gospel as public truth it is challenging the whole of society to wake out of the nightmare of subjectivism and relativism, to escape from the captivity of the self turned in upon itself.'[40])

The point is that, not only is it an illusion to associate the West's social justice with some tradition-transcending pluralistic commitment, but that it is also dangerous to do so, since justice and freedom cannot be based on any universal human reason, only the religious imaginings of the Platonic Good, Jewish God or Christian Trinity.[41] (We noted in Chapter 4 Walzer's insistence, too, that justice cannot be rooted in a rationality which appears to transcend the traditions: rather, the tradition of the Jewish Jesus gives material criteria by which we may enact anti-domination.[42]) For Milbank, while liberals' pluralism attempts to root such justice in its own Enlightenment imperialism, it is the Christian social project which truly envisages perfect reconciliation (not mere mutual toleration) together with liberty and equality. For even though the West has sought to deny otherness, other cultures have done so too, and the West alone offers the antidote, *because of* the Jewish-Christian tradition: not mutually tolerating the other but respecting each other's unique contribution to Being. So, according to Milbank, Panikkar's attempt to combine neo-Vedantic and trinitarian mysteries fails, because the Vedantic is 'indifferent' where the Trinity is 'ethical'; the Vedanta is 'agonistic' (nihilistic) where the Trinity is peaceful, non-violent; the Vedanta constitutes infinite resignation to war, allowing for the persistent conflict of the market (to which Western liberals are susceptible) which is unable to resist imperialism and excuses inequalities, whereas only the Christian reading of religion enables not perpetual conflict (holding the others at bay) but reconciliation (respecting others while fulfilling their otherness).[43]

---

[38]   Ibid., p. 190.

[39]   Ibid., pp. 186–7.

[40]   Lesslie Newbigin, *Truth to Tell: The Gospel as Public Truth* (London, 1991), p. 13.

[41]   Milbank, 'The End of Dialogue', pp. 186–8.

[42]   See pp. 85–6.

[43]   Milbank, 'The End of Dialogue', pp. 188–90.

Surin: Criticisms of Western Cultural Hegemonism

Surin's outlook is not that of Milbank's radical orthodoxy, but his criticisms of Hick's brand of pluralism are similar. In fact he accuses Kraemer, Rahner, Hick and Cantwell Smith *all* of operating from the optimistic end of colonialism and post-colonialism, where 'pluralism incorporates and therefore dissolves the localized spaces' – that is, the local is 'subsumed under the regime of the universal'.[44] As outlined above, Hick's local 'phenomena' act as mere mythical ciphers pointing us to the universal 'noumenon'. So the problem, as Surin puts it, is that this post-colonial 'global gaze' from the West 'systematically overlooks real relations of dominance and subordination' such that '*no equation of liberation with this project can be sustained*'.[45] This is a devastating criticism of Hick's optimistic pluralism. It suggests that, to whatever extent he intends to be committed to liberation and justice, he can never realize that commitment, because of the Western captivity of his monological pluralism. For Surin insists that Hick's pluralism *is* monological, as it does not truly speak *with* others, but only *of* them, in fact subsuming and relativizing all others according to his global ideology. It is, in Surin's view, the same ideology which makes McDonald's the global food. For the young, educated pluralists 'consume' a certain way of life together with this 'universal' movement; attempts to resist it are akin to the resistance against McDonald's: 'It is to seek to resist the worldview which makes both possible.'[46] He argues that pluralism flows from 'western cultural hegemonism' – so it is no wonder that Third World pluralists, who tend to belong to Western-trained elites, possess pluralism as a constituent of their ideological identity.[47]

Also, just as Cantwell Smith argues that religious traditions are reified abstractions of their flows of practices, convictions, events, texts, so Surin adds that pluralism compounds this reification by submitting the traditions to a 'more elevated abstraction', represented by a comprehensive, homogenizing scheme – like Hick's – which undertakes their 'translation' into culture-specific manifestations of a common universality.[48] The problem with this translation, in reference to liberation and justice, is that Hick thereby discounts or de-emphasizes significant political, social or cultural differences, as Milbank argues too, by virtue of his 'common soteriological structure' which cannot distinguish adequately

---

[44]   Surin, 'A "Politics of Speech"', pp. 194–6. See also Kenneth Surin, 'Towards a Materialistic Critique of Religious Pluralism: A Polemical Examination of the Discourse of John Hick and Wilfred Cantwell Smith', in Ian Hamnett (ed.), *Religious Pluralism and Unbelief: Studies Critical and Comparative* (London and New York, 1990), pp. 114–29.

[45]   Surin, 'A "Politics of Speech"', p. 196 (my emphasis).

[46]   Ibid., pp. 200–201.

[47]   Ibid., p. 203, referring to Arif Dirlik, 'Culturalism as Hegemonic Ideology and Liberating Practice', *Cultural Critique*, 6 (1987): pp. 13–50 on 'cultural hegemonism'.

[48]   Surin, 'A "Politics of Speech"', pp. 203–4, again referring to Dirlik.

between Hindus and Christians in their relation to the Real.[49] Therefore, political hermeneutics and the semiotics of the myths of power and knowledge are discounted, and pluralists, though they criticize colonialism, tend not to criticize neo-colonialism, being optimistic about world history: an optimism surely to be humbled in the light of current divisions, suspicions and conflicts.

Although Hick may be right that the Christian world is not just while the non-Christian world is unjust, such an argument is nevertheless 'propaganda', which is addressed to any self-righteousness of Christians while speaking only *of* the others.[50] As Surin puts it: 'Hick's discursive space is the space typical of an educated liberal Westerner', who 'ceaselessly dissolves' the particularities because he is committed to the 'abstract equivalence' of all spaces. It is as though Hick is saying that the differences are not all that different; an approach which renders 'the powers' invisible and unchecked.[51] In my terms, universal pretenders are not being held to account. This was reflected also in conversation with Hick: for he refutes Milbank's critique, insisting his support for Gandhi demonstrates he is no Western imperialist.[52] In fact, he dismisses the critique as 'guilt by association'; he says that pluralism and global capitalism simply share a 'global awareness' but nothing more sinister than that.[53] He notes that Surin questions his 'ruthless assimilation of the other', but his response is not clear, simply asserting that all traditions *are* '*generically* the same', all answering the same question (in 'traditional Christian language'): 'what must I do to be saved?'[54] Surin thus urges us to 'move beyond the faded ... modernist intellectuals' who purport to tell the human story but whose narrative 'remorselessly homogenizes' the particularities, perhaps unwittingly excusing the dominance and hegemony of persistent neo-colonialism.[55]

We noted previously Hodgson's assertion that Milbank and Surin overstate the problems with pluralism, caricaturing it, as though it is unaware of the dangers of *naïveté*, optimism, essentialism, power imbalances and homogenization.[56] Hodgson also argues that being Western does not automatically invalidate a perspective[57] – and Milbank would agree, because he urges Hick to assert that the Judaeo-Christian narrative is inescapably Western. I suggest, then, as Hodgson hints, that part of the problem, as Griffin identifies it, is that pluralism is criticized as though it consists of only one, not really very pluralistic, model. Milbank's and Surin's warnings remain potent for Hick's pluralism, because it is hard to

---

[49]   Ibid., pp. 204–5. See Hick, *An Interpretation*, p. 380, for his optimistic conclusion.

[50]   Surin, 'A "Politics of Speech"', p. 208, citing John Hick, 'The Non-Absoluteness of Christianity', in Hick and Knitter (eds), *The Myth of Christian Uniqueness*, p. 24.

[51]   Surin, 'A "Politics of Speech"', p. 209.

[52]   In personal conversation with John Hick, 14 November 2005.

[53]   John Hick, *The Rainbow of Faiths* (London, 1995), p. 39.

[54]   Ibid., pp. 40–41 (his emphasis).

[55]   Surin, 'A "Politics of Speech"', pp. 209–10.

[56]   Hodgson, *Winds of the Spirit*, p. 305.

[57]   Ibid.

deny that its ability to criticize universal pretenders, powers of domination or great evils is substantially blunted *by virtue of its Western liberalism*. Those warnings do not, however, apply with as much potency to other pluralistic models, such as Cobb's, since it is arguable that to pursue liberation and justice involves resisting *both* the relativism of Western liberalism *and* the absolutism of, say, Newbigin's revelational positivism, which Cobb explicitly sets out to do.[58]

Nevertheless, the insights of Milbank and Surin must be borne in mind when envisioning the nature and actions of the Shaken One. It is necessary to be wary of implicit hegemony, which would distort good intentions, and be self-critical of universal projections. The Shaken One's shakenness ought to facilitate such wariness.

The Shaken One and Western Mediation: The Quest for Mutual Liberation

With those critiques in mind, I commend Ustorf's approach. As I understand it, his christology rejects any easy mutuality which impatiently seeks out, or contrives, common ground; rather, we need a means of 'mediating' between contrasting images, experiences and visions if we are aiming for transformation – not only of 'others', but as a solidarity of others, mutually shaken. He argues that a 'disestablished Christ' makes much-needed 'mediation', therefore deeper mutuality, particularly realizable. He is concerned with elaborating a christology which addresses both the question of the Church's violence – its historical negatives (or shadow side) in general – and the dynamic tension between the ego (a distorted or inflated self) and the true self, a tension which is sometimes creative, sometimes destructive in its delineation of God and others.[59] His point is that, to the extent that it is Christ who represents what mediation entails, this is only appropriate if we affirm both Christ's 'dark' as well as 'light' sides; that is, if we de-idealize him and see his life as 'scandalously human', itself struggling towards human 'maturity' and 'integration'.[60] It is about becoming more fully human in and through relation with others, including other aspects of oneself.

Such a vision of Christ is 'disestablished' because the process of maturation and integration is not exclusive to Jesus: he symbolizes the mediating trajectory.[61] While it is incarnational in the sense that it concerns the encounter between the divine and the human, it is the same aim for us all – to struggle to be mature, recognizing that every attempt to be ethical will cast shadows as well. (This is because, as I argued above, the interpenetration of reality means that any action

---

[58]   John B. Cobb Jr, *Transforming Christianity and the World: A Way beyond Absolutism and Relativism* (Maryknoll, NY, 1999).

[59]   Ustorf, 'Emerging Christ', pp. 129–32.

[60]   Ibid., pp. 131, 137–41.

[61]   Ibid., pp. 141–3.

will have unintended consequences: even good intentions cast shadows.) It will involve, for Ustorf, engagement with other traditions and the risk of *mutual conversion*; the willingness to overcome our anxieties and aggressions in the face of the other/s, to be bridge-builders concertedly, with implications for the whole cosmos: love and reconciliation, community and peace, justice and service.[62]

In Min's terms, this demanding process of mutual conversion and transformation will consist of mutuality between and solidarity of *plural liberation movements* – with feminists and ecologists, black and Asian theologies all co-operating together, transcending each particularity in pursuit of ever greater solidarity and liberation.[63] It is about recognizing and affirming the interconnectedness of these struggles. For Min, this is an expression of appropriate resistance to both relativism and absolutism, of being true to the particularity of one's tradition (much like Shanks's sanctity), rather than falling into relativism, while being open to others (like Shanks's transgression), rather than absolutizing one's own perspective.[64] This concern to find a way between relativism and absolutism is shared also by Hodgson and Cobb.[65] It is embodied in my notion of 'critical humility', which we encountered briefly in Chapter 6; that is, the willingness to criticize dehumanizing processes while exposing oneself humbly to the criticisms of others.

The point here, for Min, is that difference as such is not the ultimate reality, since the absolutization of difference leads to relativism; rather we should prioritize *solidarity* of the different. Thus difference is important, in contrast to the absolutization of any particular tradition; but solidarity of the different is more important, in this postmodern context, in contrast to the relativism of radical postmodernism. He grounds this solidarity of the different in philosophical, historical and strategic concerns.[66] Firstly, the differences between humans and cultures are not philosophically absolute; there are points of contact, communication, mutual understanding. While we clearly live with prejudices and misconceptions which are embedded in our distinct language-systems and cultures, we are not defined solely by such conditioning. For the purposes of our living in the world it is essential that we understand ourselves as not being confined to the realms of thought, language or interpretation; more basically we are people who must face choices and act, and such a realization invites us to de-emphasize our differences and to see the

---

[62]   Ibid., p. 144.

[63]   Anselm Min, *A Solidarity of Others in a Divided World: A Postmodern Theology after Postmodernism* (New York and London, 2004), pp. 3, 111–15, 135–8, 150. This coming together of liberationist movements is also reflected by Ivan Petrella, *Beyond Liberation Theology: A Polemic* (London, 2008).

[64]   Min, pp. 79–80.

[65]   Hodgson, *Winds of the Spirit*, pp. 106–8, 309: the task of 'exposing idolatries' is against relativism, and the task of drawing out 'convergent truths' is against absolutism; Cobb, *Transforming Christianity* – the book's subtitle, '*A Way beyond Absolutism and Relativism*', expresses this intent, focusing on the dialogical and the mutually liberative.

[66]   Min, pp. 66–73.

potential for solidarity. Secondly, we can see that differences and solidarities are interweaving, interrelated features of a shared historical experience: human beings have kept working at ways of living peaceably with their differences, and as much as we have often failed, the quest for 'togetherness' is resilient. It seems that to work for the liberation either of one's own or another's group entails attentiveness to historical details; these pursuits share things in common and are interdependent. So, thirdly, it is essential that various liberation movements learn to 'de-emphasize difference and emphasize solidarity in action' instead. Strategically, structural injustices cannot be defeated by a single-issue group; the interconnected nature of our globalized world demands interconnected action; and the complex of issues we face as human beings require us to find creative ways of acting together.

Thus the world's various liberationist movements must interact with and enrich each other. Their norms, concerned with the flourishing of human life in its fullness, must complement one another. How, though, are the norms of the various religious traditions to be understood and measured? How can we resist relativism without adopting absolutism with regards to our own tradition?

For Cobb, it is wholly inappropriate to expect to be able to judge all traditions by one 'normative essence' alone.[67] Each tradition has norms of its own, which, by virtue of the Shaken One's nurture of our openness to the other, we ought to be humble enough to hear. Nonetheless, Cobb does identify a universal vision in the particularity of the Christian tradition; he presumes to evaluate the traditions in terms of their contribution to, in Sölle's words, 'the indivisible salvation of the whole world', as witnessed in the hope for what Jesus called *basileia tou theou* (the kingdom of God).[68] This vision, or measure of ourselves and others, gives us our material criteria, which are resistant to relativism: for the *basileia*, though present somewhat elusively, consists of particular kinds of transformation, especially in solidarity with those who are relatively poor and oppressed, those regarded as 'the last' or 'the least'. As Cobb puts it, we should not use the symbol 'Christ' for anything less than 'the power that works savingly in this comprehensive way. Christ must be the life that struggles against the death-dealing powers that threaten us and the way that leads through the chaos of personal and global life to just, participatory, and sustainable society in which personal wholeness is possible'.[69]

Griffin thus suggests that Cobb gives a language for those Christians whose worldview has become pluralistic; his 'complementary pluralism' is a distinctive Christian perspective, because it remains avowedly non-relativistic.[70] (As Griffin notes, Cobb asserts that his Whiteheadian ontology is 'a Christian natural theology', and that he can still maintain the normativeness of Jesus, not only for

---

[67] Cobb, *Transforming Christianity*, pp. 121–2, 185–6, 62–6.

[68] Ibid., p. 182; Dorothee Sölle, *Political Theology* (Philadelphia, PA, 1971), p. 60.

[69] John B. Cobb Jr, 'Christ beyond Creative Transformation', in Stephen T. Davis (ed.), *Encountering Jesus: A Debate on Christology* (Atlanta, GA, 1988), p. 143.

[70] Cobb, *Transforming Christianity*, pp. 58–9.

Christians but for our engagement with others.[71]) Cobb explains that all great religious traditions make 'some claim to the universal value of their particular insights' which explicitly renders ridiculous any 'sheer conceptual relativism'. For although each tradition also affirms 'a certain humility' regarding its grasp of the depths of reality, not least in the light of mutual enrichment through engagement with others, any consequent relativism would mean that a tradition's message is true for its own believers but irrelevant for others – a position which no religious tradition ought to take.[72] As he says, 'To the true relativist, bigotry and closed-mindedness are no worse than any other stance.'[73]

Although Cobb resists relativism, he does not do so by imperialistically projecting a Christian norm into all other spaces, or by subsuming all local spaces within a universal rationality abstracted from every religious tradition. As he notes, even where there are common norms found within the different traditions, it is unlikely that they have the same importance in each, so to distil 'justice' as *the* criterion would be a mistake.[74] Instead, we can each have our norms, believe they are of universal value, judge others accordingly, but must be prepared for their judgments on us: I believe this is what the praxis of 'critical humility' entails. The fact that such critical engagement between 'others' might also lead to new developments, even transformations, in any or all traditions, simply underscores that this is not a relativistic 'live and let live' ethos, but a genuine process of 'mutual enrichment', resistant to relativistic indifference and to absolutism. As Cobb emphasizes, each moment of the Christian tradition/s is relativized by subsequent moments, all traditions being living movements, without relativizing 'the process of creative transformation by which it lives and which it knows as Christ'.[75]

In my terms, the Shaken One generates particular forms of social transformation, being shaken by those regarded as 'the least' to foster an ever greater solidarity of others. This dynamic is concertedly non-relativistic, shaking its participants to recognize the dysfunctional and distorted nature of our social relations. Nevertheless, it is not resistant to criticism, but is consciously open to the values and visions of others, including those of other traditions whose understanding of the ultimate is different, but especially those others rendered relatively invisible to the traditions whose predicaments expose our own 'kyriarchal' and dehumanizing tendencies. The Shaken One thereby shakes others and is shaken by others: this is the praxis of critical humility.

---

[71]   Griffin, *Deep Religious Pluralism*, p. 57; citing Cobb, *A Christian Natural Theology: Based on the Thought of Alfred North Whitehead* (Philadelphia, PA, 1965).

[72]   Cobb, *Transforming Christianity*, pp. 67–8.

[73]   Ibid., p. 102.

[74]   In Leonard Swidler, John B. Cobb Jr, Paul F. Knitter and Monika K. Hellwig, *Death or Dialogue? From the Age of Monologue to the Age of Dialogue* (London, 1990), pp. 181, 11; Cobb, *Transforming Christianity*, p. 137.

[75]   See Cobb, *Transforming Christianity*, pp. 44–7.

Conclusion: A Western Contribution to a Universal Quest

We have been considering the Western conditioning of my universal vision: Is the goal of mutual liberation, and an ever greater solidarity of others, limited by an implicit ideological correctness? Or is there space for truth-as-Honesty rather than truth-as-correctness, in the sense that my Western perspective is sufficiently attentive to and shaken by others – those within, those beyond and those relatively invisible? I do not deny the Western dimension of this project, susceptible as Western culture is to constructing meta-narratives. However, the universal quest for people's mutual liberation and mutual humanization, overcoming the distorting effects of the 'Domination System', is a meta-narrative rooted in the Judaeo-Christian prophetic tradition – a tradition which itself feeds Western notions of the worth of all people. While Western culture tends to distort the individual's worth by way of individualism, as though we are not socially constituted, and is less consistent in its practice than it intends to be, my project emphasizes the relationality of human freedom and worth. Unlike Western objectification, this universal quest aims to resist the dichotomies between subject and object, individual and community, by being purposefully attentive to the persistent otherness of the other. There is, then, a relation between this project and Western culture, but the relation is complex and critical; it is a Western contribution to a universal quest, but open to other contributions.

For example, Pieris, from an Asian perspective, adds to the vision of Jesus as the Shaken One in the following terms.[76] Firstly, Jesus' baptism is an immersion into liberative *religion*, a choice for John the Baptist's movement rather than the separatism of the Essenes or the conservatism of the Temple Establishment. Secondly, Jesus' death is a baptism *with the poor*, a choice for solidarity with the oppressed – of whatever religion. So he argues that Jesus' story is pre-eminently the story of the God of the poor, with the poor, for the poor; thus liberation movements must act in mutuality, otherwise the liberation of all will be jeopardized by the particular liberation of some. So he affirms 'religion' as such, reclaiming it from its Western critics – both from Barth, for whom it prevents salvation, and from Marx, for whom it obstructs liberation – and he insists that, to be liberative, religion must not only criticize and outgrow its particularism (including the Western captivity of 'liberation theology' as shaped by Marx), but must recognize that other traditions *can* be liberative, too.[77] That is to say, Jesus the Shaken One determines our material criteria, focused especially on the transformation of social injustices, but is also subject to the liberative and humanizing criteria of other traditions. He shakes but is also shaken.

In Fiorenza's terms, the embodiment of Divine Wisdom in the anti-domination *basileia* community is constituted not by an idealized, individual Jesus – though as an emancipatory movement rooted in the Jewish prophets, it is anchored in

---

[76]   Aloysius Pieris SJ, *An Asian Theology of Liberation* (Edinburgh, 1988), pp. 62–5.

[77]   Ibid., pp. 94–6, 87–93.

his story. The question is whether Jesus *determines* the shape and content of the liberation and justice we should seek – as for Newbigin – or whether Jesus himself *pursues* a justice which transcends his historical particularity – as for Hick. There is a risk that to frame the issues in such terms, I may be projecting postmodern concerns (or Western anxieties) on to a pre-modern prophet. We saw in Chapter 4, however, through the work of Stassen, that the Jewish Jesus does resonate with such concerns: his focus on subverting domination finds points of contact with others who also resist domination, even as the identity and trajectory of Jesus is historically and politically distinctive.

The point is, as argued in Chapter 4, Jesus does not wholly determine the content or direction of liberation and justice, but neither does he merely reflect a universal pursuit of justice. Rather, Jesus as the Shaken One generates the particular content and direction of the Christian tradition's universal vision of mutual liberation and an ever greater solidarity of others, but only by virtue of those who were before him, those by whom he was shaken and with whom he engaged. Since his reconstructions consist of more than the historical Jesus of Nazareth, his meaning and significance continues to be shaken in relation to ever new ways in which we dehumanize each other. In terms of Cobb's christocentric catholicity, the scope of Jesus' praxis evolves as the need for engagement with social practices evolves; in the light of our experiences of distorted social relations we identify in Jesus, as the Shaken One, new causes of our exposure, regulation and transformation of such distortions.

This universal liberative quest is thus constituted by Jesus (a prophetic Jew) in community (namely the Body of Christ), but engaging also with others, anticipating both that we will be shaken again and again (for dialogue is demanding and disturbing) and that we will be the cause of others' shakenness (for we have a gospel to demonstrate), so together realizing mutual humanization. This vision of the ultimate jubilee, at which point all liberation movements are mutually fulfilled in the final undoing of the 'Domination System', therefore gives us our criteria by which we engage with others within our tradition, with others beyond, and with the relatively invisible others today.

Chapter 8
Conclusions and Recommendations

The Shaken One: Constructive Christology, Ecclesiology and Missiology

In this final chapter I attempt to draw together the traces and implications of the vision of Jesus as 'the Shaken One'. In particular, I hope to generate resources for discipleship communities of the Shaken One, to relate christology and ecclesiology to the demands of missiology: what does it mean to see Jesus the Shaken One as normative for communal life today?

With that in mind, while I have attempted to attend to the christologies of Hick and Newbigin on their own terms, not to dehumanize them in the shadow of a wider discussion, the point was nevertheless always constructive, to bring them into dialogue for the purpose of sketching the contours of an alternative proposal. The presence of their theologies in the thinking and behaviour of churches, even if mostly Free Churches, underpins part of my interest in them, but in particular it is their contrasting approaches to the challenges of identity, difference and solidarity, and their location on the frontiers between the modern and the postmodern, which determine their relevance for this project. With Hick's 'expressive' christology and Newbigin's 'constitutive' christology, they helpfully represent a dichotomy or tension evident in churches. I suggest that both such approaches foster the idealization of Jesus and illustrate the predominance of docetic christology (even Hick's Jesus only 'appears' human in the sense that his socially constituted human nature is not properly affirmed). This idealization, reflecting the objectifying tendencies of human beings in general (and our impatient desire for truth-as-correctness), is connected to their primary concern with Jesus' relation to God. I argued that, in Western cultures, such idealization of Jesus leads also to the Church's insularity, indifference and impotence.

How, then, does a constructive christology focused primarily on 'the human concern', the challenge to embody 'the myth of the Human Being' with each other, engage such social dynamics? It is about Jesus expressing and constituting what it is to be fully human, not as an idealized individual but in community. Although, with Wink, I understand this embodiment as being an embodiment of *God*'s humanity, the point is that the primary focus of such christology is Jesus' relation to Being Human. This demands attentiveness to human social relations and practices, those norms and forces which both feed our objectification of each other and enable our resistance to such objectification. For Jesus does not become fully human in a vacuum but in and through messy and unpredictable relations with human 'others' – others within his/our (Jewish/Christian) tradition, others beyond the tradition, and others rendered relatively invisible to the traditions. We, too, become fully human only in and through each other.

As the focus of the Christian tradition, the question is how the personal and corporate vision and practice of this prophetic Jew shapes, and shakes, his Body's contemporary mission? In Shanks's terms, it is a matter of demonstrating 'sanctity' to our tradition while also 'transgressing' its finalities and working for an ever greater 'solidarity of the shaken'. As Min suggests, the challenge is to see our tradition as a solidarity of others, a Body particularly committed to recognizing and valuing its internal diversity, while engaging dialogically (and deeply) with other traditions and engendering solidarity amongst the world's various liberationist movements. Ultimately, I propose, it is a vision of mutual humanization, given particular shape by the person and Body of Christ, but through persistent engagement also with plural other traditions, criticizing them on our terms but humbly being subject to them on theirs.

I do not pretend that my christological vision is wholly free from objectification, since my language and presuppositions are inevitably shaped by Western ideologies, particular experiences and political assumptions about what is good for 'others'. Rather, I affirm that what is required is a demanding process of self-criticism energized by the repeated experience of shakenness. It is of the nature of this vision, shaped by Jesus' *basileia* practice, that it intends not to conform to the dichotomous ways of the 'Domination System' which polarize the good from the bad. It is a tradition which insists instead that we ought to recognize our own 'kyriarchal' tendencies and seek out the humanity even of those demonized – both those excluded or oppressed and those who exclude or oppress. This is what it means to love enemies as well as neighbours: to accept that all people and communities have shadow sides and light sides, and that by reintegrating our full humanity through an ongoing process of maturation, as Jesus demonstrates, we can heal each other of the dehumanizing effects of the 'Domination System' and work together for its transformation.

We can but trust that the goal to which we are heading is reflected in the process: so whilst our conceptions of 'humanization' will always be shaped by our temporal and cultural contexts, we are called as followers of Jesus the Shaken One to assess our practices by their contribution to our mutual humanization as a solidarity of others. This tension, between the process and the goal, the 'now' and the 'not yet', or between God's *basileia* partially manifested in the present and God's ultimate *basileia* fulfilled in the future, is to be understood in the light of the distinction between truth-as-correctness and truth-as-Honesty. For each attempt to realize the *basileia* remains susceptible to the demands for 'correctness' defined by the ideological conditioning of contemporary social relations, even as we strive to expose and transform their distortions; whereas true Honesty is ultimately free from the grip of all such ideological conditioning. It is the experience of shakenness which makes this a creative tension, confronting us with our ideological distortions and making an ever greater solidarity of others possible. Jesus the Shaken One thus has normative, eschatological power, defined by his being shaken and his capacity to shake; his identity in community inviting us to engage in deeper ecumenical theology, that is, with others within the tradition, deeper dialogical theology, that is, with others beyond this tradition, and deeper political theology, that is, in solidarity with others rendered sociopolitically invisible.

In that light, I consider the implications of this constructive christology for Christian communities. I begin with a word about the method, its two dimensions, before considering ecumenical, dialogical and political theologies and praxes in turn. I close with a word which is not the last.

The Shaken One and Methodology: Mediation and Agitation

The task of outlining a christological vision which resists relativism, on the one hand, and absolutism, on the other, requires constant methodological attention to these two dangers. Although 'critical humility' is the term I use to express the praxis demonstrated by Jesus the Shaken One, a praxis into which followers of the Shaken One are beckoned, it is worth acknowledging briefly the two related roles which we must play to nurture this praxis. The first is that of 'mediator' or 'peace negotiator', as Giles Fraser describes Andrew Shanks, and the second is that of 'agitator', as Fraser describes himself.[1]

The point is that the dialogue encouraged here is not interested simply in truth; it is not only a quest for mutual and greater understanding, whether within the Church or between religious traditions. The dialogical approach is integrated with a political bias, to act in solidarity especially with those 'others' who are treated as 'the last' or 'the least'. In other words, the particular nature of the Christian tradition which I am fostering here is concerned both with dialogue as an essential reality in itself and with liberative action. For the sake of self-criticism as much as other-criticism, we must not exist solely for deep dialogue, even though deep dialogue can itself expose us to alternative and awkward readings of reality and its ideological captivity, but must also determine to root out and transform the damage done to each other by the dominating powers of ideologies, cliques and empires, whether active in our own tradition or others.

To use Fraser's terms, we need 'mediators' to referee between our unequal relations, to facilitate dialogue between different voices in an unjust world. It involves considerable effort to attend to the real complexity of those who are 'other' to us, and we tend to prejudge and objectify them. We need tools and traditions to help us to be more attentive, including mediators to enable mutual listening. It is important, then, for the Christian tradition itself to foster mediation methodologically, to make engagement with others a vital quality of its life, both within itself, between Christians who see things differently, and between it and other traditions or worldviews. Mediators alone are not enough, however;

---

[1]   Giles Fraser, 'Foreword', in Andrew Shanks, *Against Innocence: Gillian Rose's Reception and Gift of Faith* (London, 2008), pp. vii, xii.

for we need 'agitators', or campaigners, to confront the inequalities and alert us all to the need for transformed relations and liberated co-participants. In Wink's understanding, we must engage the powers of domination, so as to repent of our collusion in the dehumanizing 'Domination System' and heal one another of the damage done to our humanity by such powers. It is about fostering in the Church a concern to agitate our social practices and structures which are taken for granted and which obstruct peaceful and just social relations. This involves being sensitive to the distortions in our own vision of Jesus and each 'other' and acting in such ways as to affirm the humanity of one another. (For example, this project itself needs others to expose how my vision and practice is distorted by forces I have not identified.)

In essence, it is about mediating between different people, traditions and communities, so as to nurture the 'solidarity of the shaken' (amongst those who are being shaken out of their 'dishonesties'), while also agitating for new solidarities, acting politically so as to shake each other out of our respective dishonesties. Dialogue, done properly, ought to bring to light those whose participation is impeded or denied, but only agitation will enable such people or groups to participate. Mediation and agitation are thus both marks of shakenness: they confront us with other others with whom we should engage, in dialogue and in action, if we are to generate an ever greater solidarity of others.

It is not irrelevant that this method reflects concerns of the philosopher Hegel. Both Hodgson and Shanks are Hegelians, and whilst I do not claim to be deeply conversant with Hegel's thought, or to argue for his role in this project, I acknowledge his role in their thinking, because this project builds upon their work. This explains the flavour of Hegelianism in the ever-unfolding implications of Jesus the Shaken One, whose particularity draws us into dialogue with plural other particularities, in pursuit of an ever greater, and ultimately universal, solidarity of others. Although Hodgson clearly articulates his awareness that Hegel's context is very different from today's postmodern climate, he nevertheless acknowledges that Hegel's method provides the resources for his constructive, revisionist approach to theology.[2] Hegel speaks of identity, difference and mediation, and it is Hegel's insight that the *identity* of God as Love remains abstract *apart from the world;*[3] that is, whilst God is necessarily *different* from the world, God's Spirit necessarily *mediates* (or makes 'solidarity' possible) between God and the world. The themes of dialogue and liberation also reflect Hegel's concerns, for Hodgson understands God, who is 'the One who Loves in Freedom' (a Barthian phrase), in terms of relationality and freedom,[4] which are inseparable. Our connectedness, thus the

---

[2]   Peter C. Hodgson, *Winds of the Spirit: A Constructive Christian Theology* (London, 1994), p. 336.

[3]   G.W.F. Hegel, *Lectures on the Philosophy of Religion*, 1:307–9, 323–4; 3:271–4, 291–4 (Berkeley and Los Angeles, CA and London, 1985, 1987).

[4]   Hodgson, *Winds of the Spirit*, p. 47 (citing Barth, *Church Dogmatics*, II/1 (Edinburgh, 1957), p. 28), and p. 84.

possibility of mediation between us, and our freedom are deeply related and are rooted in the One who Loves in Freedom.

Shanks, too, specifically draws on Hegelian thinking in his theology and his emphasis on our being shaken out of closed-mindedness towards a greater solidarity is rooted in Hegel's vision.[5] For the spiritual community of the Church shakes its own authoritarianism,[6] opening us to the diverse individual revelations of Christ within the tradition. The universality of God's being shakes the closed-mindedness of the particularistic herd, opening us to the plural other. The particularity (singularity) of Christ shakes the closed-mindedness which dominates, manipulates and oppresses the other, opening us to free-spiritedness and solidarity. That is, the particular, the plural and the universal interrelate dynamically; there is an ever unfolding vision of reality, worked out through dialogue and liberative action, as Shanks understands Hegel to mean. In essence, the point is that both Hodgson and Shanks are resistant, as Hegel was, on the one hand, to absolutism, for there is always more to be discovered through ongoing engagement with 'others', and, on the other hand, to relativism (or any lazy agnosticism), since freedom demands that we cannot be indifferent to the predicament of each other.

I am not proposing, however, that churches adopt the Hegelian methodology wholesale, insofar as it can foster an entire way of being in the world. I simply acknowledge Hegel's contribution to this project, but urge churches to generate the two elements of mediation and agitation, or dialogue and liberation, if our fundamental concern is indeed the realizing of an ever greater solidarity of others, or our mutual humanization.

This dual task can be illustrated with reference to another trace of Jesus the Shaken One in the biblical witness. In Mark 8:22–6, we encounter a man who is blind whose friends bring him to Jesus for healing. However, Jesus leads him out of the village, as though transformation is only possible if we dare to move beyond the finalities of our own herd. He places saliva on the man's eyes and asks what he can see. 'I can see people, but they look like trees, walking', the man replies. Only after the second attempt does the man 'see everything clearly', at which point Jesus instructs him to go another way, as though to have renewed vision means we cannot retrace our steps; our world, or worldview, is transformed. It is, though, the vision of 'walking trees' which grabs my attention: for this attests to our objectification of one another, our misreading and mistreatment of others' humanity and the implication that we must learn ways of seeing beneath each other's bark. The point is: such learning entails mediation, so as to nurture dialogical habits which go deeper than the superficial similarities and differences, to uncover the 'hard kernel', as Žižek describes it, or the untranslatable otherness

---

[5]   See, for example, Andrew Shanks, *Hegel's Political Theology* (Cambridge, 1991), pp. 61–2.

[6]   Ibid., reflecting Hegel's vision of the spiritual community as anti-authoritarian. See also David MacGregor, *Hegel and Marx after the Fall of Communism* (Cardiff, 1998), p. x, confirming Hegel's anti-authoritarian sensibilities.

of one another.[7] However, mediation alone will not suffice. For our dialogue does not itself subvert the forces which define people as outsiders; we cannot overcome our partial sightedness simply through conversation. There is also the need for agitation: action which shakes the *status quo* and restores *shalom*, as illustrated by Jesus' healing of this man – a sign of our mutual healing of the effects of the 'Domination System' and a call to us to participate in such shaking action.

Jesus the Shaken One calls his Body, the Church, to generate and nourish practices of mediation and agitation, to encourage dialogue within and beyond the faith community and to fuel liberative action, in pursuit of an ever greater solidarity of others.

The Tradition of Hick, Newbigin and the Shaken One: Attentive to Context

In Chapter 5 I argued that the particularity of the Jesus-tradition, rooted in the prophetic Jewish tradition, is marked by a self-criticism and ongoing reflexivity with regards to history, knowledge and power relations. This is obviously a particular reading or interpretation of the tradition, but it is critical for an understanding of Jesus as the Shaken One.

The point is that, when we purport to define the tradition, we cannot simply 'start' in the Bible, or, conversely, in the contemporary experience of our cultural context, as though each starting-point is not related to prior assumptions and experiences we bring to it, including unidentified ideological presuppositions. Cobb, for instance, insists that responsible theologians take seriously biblical history and contemporary insights simultaneously;[8] we have seen how he also understands 'speculation' to have a role, much as Wink too recognizes that we inevitably, and not necessarily inappropriately, 'project' hopes or ideals on to Jesus or God.[9] The danger is that we may be indifferent to such possibilities or pretend we are free from such psycho-social dimensions. We need to be constantly reflexive, revisiting our history, our claims to knowledge and re-examining our power relations, in dialogue with each other – including those 'others' within the tradition whose presence and voices may be suppressed.

What, for example, of the sheer fact of Jesus the Jew straddling two Testaments? While it may be naive to conclude that he innately evokes a dialogical praxis, simply by virtue of his Jewish roots and his being definitive for Christian faith,

---

[7]   Slavoj Žižek, *Did Somebody Say Totalitarianism? Five Interventions in the (Mis)Use of a Notion* (London, 2001), p. 58.

[8]   John B. Cobb Jr, 'Christ beyond Creative Transformation: Response', in Stephen T. Davis (ed.), *Encountering Jesus: A Debate on Christology* (Atlanta, GA, 1988), p. 176.

[9]   John B. Cobb Jr, 'Critiques', in Davis (ed.), *Encountering Jesus*, p. 29; Walter Wink, *The Human Being: Jesus and the Enigma of the Son of the Man* (Minneapolis, MN, 2002), pp. 128–30.

it is no less naive to pretend that his Jewishness does not problematize Christian readings of him. Rather, to understand and interpret Christian tradition/s as fully as possible, it is essential that we dialogue deeply with Jewish tradition/s, no less than the Jewish Jesus prompted engagement with Gentiles.[10]

It is inevitable, though, that an individual theologian or interpretive community would not engage with all possible dialogue-partners. We have seen this with regards to both Hick and Newbigin. Hick prioritizes dialogue with relatively like-minded liberals and Newbigin implicitly prioritizes dialogue with relatively like-minded Christians. Arguably, therefore, neither of them facilitates a truly dialogical 'solidarity of the shaken': for while Hick is shaken more by the moral threat posed by exclusivism, and Newbigin is shaken more by the moral threat posed by Western relativism, neither is shaken by both such threats nor by the threat of their own sectarianism.

These failures are rooted in weak, objectified versions of relationality. Although Hick attempts to show how different traditions are related, he engages in monological (superficial) pluralism, speaking more *of* or *for* 'the others' than with their genuine (deep) otherness. He objectifies relationality too neatly, presuming the identification of 'Jesus' with 'the others'. Although Newbigin affirms that Christians should dialogue with each other and with other disciplines and traditions, his prior 'knowledge' that Jesus will be shown to be the measure of us all and the others undermines such openness. He objectifies relationality too neatly, presuming an absolute discontinuity between 'Jesus' and 'the others'. In effect, they are insufficiently shaken by otherness – whether the otherness within the tradition, the otherness of other traditions, or the otherness of the System's victims.

Nevertheless, it is vital that we note the positive contributions of both Hick and Newbigin, not least their engagement with culture and attentiveness to context. As such, they are partly shaken. Although Hick's theology appears to be subsumed within the culture of Western rationalism and Newbigin's approach to (Western) culture seems unduly negative, they still represent the importance of faith's relation to its cultural context. Even as Hick is more reliant than he realizes on Kantian presuppositions and Western dichotomies, as a second-order explanatory framework of religious plurality his hypothesis *is* a religious interpretation of religion.[11] While his schema has room for secular humanists and it diminishes the distinctiveness of each tradition, he remains a person of faith, whose image of Jesus arguably determines his universal criterion of saintliness. The point is: he is committed to being attentive to Western culture, religious plurality and the reality of faith, bringing these interrelated facets of contemporary life into creative dialogue. Though he intends also to resist cultural imperialism, it is the ease with

---

[10]   Cobb, 'Christ beyond Creative Transformation: Response', p. 149: Christians can hope Jews may reappropriate Jesus, a prophetic Jew, but without having to depart from Judaism, just as Jews can hope Christians reappropriate their Jewish roots.

[11]   John Hick, *An Interpretation of Religion: Human Responses to the Transcendent*, 2nd edn (Basingstoke, 2004), p. 1.

which his schema can be read as a first-order discourse, committed to reinterpreting each tradition in terms of this universal vision, which illustrates the negation of such intent. It is wrong to accuse him, then, as some do, of secular humanism,[12] because he means to be open to the reality of the transcendent but in the context of Western, pluralist culture. The intention is a sign of his shakenness.

Meanwhile, for Newbigin, Jesus stands over and against any other authority, including that of both religion and culture, but Newbigin is insufficiently attentive to the interrelatedness of the Judaeo-Christian tradition and Western modernity. In other words, even as Hick is accused, only half fairly, of sanctifying the Enlightenment at the cost of faith, Newbigin seems to belittle the Enlightenment while relying on its gifts to him: that is, Hick is more religious than some assume, and Newbigin is more culturally conditioned than he assumes, such that they share more space than either recognizes.

Essentially, we need to foster deeper engagement between religion and culture, including between Christian faith and Western post-Enlightenment, pluralistic culture; engagement which is alert to the sacralization of cultural norms and the secularization of religious practice; engagement which is critical *and* humble. Both Hick and Newbigin point the Church towards such engagement, to appreciate the interrelation between faith and context, even as their understandings of the interrelation are marked by insufficient self-criticism. How, then, should we criticize and regulate our religious engagement with our cultural context? We note that Jesus the Shaken One, historically embedded in a pluralistic culture, engaged in various ways with its fluidities and supposed finalities. Whether it is an indication of his shadow side or simply of human realism, he commends 'dusting off one's feet' in the face of rejection (Mark 6:11); and elsewhere he retreats, urges silence, even explicitly demands non-interference with an 'other' exorcist whom his disciples jealously seek to dehumanize to the point of destruction (Mark 9:39–41). Even his exhortation to 'turn the other cheek' illustrates a strategy of indirect, not direct, engagement with the other (Matthew 5:39): for it does not presume the aggressor will dialogue, but exposes the moral bankruptcy of violence and refuses to co-operate with or succumb to it.[13] It even embodies a refusal to be shaken by the violent exercise of power, so provocatively 'shakes' the System's own cultural expectations. It is possible, then, to remain committed to the task of engagement, of attentiveness to others within one's cultural context, even of love for enemies, without naively believing that everyone is ready for peaceful and mutually respectful dialogue. We saw in Chapter 4 that Jesus himself had to be shaken out of his cultural norms by a

---

[12] For example: Matthew Siebert, 'What Should We Do about Religious Pluralism? A Response to John Hick's Interpretation of Religion', *Society for the Study of Theology*, Annual Conference, 4 April 2006. See also Christopher Sinkinson, *The Universe of Faiths: A Critical Study of John Hick's Religious Pluralism* (Carlisle, 2001), pp. 52, 77, 84, 124 ('implicit atheism'), 157.

[13] Walter Wink, *Engaging the Powers: Discernment and Resistance in a World of Domination* (Minneapolis, MN, 1992), pp. 175–7.

feisty Syro-Phoenician woman, as though he was not ready for engagement, and she persuaded him of the universal implications of his purported vision.

For the Church, this means we should be willing for the limits on our engagement with culture to be shaken, while also accepting there will be times and places when the System or our own human needs will compel us to engage indirectly at most. Occasionally, for the sake of our mutual humanization, we must temporarily withdraw from engagement and maintain some distance. In Benhabib's terms, we will sometimes need to 'generalize' about others, because we do not always have the means or strength to appreciate others' concreteness;[14] and in order to be energized for re-engagement, especially for the sake of those relatively invisible in our culture who most need social relations to be transformed, we must be mindful of our fragility. The Church is thus called to attend to itself. As the earlier discussion of metaphorical language illustrates, we must recognize the interpenetration of the 'is' and the 'is not', the truth and the untruth, the uniqueness and the incompleteness of our identity. To demonstrate 'sanctity' to our tradition, we need to engage the 'shadow side' and diversity of our history, to recognize the distinctiveness and conditioning of our knowledge, to be self-critical regarding our power relations, to appreciate the variety and value of trinitarian traditions, to examine our dependence and impact on culture, and all such engagements involve fostering deeper dialogue and solidarity ecumenically.

As such, the Shaken One encourages us to nurture communities of mediation in which we facilitate deeper conversation with each other, so as to affirm the Christian tradition's scandalously distinctive vision and practice of universal, mutual humanization, while also recognizing that our tradition does not exhaust the universal quest. In particular, we must act 'from the outside in', that is, with a political bias regarding others treated as 'the last' or 'the least', to which I will return below.

The Dialogue of the Shaken One: Resistant to Closure

It is not only because the history of Jesus remains unsettled that we must continue to dialogue with regards to the contrasting visions of him. Certainly, the reality of the mythicization of his history and his historicization of the myth of God's ultimate rule, to which Theissen directs us, together with Wink's insistence on the open-endedness of historical inquiry, urge us to sustain interest in the question of Jesus' historical nature. It is also, however, the reality of different theological versions of him, rooted not only in various theological and ideological traditions throughout history, but also in the biblical witness, which demands of us an ecumenical and dialogical approach to christology; that is, conversation within the Church and conversation between the Church and other traditions.

---

[14]   Seyla Benhabib, *Situating the Self: Gender, Community and Postmodernism in Contemporary Ethics* (Oxford, 1992), pp. 152–69.

We noted in Chapter 6 that Knitter recommends appreciation of what exclusivism, inclusivism and pluralism each offer to such dialogical christology. For there are features of the witness to Jesus which suggest a figure strong enough to expose and confront sin, as in exclusivism; and there are features which suggest an inclusivist understanding, by virtue of his willingness to see the good in the other. The activist-scholar Myers, for example, argues that the implications of Jesus' positive non-interference with the other exorcist are that he would be regarded as an inclusivist today.[15] Dunn, too, assesses the biblical material as evidence for Jesus' understanding of himself as definitive for world history,[16] even if he is also open to discern the movement of God's Spirit beyond his own immediate community. What, though, is the basis for a pluralistic vision of Jesus? We observed Griffin's suggestion that, with regards to the move from exclusivism and inclusivism to pluralism, there is an ontological shift in worldview from supernatural theism to naturalistic theism. Thus, even if the historical Jesus had a self-understanding consistent with constitutive christologies, by which his very being is deemed to problematize the supposedly 'natural' course of history, the point is that naturalistic theism raises questions regarding such a self-understanding. In terms of Jesus' being 'the Shaken One', namely, this possible self-understanding can be viewed as a sign of Jesus' historical conditioning within a particular cultural and ideological matrix. It will certainly be shaped by religio-cultural assumptions about the significance of Jewish history for world history and the prophetic tradition's vision of universal human well-being. The sociality of being human means that Jesus and his self-understanding are inseparable from others' visions of him. Not only will his self-understanding have been shaped, therefore, by others before and contemporaneous with his historicity, but his personhood and meaning will have been constantly shaped and reshaped by others. For any ongoing grasps of his historical decisiveness will be connected with the various ways in which we and others interpret his history/ myth in the light of current ideologies. In Lochhead's terms, then, it is possible that exclusivist visions of Jesus are determined by ingrained suspicions of and hostility between competing religious traditions, as much as superficially pluralist visions of him are constructed on the basis of liberal imperialism.

Deep pluralism, by contrast, urges us to attend to the ideological conditioning of any vision of Jesus (and other religious icons). We must concern ourselves with historical and ideological inquiry, to become as aware as possible of the way in which we are interpreting Jesus' being and significance. In fact, the reality of shakenness demands that, even if the 'historical' Jesus could ever be proven to be non-pluralist, Jesus the Shaken One problematizes the limits of his original context; the demands of shakenness in the direction of truth-as-Honesty compel

---

[15]   Ched Myers, *Binding the Strong Man: A Political Reading of Mark's Story of Jesus* (Maryknoll, NY, 1998), p. 262.

[16]   James D.G. Dunn, *Christology in the Making: An Inquiry into the Origins of the Doctrine of the Incarnation*, 2nd edn (London, 1989), pp. 253–4, 262. Wink, *Human Being*, p. 22, confirms that Jesus was not modest!

us to imagine at least the possibility that Jesus not only recognizes the good in the other which conforms to his tradition's own good but is willing to be shaken by the good of the other on its own terms. His very openness to others, including those regarded as enemies, implies that his tradition ought self-critically to root out all ideological conditioning especially for the sake of any others who suffer the consequences of the powers of domination.

My argument is, in essence, that the particularity of the Jesus tradition does indeed offer a scandalously universal vision, rooted in the prophetic Jewish heritage, which reaches beyond those committed to it. It is a vision which seeks to affirm all people's inherent worth and dignity as human beings, or children of God who can and do reflect God's humanity. Such an affirmation necessarily entails, as Wink illustrates, Jesus' understanding of his own embodiment of 'the myth of the Human Being' but that he does not fulfil it alone. We become more fully human in and through relationship with each other. For example, by Jesus' inclusion of children, tax collectors, sinners, 'the unclean', and, as Fiorenza argues, 'wo/men',[17] in the *basileia* community, he demonstrates that the *basileia* itself undergoes a deeper shakenness, even explicitly inviting criticisms of its various temporal forms, such that all powers of domination will in the end be named, engaged and transformed. The reality of shakenness indicates, therefore, that it does not only extend from 'us' *to* 'the others' but is experienced *by* 'us' in our encounter *with* 'them'; this is to say, our tradition alone is not all-determinative for the contours of our humanization in solidarity with each other; rather our tradition teaches us to remain open to the shaking power of others' traditions.

What this means for the Church is that our readiness to be 'critical' must be tempered by due 'humility'. While we are free, like inclusivists, to engage with others, to see truth and goodness in others, and to criticize their shortcomings by our own norms, we are also prompted, by virtue of our discipleship of Jesus the Shaken One, to practise humility, not so as to deny our scandalous distinctiveness, but accepting that others may shake us out of unidentified ideological captivity and unrecognized oppressive behaviour, especially for the sake of any others excluded from such humanizing regard. For the tradition's plural visions of Jesus demand of us an appreciation of the tradition's plural visions of the religious others as well (Jesus himself being 'other' to those others), not merely for the sake of mediating between the differences but agitating towards an ever greater solidarity of others.

---

[17] Elisabeth Schüssler Fiorenza, *Jesus – Miriam's Child, Sophia's Prophet: Critical Issues in Feminist Christology* (London, 1995), p. 191: 'my unorthodox writing of the term [underscores that] those kyriarchal structures that determine women's lives and status also have an impact on men of subordinated races, classes, countries and religions, albeit in a different way ... "Wo/men" must therefore be understood as an inclusive expression rather than as an exclusive universalized gender term.'

The Solidarity of the Shaken One: Action as Victim/Victor

If it is true that a constructive christology, focused on a vision of Jesus as the Shaken One, demands of the Church a praxis of 'critical humility' in our engagement with each other and those beyond our own tradition, how should we exercise the specifically political dimension of this praxis? Repeatedly I have argued that this pluralistic approach to Jesus, in community, is not relativistic; that it is concerned deeply with the differences between each 'other' rather than retreating into indifference; and that it is possible to be open to the otherness of the other while sustaining a vision of moral force. What, then, of the implications of such a trajectory for the Church today, being committed to solidarity especially with those treated as invisible? How should we engage the 'Domination System', to heal each other of its dehumanizing power and liberate one another of our complicity with it?

First, we should see that reality is not fixed; in Žižek's terms, there is an ontological gap, a crack, at the heart of reality, a readiness to realize its own incompleteness.[18] The point of this is to allow for grander visions of possibility. For our relationships of critical humility must not be unchanging; there must instead be a readiness to see existing movements between the centres of power and the margins, to recognize within our tradition and those of others that some participants are usurping or belittling the place of others, and that even those on the margins can be manipulative or can use their position to resist greater solidarity. No one is free from the temptations to dominate or manipulate, or to deny the histories of others; thus we must be ready to identify the exercise of such forces wherever they may be and to redirect their energy in pursuit of the ever greater solidarity of others.

Secondly, since such powers of domination affect and infect our visions of Jesus, we should beware idealizations of him and his history. As Wink puts it, we should reject the 'superman' christologies which draw all the attention to Jesus' power and thus disempower us; instead we should encourage and cherish 'broken wholeness':[19] that is, we should recognize Jesus' embeddedness in the fragility and brokenness of human social relations and his capacity to facilitate our healing from such distortions, as defined by his (corporate) embodiment of 'the myth of the Human Being'. Wink suggests, after all, that 'Jesus seems to have expected people to begin behaving differently *now*', not that he would resolve the world's problems single-handedly.[20] The vision of Jesus as the Shaken One, who enables our participation in a wider social movement, is thus, in Wink's terms, 'the myth of the human being, imperfect but exemplary, victim but victorious ... who gambled all on the reality of God and reveals and catalyses true humanity'.[21]

---

[18] Žižek, pp. 166, 174.
[19] Wink, *Human Being*, p. 32.
[20] Ibid., p. 162.
[21] Ibid., pp. 259–60.

Whilst the original disciples and followers of Jesus throughout history tend to project power on to him, Wink argues that Jesus did and would break such projections, illustrating the conflict between the myth of the superhuman and the myth of the truly human.[22] This does not negate his distinctive role in history; he remains the Shaken One whose vision and practice energizes the shape and life of God's *basileia*. However, if we are to rediscover the permission and the call to act for social change, even in the face of the unintended consequences of such action, we can look to Jesus' example as evidence that shadows may be cast but still it is worth engaging the powers. Even though there are costs, known and unforeseen, it is better to identify and enact the direction of anti-domination than to adopt a stance of innocent disengagement. We had better learn, therefore, how to de-idealize the biblical witness to Jesus and emphasize instead the traces of his shakenness, his indebtedness to others and his building of a movement of social transformation.

Thirdly, in terms of Jesus' being both victim and victor, this has particular implications for the Church's social practice. The nature of the movement of social transformation effected by Jesus is not designed for efficient or straightforward progress. It is, in fact, an awkward movement, inclusive of people who will not make things easy. Certainly Hick is resistant to Christian superiority-complexes, in solidarity with those who have been their victims, and Newbigin insists on the costly manner of Jesus' absoluteness – the Christian tradition should express solidarity with victims. However, Jesus the Shaken One goes further than the visions of either Hick or Newbigin: for as much as the role of victor is not to be idealized, so the role of victim must not be idealized; Jesus in fact affirms and problematizes both roles, transforming all such dichotomies. As we saw in Chapter 4, in the analysis of James Alison, Jesus demonstrates that the judged become the judges, the victims become the victors, the outsiders become the insiders, the last become the first. While Newbigin argues that outsiders are chosen by God to humble us of our self-righteousness, it is not clear that he emphasizes the sociopolitical implications: for this gospel imperative is not to be limited to the realm of spiritual truths, so as to prevent Christian self-aggrandizement, whether as understood by Hick or Newbigin, but is awkwardly and profoundly political.

The movement of social transformation, directed towards the realization of God's *basileia*, which Jesus envisions and enables, is a community of victims and victors in which we are each an element of both. We are complicit with social practices which render others 'victims', while also participating in the tradition's alternative practices which affirm the dignity of all people and turn former victims of the dehumanizing effects of the 'Domination System' into 'victors'. The Church, therefore, cannot expect to be socially victorious; we will not be successful in worldly terms, in the sense of embodying our principles perfectly or growing easily in faith, hope or size. Conversely, we should not wallow in victimhood, by demonizing those who would marginalize our influence. Rather, we should act in

---

[22]   Ibid., pp. 132–44, 250–56.

solidarity with victims of the 'Domination System', seek to build a community of 'the last' and 'the least', a solidarity of domination survivors, without self-righteously excluding 'the first' and the powerful. As all can potentially experience shakenness, we should expect to be a community of all kinds of people, mediating between all our differences and agitating for new solidarities.

Jesus the Shaken One: Not the Last Word

When two 'others' meet and experience what Žižek understands as a 'traumatic encounter' (or shakenness), there is, he suggests, a 'vanishing mediator', in the sense that a certain kind of space, gap or freedom is fostered between what is and what could be.[23] To be shaken by an other is to be on the cusp of new possibilities – of self-understanding, other-understanding and actions which embody solidarity with each other. This resonates with Sölle's image of Jesus as the Teacher, one who invites us to step into the space where he has provisionally stood.[24] Rather than a teacher who is simply an exemplar of moral behaviour, who *could* be 'replaced' by mere 'learning machines' so *should* be replaced, Jesus truly gives of himself in the act of teaching, truly identifies and is interrelated with his students, so represents us provisionally in the learning-process toward maturation.[25] As such, he does not simply 'express' what must be taught, but 'constitutes' it such that we too may constitute it. Specifically, he expresses *and* constitutes what it is to be fully human, in and through relationship with others, in such a way as to draw us into the process of mutual humanization in solidarity with each other. As Sölle argues: not being our 'substitute' or 'replacement', since that would belittle and dehumanize us, but our temporary 'representative' and God's representative before us (so acting more as the 'vanishing mediator'), Jesus enables us to appreciate his identification with God and us *and* its incompleteness.[26]

In a striking passage, Sölle puts it thus:

> If Christ were identical with God, we would have nothing to expect, except Christ. But because he only represents God, only acts in place of God, only plays God's role – helps out the absent one, supports the helpless one – this difference keeps open the possibility that what Christ achieved here and now is not exhaustive. By its provisionality, representation makes hope possible. As identification, it is love in the pregnant sense of existence for others. But because

---

[23]   Žižek, p. 59.

[24]   Dorothee Sölle, *Christ the Representative: An Essay in Theology after the 'Death of God'* (London, 1967), pp. 113–22.

[25]   Ibid., p. 116.

[26]   Ibid., pp. 102–5, 130ff.

Christ remains dependent on the acceptance or rejection [not only of us, but] of the God he represents in the world, he needs, as his representative, faith.[27]

Perhaps we can understand God's 'absence' here as the relative absence of the embodiment of God's humanity, such that Jesus is Christ, the Shaken One, by virtue of his 'making present', or his embodiment, of God's humanity, in community with others. It is a provisional role, in the sense that it is unfinished; Jesus acts *in faith*, trusting that God continues to resource the making present of Being Human *and* trusting that others will follow, that we too may 'graduate' from Christ's school to God's kingdom.[28]

Of course, the 'Domination System' makes us suspect it is impossible; humanity's shadowy history of objectifying each other, of mishandling difference and oppressing certain others, suggests the distorted relations of religion and rationality cannot be transformed; and christology can appear to be a choice between a liberal Jesus who broadly does what other icons do and an absolute Christ who is starkly distinguished from social relations. Nevertheless, the vision and tradition of Jesus the Shaken One offers a distinctive but interrelated contribution to these challenges. It is a constructive christology which requires the Church to be both ecumenical and dialogical: to engage deeply with the tradition's many diverse images and experiences of Jesus and with other traditions' diverse narratives of what is ultimately significant, in a spirit of critical humility. That is, it is a way of being human, as Jesus is human in community, which involves criticism of each vision's cultural and ideological limitations or imperialism, and humility in the face of others' criticisms of one's own vision, especially for the sake of those who suffer the most other-disregard.

This is a particular reading of the Christian tradition which demands openness to and engagement with plural other readings and traditions. Without such engagement, its scandalously universal vision of the ultimate solidarity of all others is not realizable: for the point at which God and the world are mutually perfected, as Hodgson envisages it,[29] is the point at which God's humanity is embodied in our relationships *with each other*.

---

27 Ibid., p. 143 (my addition).
28 Ibid., pp. 123, 117.
29 Hodgson, *Winds of the Spirit*, pp. 330–31.

Bibliography

Alison, James, *The Joy of Being Wrong: Original Sin through Easter Eyes* (New York: Crossroad Publishing, 1998).

Apczynski, John V., 'John Hick's Theocentrism: Revolutionary or Implicitly Exclusivist?', *Modern Theology*, 8/1 (January 1992): 39–52.

Armstrong, Karen, *The Battle for God: Fundamentalism in Judaism, Christianity and Islam* (London: HarperCollins, 2000).

Badham, Paul (ed.), *A John Hick Reader* (London: Macmillan, 1990).

Baillie, Donald M., *God Was in Christ: An Essay on Incarnation and Atonement* (London: Faber & Faber, 1948).

Barnes, Michael, *Theology and the Dialogue of Religions* (Cambridge: Cambridge University Press, 2002).

Barnes, L. Philip, 'Continuity and Development in John Hick's Theology', *Studies in Religion*, 21/4 (1992): 395–402.

Barth, Karl, *Church Dogmatics*, I/2: *The Doctrine of the Word of God* (Edinburgh: T&T Clark, 1956).

——, *Church Dogmatics*, II/1: *The Doctrine of God* (Edinburgh: T&T Clark, 1957).

——, *Dogmatics in Outline* (London: SCM, 2001).

Bauman, Zygmunt, *Globalisation: The Human Consequences* (Oxford: Polity/Blackwell, 1998).

Benhabib, Seyla, *Situating the Self: Gender, Community and Postmodernism in Contemporary Ethics* (Oxford: Polity/Blackwell, 1992).

Bennett, Clinton, *In Search of Jesus: Insider and Outsider Images* (London: Continuum, 2001).

Berger, Peter L., *The Heretical Imperative: Contemporary Possibilities of Religious Affirmation* (Garden City, NY: Anchor Press/Doubleday, 1979).

Bliese, Richard H., 'Globalization', in K. Muller and T. Sundermeler, et al. (eds), *Dictionary of Mission* (Maryknoll, NY: Orbis, 1997).

Bonhoeffer, Dietrich, *Christ the Centre*, trans. E.H. Robertson (New York: Harper and Row, 1978).

Borg, Marcus J. (ed.), *Jesus and Buddha: The Parallel Sayings* (Berkeley, CA: Seastone, 1997).

——. (ed.), *Jesus at 2000* (Oxford: Westview Press, 1997).

Buber, Martin, *Between Man and Man* (London: Fontana, 1947).

——, *I and Thou* (New York: Scribner's, 1958).

Bultmann, Rudolf, 'New Testament and Mythology', in H.W. Bartsch (ed.), *Kerygma and Myth*, vol. 1 (London: SPCK, 1953).

——, 'On the Problem of Demythologizing', in Schubert Ogden (ed.), *New Testament and Mythology and Other Basic Writings* (London: SCM, 1985).

——, 'Jesus Christ and Mythology', in Roger Johnson (ed.), *Rudolf Bultmann: Interpreting Faith for the Modern Era* (London: Collins, 1987).

Carruthers, Gregory H., *The Uniqueness of Jesus Christ in the Theocentric Model of the Christian Theology of World Religions: An Elaboration and Evaluation of the Position of John Hick* (Lanham, MD: University Press of America, 1990).

Cheetham, David, *John Hick: A Critical Introduction and Reflection* (Aldershot: Ashgate, 2003).

Clooney, Francis X., 'Reading the World in Christ: From Comparison to Inclusivism', in Gavin D'Costa (ed.), *Christian Uniqueness Reconsidered: The Myth of a Pluralistic Theology of Religions* (Maryknoll, NY: Orbis, 1990).

Cobb, John B., Jr, *A Christian Natural Theology: Based on the Thought of Alfred North Whitehead* (Philadelphia, PA: Westminster, 1965).

——, *Beyond Dialogue: Toward a Mutual Transformation of Christianity and Buddhism* (Philadelphia, PA: Fortress Press, 1982).

——, 'Christ Beyond Creative Transformation', in Stephen T. Davis (ed.), *Encountering Jesus: A Debate on Christology* (Atlanta, GA: John Knox Press, 1988).

——, 'Critiques', in Stephen T. Davis (ed.), *Encountering Jesus: A Debate on Christology* (Atlanta, GA: John Knox Press, 1988).

——, 'Beyond "Pluralism"', in Gavin D'Costa (ed.), *Christian Uniqueness Reconsidered: The Myth of a Pluralistic Theology of Religions* (Maryknoll, NY: Orbis, 1990).

——, 'Dialogues' and 'Responses', in Leonard Swidler, John B. Cobb Jr, Paul F. Knitter and Monika K. Hellwig (eds), *Death or Dialogue? From the Age of Monologue to the Age of Dialogue* (London: SCM; Philadelphia, PA: Trinity Press, 1990).

——, *Transforming Christianity and the World: A Way beyond Absolutism and Relativism* (Maryknoll, NY: Orbis, 1999).

——, 'Some Whiteheadian Assumptions about Religion and Pluralism', in David R. Griffin (ed.), *Deep Religious Pluralism* (Louisville, KY: Westminster John Knox, 2005).

Conway, Martin, 'God-Open, World-Wide, and Jesus-True: Lesslie Newbigin's Faith Pilgrimage', *Mission Studies*, 11/2 (1994): 191–202.

Cook, Robert, 'Postmodernism, Pluralism and John Hick', *Themelios*, 19/1 (1993): 10–12.

——, 'Response to John Hick', *Themelios*, 19/3 (1994): 20–21.

Coventry, John, 'The Myth and the Method', *Theology*, 81/682 (July 1978): 252–61.

Crossan, John Dominic, 'Jesus and the Kingdom: Itinerants and Householders in Earliest Christianity', in Marcus J. Borg (ed.), *Jesus at 2000* (Oxford: Westview Press, 1997).

Cupitt, Don, *The Debate about Christ* (London: SCM, 1979).

Davis, Stephen T. (ed.), *Encountering Jesus: A Debate on Christology* (Atlanta, GA: John Knox press, 1988).

D'Costa, Gavin, *John Hick's Theology of Religions: A Critical Evaluation* (Lanham, MD: University Press of America, 1987).

—— (ed.), *Christian Uniqueness Reconsidered: The Myth of a Pluralistic Theology of Religions* (Maryknoll, NY: Orbis, 1990).

——, 'Christ, the Trinity and Religious Plurality', in Gavin D'Costa (ed.), *Christian Uniqueness Reconsidered: The Myth of a Pluralistic Theology of Religions* (Maryknoll, NY: Orbis, 1990).

——, 'John Hick and Religious Pluralism: Yet Another Revolution?', in Harold Hewitt Jr (ed.), *Problems in the Philosophy of Religion: Critical Studies of the Work of John Hick* (London: Macmillan; New York: St. Martin's Press, 1991).

——, *The Meeting of the Religions and the Trinity* (Edinburgh: T&T Clark, 2000).

DiNoia, J.A., 'Pluralist Theology of Religions: Pluralistic or Non-Pluralistic?', in Gavin D'Costa (ed.), *Christian Uniqueness Reconsidered: The Myth of a Pluralistic Theology of Religions* (Maryknoll, NY: Orbis, 1990).

Dirlik, Arif, 'Culturalism as Hegemonic Ideology and Liberating Practice', *Cultural Critique*, 6 (1987): 13–50.

Doniger, Wendy, *The Implied Spider: Politics and Theology in Myth* (New York: Columbia University Press, 1998).

Duffy, Stephen J., 'A Theology of Religions and/or a Comparative Theology?', *Horizons*, 26 (1999): 106.

Dulles, Avery, *Models of Revelation* (London: Gill & Macmillan, 1992).

Dunn, James D.G., *Christology in the Making: An Inquiry into the Origins of the Doctrine of the Incarnation*, 2nd edn (London: SCM, 1989).

——, *Unity and Diversity in the New Testament: An Inquiry into the Character of Earliest Christianity*, 2nd edn (London: SCM, 1990).

Dupuis, Jacques, 'Trinitarian Christology as a Model for a Theology of Religious Pluralism', in T. Dayanandan Francis and Israel Selvanayagam (eds), *Many Voices in Christian Mission: Essays in Honour of J.E. Lesslie Newbigin* (Madras: Christian Literature Society, 1994).

——, *Toward a Christian Theology of Religious Pluralism* (Maryknoll, NY: Orbis, 1997).

——, '"The Truth Will Make You Free": The Theology of Religious Pluralism Revisited', *Louvain Studies*, 24 (1999): 211–63.

Fackre, Gabriel, 'The Scandals of Particularity and Universality', *Mid-Stream*, 22/1 (1983): 32–52.

Farley, Edward, and Peter C. Hodgson, 'Scripture and Tradition', in Peter C. Hodgson and Robert H. King (eds), *Christian Theology: An Introduction to its Traditions and Tasks*, 2nd edn (Philadelphia, PA: Fortress Press, 1985).

Farmer, H.H., 'The Bible: Its Significance and Authority', in *Interpreter's Bible*, 1 (Abingdon: Cokesbury, 1952).

——, *Revelation and Religion* (New York: Harper and Brothers, 1954).

Ferguson, David, *Rudolf Bultmann* (London and New York: Continuum, 1992).
Fiorenza, Elisabeth Schüssler, *In Memory of Her: A Feminist Theological Reconstruction of Christian Origins*, 2nd edn (London: SCM, 1995).
——, *Jesus – Miriam's Child, Sophia's Prophet: Critical Issues in Feminist Christology* (London: SCM, 1995).
——, *Jesus and the Politics of Interpretation* (London: Continuum, 2000).
Firestone, Chris L., 'Kant and Religion: Conflict or Compromise?', *Religious Studies*, 35/2 (June 1999): 151–71.
Forrester, Duncan B., 'Lesslie Newbigin as Public Theologian', in Thomas F. Foust, George R. Hunsberger, J. Andrew Kirk, Werner Ustorf (eds), *A Scandalous Prophet: The Way of Mission after Newbigin* (Grand Rapids, MI: Eerdmans, 2002).
Foust, Thomas, 'Lesslie Newbigin's Epistemology: A Dual Discourse?', in Thomas F. Foust, George R. Hunsberger, J. Andrew Kirk, Werner Ustorf (eds), *A Scandalous Prophet: The Way of Mission after Newbigin* (Grand Rapids, MI: Eerdmans, 2002).
Foust, Thomas F., George R. Hunsberger, J. Andrew Kirk and Werner Ustorf (eds), *A Scandalous Prophet: The Way of Mission after Newbigin* (Grand Rapids, MI: Eerdmans, 2002).
Francis, T. Dayanandan and Israel Selvanayagam (eds), *Many Voices in Christian Mission: Essays in Honour of J.E. Lesslie Newbigin* (Madras: The Christian Literature Society, 1994).
Fraser, Giles, 'Foreword', in Andrew Shanks, *Against Innocence: Gillian Rose's Reception and Gift of Faith* (London: SCM, 2008).
Fredericks, James L., *Faith among Faiths: Christian Theology and Non-Christian Religions* (New York: Paulist Press, 1999).
Freire, Paulo, *Pedagogy of the Oppressed*, rev. edn (London: Penguin, 1996).
Gilkey, Langdon, 'Plurality and Its Theological Implications', in John Hick and Paul Knitter (eds), *The Myth of Christian Uniqueness* (London: SCM, 1988).
Gillis, Chester, *A Question of Final Belief: John Hick's Pluralistic Theory of Salvation* (London: Macmillan, 1989).
Gingerich, Ray, and Ted Grimsrud (eds), *Transforming the Powers: Justice, Peace and the Domination System* (Minneapolis, MN: Fortress Press, 2006).
Goheen, Michael W., 'Toward a Missiology of Western Culture', *European Journal of Theology*, 8/2 (1999): 155–68.
Goulder, Michael, *Incarnation and Myth: The Debate Continued* (London: SCM, 1979).
Graham, Elaine, and Heather Walton, 'A Walk on the Wild Side: A Critique of *The Gospel and Our Culture*', *Modern Churchman*, 33/1 (1991): 1–7.
Green, Michael, 'Preface: Scepticism in the Church', in Michael Green (ed.), *The Truth of God Incarnate* (London: Hodder and Stoughton, 1977).
Greene, Colin J.D., 'Trinitarian Tradition and the Cultural Collapse of Late Modernity', in Thomas F. Foust, George R. Hunsberger, J. Andrew Kirk,

Werner Ustorf (eds), *A Scandalous Prophet: The Way of Mission after Newbigin* (Grand Rapids, MI: Eerdmans, 2002).

——, *Christology in Cultural Perspective: Marking out the Horizons* (Carlisle: Paternoster, 2003).

Grey, Mary C., *Sacred Longings: Ecofeminist Theology and Globalization* (London: SCM, 2003).

Griffin, David R. (ed.), *Deep Religious Pluralism* (Louisville, KY: Westminster John Knox, 2005).

Griffin, David R., and Huston Smith, *Primordial Truth and Postmodern Theology* (Albany, NY: State University of New York Press, 1989).

Griffiths, Paul J., 'The Uniqueness of Christian Doctrine Defended', in Gavin D'Costa (ed.), *Christian Uniqueness Reconsidered: The Myth of a Pluralistic Theology of Religions* (Maryknoll, NY: Orbis, 1990).

Gunton, Colin, *Yesterday and Today: A Study of Continuities in Christology* (London: Darton, Longman and Todd, 1983).

——, *The One, the Three, and the Many: God, Creation and the Culture of Modernity* (Cambridge: Cambridge University Press, 1993).

Habermas, Jürgen, *Theory and Practice* (London: Heinemann, 1974).

Haight, Roger, *Jesus the Symbol of God* (Maryknoll, NY: Orbis, 1999).

Hamnett, Ian (ed.), *Religious Pluralism and Unbelief: Studies Critical and Comparative* (London and New York: Routledge, 1990).

Hardy, Daniel W., 'Theology through Philosophy', in David F. Ford (ed.), *The Modern Theologians: An Introduction to Christian Theology in the Twentieth Century*, vol. 2 (Oxford: Blackwell, 1989).

Hardy, Daniel W. and P.H. Sedgwick (eds), *The Weight of Glory – A Vision and Practice for Christian Faith: The Future of Liberal Theology* (Edinburgh: T&T Clark, 1991).

Hartshorne, Charles, *The Divine Relativity* (London: Yale University Press, 1948).

Hegel, G.W.F., *Lectures on the Philosophy of Religion* (Berkeley and Los Angeles, CA and London: University of California Press, 1985, 1987).

Heim, S. Mark, *Salvations: Truth and Difference in Religion* (Maryknoll, NY: Orbis, 1995).

——, 'Review of *Bearing the Witness of the Spirit* by George R. Hunsberger', *Theology Today*, 56/2 (1999): 266–268.

——, *The Depth of Riches: A Trinitarian Theology of Religious Ends* (Grand Rapids, MI: Eerdmans, 2001).

Hewitt, Harold, Jr (ed.), *Problems in the Philosophy of Religion: Critical Studies of the work of John Hick* (London: Macmillan; New York: St. Martin's Press, 1991).

Heywood Thomas, J., *Tillich* (London and New York: Continuum, 2000).

Hick, John, *Faith and Knowledge* (New York: Cornell University Press, 1957).

——, 'The Christology of D.M. Baillie', *Scottish Journal of Theology*, 11 (1958): 1–12.

——, 'Christology at the Cross-roads', in F.G. Healey (ed.), *Prospect for Theology: Essays in Honour of H.H. Farmer* (Digswell Place: James Nisbet, 1966).

——, *Evil and the God of Love* (London: Macmillan, 1966; 2nd edn, 1977).

——, *Christianity at the Centre* (London: SCM, 1968).

——, 'Religious Faith as Experiencing-as', in G.N.A. Vesey (ed.), *Talk of God* (London: Macmillan, 1969).

——, *God and the Universe of Faiths* (London: Macmillan, 1973).

——, *Death and Eternal Life* (London: Macmillan, 1976).

——, *The Centre of Christianity* (London: SCM, 1977).

—— (ed.), *The Myth of God Incarnate* (London: SCM, 1977).

——, 'Pilgrimage in Theology', *Epworth Review*, 6/2 (1979): 73–8.

——, 'Is there a Doctrine of the Incarnation?', in Michael Goulder (ed.), *Incarnation and Myth: The Debate Continued* (London: SCM, 1979).

——, *God Has Many Names* (London: Macmillan, 1980).

——, *The Second Christianity* (London: SCM, 1983).

——, *Problems of Religious Pluralism* (London: Macmillan, 1985).

——, 'An Inspiration Christology for a Religiously Plural World', in Stephen T. Davis (ed.), *Encountering Jesus: A Debate on Christology* (Atlanta, GA: John Knox press, 1988).

——, 'The Non-Absoluteness of Christianity', in John Hick and Paul Knitter (eds), *The Myth of Christian Uniqueness* (London: SCM, 1988).

——, 'On Grading Religions', in Paul Badham (ed.), *A John Hick Reader* (London: Macmillan, 1990).

——, 'Reply', in Harold Hewitt Jr (ed.), *Problems in the Philosophy of Religion: Critical Studies of the Work of John Hick* (London: Macmillan; New York: St. Martin's Press, 1991).

——, *Disputed Questions in Theology and the Philosophy of Religion* (Basingstoke: Macmillan, 1992).

——, *The Metaphor of God Incarnate* (London: SCM, 1993).

——, 'Response to Robert Cook', *Themelios*, 19/3 (1994): 20.

——, *The Rainbow of Faiths* (London, SCM, 1995).

——, 'A Pluralist View', in Dennis Okholm and Timothy Phillips (eds), *More than One Way?*, reissued as *Four Views on Salvation in a Pluralistic Age* (Grand Rapids, MI: Zondervan, 1995 and 1996).

——, 'The Possibility of Religious Pluralism: A Reply to Gavin D'Costa', *Religious Studies*, 33/2 (1997): 161–6.

——, *The Fifth Dimension* (Oxford: Oneworld, 1999).

——, *John Hick: An Autobiography* (Oxford: Oneworld, 2002).

——, *An Interpretation of Religion: Human Responses to the Transcendent*, 2nd edn (Basingstoke: Palgrave Macmillan, 2004).

Hick, John, and Paul Knitter (eds), *The Myth of Christian Uniqueness* (London: SCM, 1988).

Hines, Colin, *Localization: A Global Manifesto* (London: Earthscan, 2000).

Hodgson, Peter C., *Winds of the Spirit: A Constructive Christian Theology* (London: SCM, 1994).

——, *Theology in the Fiction of George Eliot: The Mystery Beneath the Real* (London: SCM, 2001).

Hoedemaker, Bert, 'Rival Conceptions of Global Christianity: Mission and Modernity, Then and Now', in Thomas F. Foust, George R. Hunsberger, J. Andrew Kirk, Werner Ustorf (eds), *A Scandalous Prophet: The Way of Mission after Newbigin* (Grand Rapids, MI: Eerdmans, 2002).

Hollenweger, Walter J., 'Towards a Pentecostal Missiology', in T. Dayanandan Francis and Israel Selvanayagam (eds), *Many Voices in Christian Mission: Essays in Honour of J.E. Lesslie Newbigin* (Madras: The Christian Literature Society, 1994).

Hopkins, Julie, *Towards a Feminist Christology* (London: SPCK, 1995).

Horrell, David G., *Solidarity and Difference: A Contemporary Reading of Paul's Ethics* (London: T&T Clark, 2005).

Hunsberger, George R., *Bearing the Witness of the Spirit: Lesslie Newbigin's Theology of Cultural Plurality* (Grand Rapids, MI and Cambridge: Eerdmans, 1998).

——, 'The Church in the Postmodern Transition', in Thomas F. Foust, George R. Hunsberger, J. Andrew Kirk, Werner Ustorf (eds), *A Scandalous Prophet: The Way of Mission after Newbigin* (Grand Rapids, MI: Eerdmans, 2002).

Hutchinson, John A., *Paths of Faith* (New York: McGraw Hill, 1969).

Hyman, Gavin, *The Predicament of Postmodern Theology: Radical Orthodoxy or Nihilist Textualism?* (Louisville, KY: Westminster John Knox, 2001).

Insole, Christopher, 'Why John Hick Cannot, and Should Not, Stay Out of the Jam Pot', *Religious Studies*, 36/1 (March 2000): 25–33.

Jackson, Eleanor, 'Reviews', *British and Irish Association for Mission Studies,* 22/6 (March 2004): 6–8.

Jeffrey, Robert M.C., 'Globalization, Gospel, and Cultural Relativism', in Thomas F. Foust, George R. Hunsberger, J. Andrew Kirk, Werner Ustorf (eds), *A Scandalous Prophet: The Way of Mission after Newbigin* (Grand Rapids, MI: Eerdmans, 2002).

Kärkkäinen, Veli-Matti, *Christology – A Global Introduction: An Ecumenical, International and Contextual Perspective* (Grand Rapids, MI: Baker Academic, 2003).

Kenneson, Philip D., 'Trinitarian Missiology: Mission as Face-to-Face Encounter', in Thomas F. Foust, George R. Hunsberger, J. Andrew Kirk, Werner Ustorf (eds), *A Scandalous Prophet: The Way of Mission after Newbigin* (Grand Rapids, MI: Eerdmans, 2002).

Kettle, David, 'Gospel, Authority, and Globalization', in Thomas F. Foust, George R. Hunsberger, J. Andrew Kirk, Werner Ustorf (eds), *A Scandalous Prophet: The Way of Mission after Newbigin* (Grand Rapids, MI: Eerdmans, 2002).

Klostermaier, Klaus K., *A Concise Encyclopaedia of Hinduism* (Oxford: Oneworld, 1998).

Knitter, Paul F., *No Other Name? A Critical Survey of Christian Attitudes toward the World Religions* (Maryknoll, NY: Orbis, 1986).

——, 'Interreligious Dialogue: What? Why? How?', in Leonard Swidler, John B. Cobb Jr, Paul F. Knitter and Monika K. Hellwig, *Death or Dialogue? From the Age of Monologue to the Age of Dialogue* (London: SCM; Philadelphia, PA: Trinity Press, 1990).

——, *Jesus and the Other Names: Christian Mission and Global Responsibility* (Maryknoll, NY: Orbis, 1996).

——, *Introducing Theologies of Religions* (Maryknoll, NY: Orbis, 2002).

Kraemer, Hendrik, *The Christian Message in a Non-Christian World* (London: Edinburgh House, 1938).

Lampe, Geoffrey W.H., *God as Spirit: The Bampton Lectures 1976* (Oxford: Clarendon Press, 1977).

Le Roy Stults, Donald, *Grasping Truth and Reality: Lesslie Newbigin's Theology of Mission to the Western World* (Eugene, OR: Wipf and Stock, 2008).

Lindbeck, George A., *The Nature of Doctrine: Religion and Theology in a Postliberal Age* (London: SPCK, 1984).

Lochhead, David, *The Dialogical Imperative: A Christian Reflection on Interfaith Encounter* (Maryknoll, NY: Orbis, 1988).

Loughlin, Gerard, 'On Telling the Story of Jesus', *Theology*, 87 (1984): 323–9.

——, 'Noumenon and Phenomena', *Religious Studies*, 23 (1987): 493–508.

——, 'Prefacing Pluralism: John Hick and the Mastery of Religion', *Modern Theology*, 7 (1990): 29–55.

——, 'Squares and Circles: John Hick and the Doctrine of the Incarnation', in Harold Hewitt Jr (ed.), *Problems in the Philosophy of Religion: Critical Studies of the work of John Hick* (London: Macmillan; New York: St. Martin's Press, 1991).

McClendon, James Wm., Jr, *Ethics: Systematic Theology*, vol. 1 (Nashville, TN: Abingdon, 1986; rev. edn 2002).

McCready, Douglas, 'The Disintegration of John Hick's Christology', *Journal of the Evangelical Theological Society*, 39/2 (June 1996): 257–70

McGrane, Bernard, *Beyond Anthropology: Society and the Other* (New York: Columbia University Press, 1989).

MacGregor, David, *Hegel and Marx after the Fall of Communism* (Cardiff: University of Wales Press, 1998).

McFague, Sallie, *Metaphorical Theology: Models of God in Religious Language* (Philadelphia, PA: Fortress Press, 1982).

McFarland, Ian A., *Listening to the Least: Doing Theology from the Outside In* (Cleveland, OH: United Church Press, 1998).

McLaren, Brian, *Church on the Other Side: Exploring the Radical Future of the Local Congregation* (Grand Rapids, MI: Zondervan, 1998).

Macquarrie, John, *Jesus Christ in Modern Thought* (London: SCM, 1990).

Maroney, Eric, *Religious Syncretism* (London: SCM, 2006).

Migliore, Daniel, *Faith Seeking Understanding: An Introduction to Christian Theology* (Grand Rapids, MI: Eerdmans, 1991).

Milbank, John, *Theology and Social Theory: Beyond Secular Reason* (Oxford: Blackwell, 1990).

——, 'The End of Dialogue', in Gavin D'Costa (ed.), *Christian Uniqueness Reconsidered: The Myth of a Pluralistic Theology of Religions* (Maryknoll, NY: Orbis, 1990).

——, 'Postmodern Critical Augustinianism: A Short *Summa* in Forty-Two Responses to Unasked Questions', in Graham Ward (ed.), *The Postmodern God: A Theological Reader* (Oxford: Blackwell, 1997).

Min, Anselm, *The Solidarity of Others in a Divided World: A Postmodern Theology after Postmodernism* (New York: T&T Clark, 2004).

Molnar, Paul D., *Incarnation and Resurrection: Toward a Contemporary Understanding* (Grand Rapids, MI: Eerdmans, 2007).

Moltmann, Jürgen, *The Crucified God* (London: SCM, 1974).

——, *The Way of Christ: Christology in Messianic Dimensions* (London: SCM, 1990).

——, 'Is "Pluralistic Theology" Useful for the Dialogue of World Religions?', in Gavin D'Costa (ed.), *Christian Uniqueness Reconsidered: The Myth of a Pluralistic Theology of Religions* (Maryknoll, NY: Orbis, 1990).

Murphy, Nancey, 'Traditions, Practices and the Powers', in Ray Gingerich and Ted Grimsrud (eds), *Transforming the Powers: Justice, Peace and the Domination System* (Minneapolis, MN: Fortress Press, 2006).

Myers, Ched, *Binding the Strong Man: A Political Reading of Mark's Story of Jesus* (Maryknoll, NY: Orbis, 1998).

Netland, H., *Dissonant Voices: Religious Pluralism and the Question of Truth* (Leicester: Apollos, 1991).

Newbigin, Lesslie, *The Household of God: Lectures on the Nature of the Church* (London: SCM, 1953).

——, 'The Present Christ and the Coming Christ', *Ecumenical Review*, 6/2 (January 1954): 118–23.

——, *Sin and Salvation* (London: SCM, 1956).

——, *A Faith for this One World?* (London: SCM, 1961).

——, *Honest Religion for Secular Man* (London: SCM, 1966).

——, *Behold I Make All Things New* (Madras: Christian Literature Society, 1968).

——, *Christ our Eternal Contemporary* (Madras: Christian Literature Society, 1968).

——, *The Finality of Christ* (London: SCM, 1969).

——, 'Jesus Christ', in Stephen Neill, Gerald Anderson and John Goodwin (eds), *Concise Dictionary of the Christian World Mission* (London: Lutterworth Press, 1970).

——, *The Open Secret: Sketches for a Missionary Theology* (Grand Rapids, MI: Eerdmans, 1978).

——, 'The Centrality of Jesus for History', in Michael Goulder (ed.), *Incarnation and Myth: The Debate Continued* (London: SCM, 1979).

——, 'Christ and the World of Religions', *Churchman*, 97/1 (1983): 16–30.

——, *The Other Side of 1984: Questions for the Churches* (Geneva: WCC, 1984).

——, *Unfinished Agenda: An Autobiography* (London: SPCK, 1985).

——, *Foolishness to the Greeks: The Gospel and Western Culture* (London: SPCK, 1986).

——, 'Response to David M. Stowe', *International Bulletin of Missionary Research*, 12/4 (1988): 151–3.

——, *The Gospel in a Pluralist Society* (London: SPCK, 1989).

——, 'Religion for the Marketplace', in Gavin D'Costa (ed.), *Christian Uniqueness Reconsidered: The Myth of a Pluralistic Theology of Religions* (Maryknoll, NY: Orbis, 1990).

——, *Truth to Tell: The Gospel as Public Truth* (London: SPCK, 1991).

——, 'Whose Justice?', *Ecumenical Review*, 44 (1992): 308–11.

Ogden, Schubert M., *The Point of Christology: The 1980 Sarum Lectures* (London: SCM, 1982).

—— (ed.), *New Testament and Mythology and Other Basic Writings* (London: SCM, 1985).

——, 'Problems in the Case for a Pluralistic Theology of Religion', *The Journal of Religion*, 68 (October 1988): 493–507.

——, *Is There Only One True Religion or Are There Many?* (Dallas, TX: Southern Methodist University Press, 1992).

Oman, John, *Grace and Personality* (Cambridge: Cambridge University Press, 1917).

——, *The Natural and the Supernatural* (Cambridge: Cambridge University Press, 1931).

Palleras, José Cárdenas, *A Poor Man Called Jesus: Reflections on the Gospel of Mark* (Maryknoll, NY: Orbis, 1985).

Panikkar, Raimundo, *The Unknown Christ of Hinduism* (London: Darton, Longman and Todd, 1964).

——, *The Trinity and the Religious Experience of Man* (Maryknoll, NY: Orbis, 1973).

——, 'The Jordan, the Tiber, and the Ganges: Three Kairological Moments of Christic Self-Consciousness', in John Hick and Paul F. Knitter (eds), *The Myth of Christian Uniqueness* (London: SCM, 1987).

——, 'The Invisible Harmony: A Universal Theory of Religion or a Cosmic Confidence in Reality?', in Leonard Swidler (ed.), *Toward a Universal Theology of Religions* (Maryknoll, NY: Orbis, 1987).

——, *The Cosmotheandric Experience: Emerging Religious Consciousness* (Maryknoll, NY: Orbis, 1993).

Pannenberg, Wolfhart, *Jesus – God and Man* (London: SCM, 1968).

——, *Basic Questions in Theology*, vol. 2 (London: SCM, 1971).

——, 'Religious Pluralism and Conflicting Truth Claims', in Gavin D'Costa (ed.), *Christian Uniqueness Reconsidered: The Myth of a Pluralistic Theology of Religions* (Maryknoll, NY: Orbis, 1990).

Patočka, Jan, 'Wars of the Twentieth Century and the Twentieth Century as War', *Telos*, 30 (1976–77).

——, 'What Charter 77 Is and What It Is Not', in H. Gordon Skilling, *Charter 77 and Human Rights in Czechoslovakia* (Winchester, MA: Allen and Unwin, 1981).

Pattison, Stephen, 'The Shadow Side of Jesus', *Studies in Christian Ethics*, 8/2 (1995): 54–67.

Peel, David R., *Ministry for Mission* (Salford: Trinity Press, 2003).

——, 'The Theological Legacy of Lesslie Newbigin', in Anna M. Robbins (ed.), *Ecumenical and Eclectic: The Unity of the Church in the Contemporary World – Essays in Honour of Alan P.F. Sell* (Milton Keynes: Paternoster, 2007).

Petrella, Ivan, *Beyond Liberation Theology: A Polemic* (London: SCM, 2008).

Pieris, Aloysius, *An Asian Theology of Liberation* (Edinburgh: T&T Clark, 1988).

——, *Fire and Water: Basic Issues in Asian Buddhism and Christianity* (Maryknoll, NY: Orbis, 1996).

——, *God's Reign for God's Poor: A Return to the Jesus Formula* (Sri Lanka: Tulana Research Centre, 1998).

——, 'Christ beyond Dogma: Doing Christology in the Context of the Religions and the Poor', *Louvain Studies*, 25 (2000): 187–231.

Polyani, Michael, *Personal Knowledge: Towards a Post-Critical Philosophy* (Chicago, IL: University of Chicago Press, 1962).

Price, Lynne, 'Churches and Postmodernity: Opportunity for an Attitude Shift', in Thomas Foust, George R. Hunsberger, J. Andrew Kirk and Werner Ustorf (eds), *A Scandalous Prophet: The Way of Mission After Newbigin* (Grand Rapids, MI and Cambridge: Eerdmans, 2002).

Quinn, Philip L., 'Religious Pluralism and Religious Relativism', *Scottish Journal of Religious Studies*, 15/2 (1994): 69–84.

Reader, John, 'Theology, Culture and Post-Modernity: In Response to Graham, Walton and Newbigin', *Modern Churchman*, 34/5 (1993): 58–63.

Redemptor Hominis, Encyclical of the Supreme Pontiff John Paul II (1979).

Ricoeur, Paul, *Freud and Philosophy: An Essay on Interpretation* (New Haven, CT: Yale University Press, 1970).

——, *The Rule of Metaphor: Multi-disciplinary Studies of the Creation of Meaning in Language* (London: Routledge and Kegan Paul, 1978).

——, *Figuring the Sacred: Religion, Narrative and Imagination* (Minneapolis, MN: Augsburg Fortress Press, 1995).

Roberts, R.H., *A Theology on Its Way? Essays on Karl Barth* (Edinburgh: T&T Clark, 1991).

Rosales, Gaudencia B. and C.G. Arévalo (eds), *For All the Peoples of Asia: Federation of Asian Bishops' Conferences Documents from 1970 to 1991*, vol. 1 (Maryknoll, NY: Orbis, 1992).

Rowe, William L., 'Religious Pluralism', *Religious Studies*, 35/2 (June 1999): 143–50.

Ruether, Rosemary Radford, 'Feminism and Jewish-Christian Dialogue: Particularism and Universalism in the Search for Religious Truth', in John Hick and Paul Knitter (eds), *The Myth of Christian Uniqueness* (London: SCM, 1988).

Runzo, Joseph, 'God, Commitment and Other Faiths: Pluralism vs. Relativism', *Faith and Philosophy*, 5 (1987): 343–64.

Rupert, Mark, *Ideologies of Globalization: Contending Visions of a New World Order* (London: Routledge, 2000).

Sanders, E.P., *Jesus and Judaism* (Philadelphia, PA: Fortress Press, 1985).

Schillebeeckx, Edward, *Jesus: An Experiment in Christology* (New York: Seabury Press, 1979, and London: Fount, 1983).

Schmidt-Leukel, Perry, 'Mission and Trinitarian Theology', in Thomas F. Foust, George R. Hunsberger, J. Andrew Kirk, Werner Ustorf (eds), *A Scandalous Prophet: The Way of Mission after Newbigin* (Grand Rapids, MI: Eerdmans, 2002).

Schreiter, Robert J., *The New Catholicity: Theology between the Global and the Local* (Maryknoll, NY: Orbis, 1997).

Schweitzer, Albert, *The Quest of the Historical Jesus*, 3rd edn (London: A&C Black, 1954).

Schwöbel, Christoph, 'Particularity, Universality, and the Religions', in Gavin D'Costa (ed.), *Christian Uniqueness Reconsidered: The Myth of a Pluralistic Theology of Religions* (Maryknoll, NY: Orbis, 1990).

Shanks, Andrew, *Hegel's Political Theology* (Cambridge: Cambridge University Press, 1991).

——, *Civil Society, Civil Religion* (Oxford: Blackwell, 1995).

——, *A Theological Context for Urban/Industrial Mission*, privately circulated paper, cited by Malcolm Brown, *New Government, New Community?* Second Andrewtide Lecture, 26 November 1997, published in association with The William Temple Foundation.

——, *God and Modernity: A New and Better Way to Do Theology* (London: Routledge, 2000).

——, *What is Truth? Towards a Theological Poetics* (London and New York: Routledge, 2001).

——, *Faith in Honesty: The Essential Nature of Theology* (Aldershot: Ashgate, 2005).

——, *The Other Calling: Theology, Intellectual Vocation and Truth* (Oxford: Blackwell, 2007).

Siebert, Matthew, 'What Should We Do about Religious Pluralism? A Response to John Hick's Interpretation of Religion', *Society for the Study of Theology*, Annual Conference, 4 April 2006.

Sinkinson, Christopher, *John Hick: An Introduction to His Theology* (Leicester: Religious and Theological Studies Fellowship, 1995).

——, 'Is Christianity Better than Other Religions?', *The Expository Times*, 107/9 (June 1996): 260–65.

——, *The Universe of Faiths: A Critical Study of John Hick's Religious Pluralism* (Carlisle: Paternoster, 2001).

Smith, Wilfred Cantwell, 'Theology and the World's Religious History', in Leonard Swidler (ed.), *Toward a Universal Theology of Religion* (Maryknoll, NY: Orbis, 1987).

——, 'Idolatry: In Comparative Perspective', in John Hick and Paul Knitter (eds), *The Myth of Christian Uniqueness* (London: SCM, 1988).

Sobrino, Jon, *Christology at the Crossroads: A Latin American View* (London: SCM, 1978).

Sobrino, Jon and Ignacio Ellacuria (eds), *Systematic Theology: Perspectives from Liberation Theology* (London: SCM, 1996).

Sölle, Dorothee, *Christ the Representative: An Essay in Theology after the 'Death of God'* (London: SCM, 1967).

——, *Political Theology* (Philadelphia, PA: Fortress Press, 1971).

Solomon, Robert, *In the Spirit of Hegel* (New York: Oxford University Press, 1983).

Soskice, Janet Martin, *Metaphor and Religious Language* (Oxford: Oxford University Press, 1985).

Stassen, Glen, *Just Peacemaking: Transforming Initiatives for Justice and Peace* (Louisville, KY: Westminster John Knox, 1992).

——, 'Michael Walzer's Situated Justice', *Journal of Religious Ethics* (Autumn 1994): 375–99.

——, 'The Kind of Justice Jesus Cares About', in Ray Gingerich and Ted Grimsrud (eds), *Transforming the Powers: Justice, Peace and the Domination System* (Minneapolis, MN: Fortress Press, 2006).

Stowe, David M., 'Modernization and Resistance: Theological Implications for Mission', *International Bulletin of Missionary Research*, 12/4 (1988): 146–51.

Suchocki, Marjorie Hewitt, 'In Search of Justice: Religious Pluralism from a Feminist Perspective', in John Hick and Paul Knitter (eds), *The Myth of Christian Uniqueness* (London: SCM, 1988).

——, *Divinity and Diversity: A Christian Affirmation of Religious Pluralism* (Nashville, TN: Abingdon, 2003).

Surin, Kenneth, 'A "Politics of Speech": Religious Pluralism in the Age of the McDonalds Hamburger', in Gavin D'Costa (ed.), *Christian Uniqueness Reconsidered: The Myth of a Pluralistic Theology of Religions* (Maryknoll, NY: Orbis, 1990).

——, 'Towards a "Materialist" Critique of Religious Pluralism: An Examination of the Discourse of John Hick and Wilfred Cantwell Smith', in Ian Hamnett (ed.), *Religious Pluralism and Unbelief: Studies Critical and Comparative* (London and New York: Routledge, 1990).

Swidler, Leonard, (ed.), *Toward a Universal Theology of Religion* (Maryknoll, NY: Orbis, 1987).

Swidler, Leonard, John B. Cobb Jr, Paul F. Knitter and Monika K. Hellwig, *Death or Dialogue? From the Age of Monologue to the Age of Dialogue* (London: SCM, 1990).

Taber, Charles R., 'The Gospel as Authentic Meta-Narrative', in Thomas F. Foust, George R. Hunsberger, J. Andrew Kirk, Werner Ustorf (eds), *A Scandalous Prophet: The Way of Mission after Newbigin* (Grand Rapids, MI: Eerdmans, 2002).

Theissen, Gerd, *The Shadow of the Galilean*, trans. John Bowden (London: SCM, 1987).

——, *A Theory of Primitive Christian Religion*, trans. John Bowden (London: SCM, 1999).

Thiselton, Anthony, *Interpreting God and the Postmodern Self: On Meaning, Manipulation and Promise* (Edinburgh: T&T Clark, 1995).

Thomas, M.M., 'A Christ-Centred Humanist Approach to Other Religions in the Indian Pluralistic Context', in Gavin D'Costa (ed.), *Christian Uniqueness Reconsidered: The Myth of a Pluralistic Theology of Religions* (Maryknoll, NY: Orbis, 1990).

Thomas, Owen C. (ed.), *Attitudes toward Other Religions: Some Christian Interpretations* (London: SCM, 1969).

Thompson, Geoff, and Christiaan Mostert (eds), *Karl Barth: A Future for Postmodern Theology?* (Adelaide: Openbook, 2000).

Tillich, Paul, *The Courage to Be* (New Haven, CT: Yale University Press, 1952).

——, *Systematic Theology* (Digswell Place: James Nisbet, 1963).

Toynbee, Arnold, 'What Should Be the Christian Approach to the Contemporary Non-Christian Faiths?', in Owen C. Thomas (ed.), *Attitudes toward Other Religions: Some Christian Interpretations* (London: SCM, 1969).

Tracy, David, *The Analogical Imagination* (New York: Crossroad, 1981).

Twiss, Sumner B., 'The Philosophy of Religious Pluralism: A Critical Appraisal of Hick and his Critics', *The Journal of Religion*, 70/4 (October 1990): 532–68.

Ustorf, Werner, 'The Emerging Christ of Post-Christian Europe', in Thomas F. Foust, George R. Hunsberger, J. Andrew Kirk, Werner Ustorf (eds), *A Scandalous Prophet: The Way of Mission after Newbigin* (Grand Rapids, MI: Eerdmans, 2002).

Volf, Miroslav, 'The Trinity is our Social Program: The Doctrine of the Trinity and the Shape of our Social Engagement', *Modern Theology*, 14/3 (July 1998): 403–23.

Wainwright, Geoffrey, *Lesslie Newbigin: A Theological Life* (New York: Oxford University Press, 2000).

Walls, Andrew, 'Enlightenment, Postmodernity, and Mission', in Thomas F. Foust, George R. Hunsberger, J. Andrew Kirk, Werner Ustorf (eds), *A Scandalous Prophet: The Way of Mission after Newbigin* (Grand Rapids, MI: Eerdmans, 2002).

Walzer, Michael, *Spheres of Justice: A Defense of Pluralism and Equality* (Cambridge, MA: Harvard University Press, 1984).

Ward, Graham, *The Postmodern God: A Theological Reader* (Oxford: Blackwell, 1997).

Ward, Heather, 'The Use and Misuse of "Metaphor" in Christian Theology', in Thomas F. Foust, George R. Hunsberger, J. Andrew Kirk, Werner Ustorf (eds), *A Scandalous Prophet: The Way of Mission after Newbigin* (Grand Rapids, MI: Eerdmans, 2002).

Ward, Keith, *A Vision to Pursue: Beyond the Crisis in Christianity* (London: SCM, 1991).

Webster, John, 'The Grand Narrative of Jesus Christ: Barth's Christology', in Geoff Thompson and Christiaan Mostert (eds), *Karl Barth: A Future for Postmodern Theology?* (Adelaide: Openbook, 2000).

Werner, Karel, *A Popular Dictionary of Hinduism* (Richmond: Curzon Press, 1994).

West, Charles C., 'Mission to the West: A Dialogue with Stowe and Newbigin', *International Bulletin of Missionary Research*, 12/4 (1988): 153–6.

Whitehead, A.N. (orig. edn, 1929), Griffin, D.R. and Sherburne, D.W. (eds), *Process and Reality: An Essay in Cosmology*, corrected edn (New York: Free Press, 1978).

Wiles, Maurice, 'Christianity without Incarnation?', in John Hick (ed.), *The Myth of God Incarnate* (London: SCM, 1977).

——, 'Myth in Theology', in John Hick (ed.), *The Myth of God Incarnate* (London: SCM, 1977).

——, 'Comment on Lesslie Newbigin's Essay', in Michael Goulder (ed.), *Incarnation and Myth: The Debated Continued* (London: SCM, 1979).

Williams, Rowan, 'Trinity and Pluralism', in Gavin D'Costa (ed.), *Christian Uniqueness Reconsidered: The Myth of a Pluralistic Theology of Religions* (Maryknoll, NY: Orbis, 1990).

——, *On Christian Theology: Challenges in Contemporary Theology* (Oxford: Blackwell, 2000).

Wink, Walter, *Engaging the Powers: Discernment and Resistance in a World of Domination* (Minneapolis, MN: Fortress Press, 1992).

——, *The Human Being: Jesus and the Enigma of the Son of the Man* (Minneapolis, MN: Fortress Press, 2002).

——, 'The New Worldview: Spirit at the Core of Everything', in Ray Gingerich and Ted Grimsrud (eds), *Transforming the Powers: Justice, Peace and the Domination System* (Minneapolis, MN: Fortress Press, 2006).

Wright, N.T., *Jesus and the Victory of God* (London: SPCK, 1996).

Yoder, John Howard, in *The Politics of Jesus* (Grand Rapids, MI: Eerdmans 1994).

——, *Body Politics: Five Practices of the Christian Community before the Watching World* (Scottdale, PA: Herald Press, 1997).

Young, Amos, *Beyond the Impasse: Toward a Pneumatological Theology of Religions* (Carlisle: Paternoster, 2003).

Young, Frances, 'Two Roots or a Tangled Mass?', in John Hick (ed.), *The Myth of God Incarnate* (London: SCM, 1977).

——, 'The Uncontainable God: Pre-Christendom Doctrine of Trinity', in Thomas F. Foust, George R. Hunsberger, J. Andrew Kirk, Werner Ustorf (eds), *A Scandalous Prophet: The Way of Mission after Newbigin* (Grand Rapids, MI: Eerdmans, 2002).

Žižek, Slavoj, *Did Somebody Say Totalitarianism? Five Interventions in the (Mis)Use of a Notion* (London: Verso, 2001).

Zub, David, 'Commitment with Confidence (Not Certainty): Observations on Lesslie Newbigin', *Touchstone*, 14 (May 1996): 50–56.

Index

absolute, absoluteness, 6, 9, 16, 24, 40,
    52–3, 56, 62, 66–7, 70–71, 73, 95,
    105, 113, 120, 147, 149–50, 161,
    173, 179, 181
    absolutism, absolutist, absolutize, 66,
    70–71, 101, 106, 120, 131–2, 150,
    152–3, 160–63, 169, 171
    deabsolutize, 37–8
agitation, 169–72, 177, 180
agnosticism, 43, 46, 66, 134, 171
Alison, James, 87–9, 179
ambiguity, ambiguous, 9, 11–12, 14, 19,
    29–30, 33–5, 37, 41, 43–4, 46, 59,
    63, 67, 96, 99, 102–3, 120, 126,
    132, 148–9, 156
Amnesty International, 15
anxiety, 9, 10
asylum, 7
attentiveness, 2, 5–6, 10, 13, 16, 22, 24, 27,
    30, 40, 45–6, 50, 64, 69, 73, 75, 77,
    79, 84, 87, 108, 113, 120, 131, 135,
    138, 162, 164, 167, 169, 173–4

Barth, Karl, Barthian, 31, 50, 53, 54–6, 59,
    61, 70, 97, 111–12, 116–17, 125–6,
    143, 153, 164, 170
basileia or kingdom, 5, 11, 12, 21, 24,
    54–6, 71, 73, 76, 79, 86, 88–92,
    113, 115, 118, 128, 136, 145, 147,
    155, 162, 164, 168, 177, 179, 181
Benhabib, Seyla, 7, 11–13, 175
Bible, biblical, scripture, scriptural, 6, 17,
    30, 45, 51, 58–9, 61, 66, 73–93,
    95–7, 103, 107, 110, 126, 129,
    171–2, 175–6, 179
Body (of Christ), 1, 6, 10, 12, 13, 16–17,
    20–21, 24, 35, 44, 47–8, 60, 63, 65,
    69, 71, 77, 82–3, 89, 95, 98, 105,
    109, 115, 117–18, 131, 137, 142–3,

146, 150, 165, 168, 172
    see also church; embody
Bonhoeffer, Dietrich, 31, 78
Buddha, 20
Bultmann, Rudolf, 34, 77

capitalism, 8, 49, 70, 149, 159
Catholic, catholicity, 107, 112–13, 128,
    141–4, 165
Chalcedon, 30–31
Christ-event, 53–5, 57, 62, 74, 119, 125–8,
    132
    see also Jesus
Christianity, 10, 33, 35, 37, 47, 54, 67, 74,
    112–13, 115, 128, 130–31, 148,
    151, 153
    see also tradition, Christian
christology 1, 2, 5–6, 8, 10–11, 13, 16–22,
    24–8, 35, 37, 40, 45, 47–8, 50, 52,
    57, 61–3, 69, 73–80, 82–3, 85, 92,
    99, 100, 104–5, 109–10, 112–13,
    117, 119–20, 125–6, 131, 135–7,
    141, 143–4, 155, 160, 167, 169,
    175–6, 178, 181
    see also incarnation; Jesus
    constitutive, 25, 35, 79–80, 100,
    113–14, 116, 125–6, 128, 131, 137,
    167, 176
    constructive, 1, 2, 5–6, 16, 18–22,
    22–4, 109, 117, 167, 169, 178, 181
    degree, 31
    dialogical, 176
    docetic, 8, 16, 128, 167
    expressive, 25, 45, 79, 167
Church, Early, 35, 83, 97
Church, universal, vii, 7–10, 15, 17, 21–3,
    48, 50, 52–3, 57–8, 60, 62, 64,
    66–7, 70, 74, 76, 78, 81, 84, 88–9,
    92, 97, 100, 105–6, 113–14, 116,

124, 126–8, 136, 155, 157, 160,
    169–71, 172, 174–5, 177–9, 181
church or churches, local, vii, 2, 6–11, 15,
    17, 25, 27, 30, 56, 69, 107, 167,
    171
church meeting, 6
Church, Western 6, 8–10, 15–16, 47, 52,
    67, 167
closed-mindedness, 15, 112, 117, 171
Cobb, John B. Jr, 2, 77, 107, 120–2, 124,
    133, 135, 138–43, 147, 154, 160–3,
    165, 172–3
community, communities, vii, 1, 2, 5, 8,
    10, 12, 16–17, 20–3, 25–7, 42,
    44–5, 50, 57–8, 70, 75–6, 81–6,
    88–9, 91–2, 96–8, 104, 106–8, 111,
    115–19, 121, 123, 129, 131–2, 138,
    143–4, 152, 154–5, 161, 164–5,
    167–73, 175–81
concrete, concreteness 7, 10, 12, 20, 26,
    44, 59, 67, 71, 73, 130, 142, 150,
    152, 175
    see also other, concrete
conditions (verb), conditioning, 2, 14, 20,
    28–30, 34, 36, 38–40, 42, 45–6, 48,
    53–4, 56, 62–3, 68, 70–71, 76, 100,
    109, 129–30, 134–5, 147–50, 153,
    161, 164, 168, 174–7
Congregational, Congregationalism,
    Congregationalists, vii, 6–8
Congregational Federation, vii, 6
conservatism, 7, 164
context, 1, 2, 6, 8, 10–12, 17–18, 20, 25,
    35, 56, 76, 78, 80, 95–6, 100, 103,
    105–6, 121, 128–9, 143, 147–8,
    161, 168, 170, 172–4, 176
    contextual theology – see theology
corporate, 1, 6, 10, 12–13, 16–17, 19, 26,
    79, 82–3, 95, 97, 100, 103, 109,
    168, 178
critical humility, 120, 143, 161, 163, 169,
    178, 181
culture, cultural, vii, 9, 14–15, 22, 24, 30,
    35, 41, 43, 45, 50, 53–4, 56, 58,
    60–64, 67–8, 73, 75–6, 83, 86, 90,
    95–6, 98, 103, 105–6, 112–13, 116,
    119, 122, 129, 133–4, 139, 148,
    154–8, 161, 168, 172–6, 181

cultural conditioning, 29–30, 34–6,
    38–40, 45–6, 48, 54, 100, 109, 134,
    147, 174
religio-cultural context, 1, 35, 42, 45,
    74–5, 174–6
theology of cultural plurality, 58–9,
    105–106
Western culture, the West 50–53, 64–5,
    67–9, 99, 103, 158–60, 164, 167,
    173–4
    see also Enlightenment

D'Costa, Gavin, vii, 27–30, 40–3, 47, 106,
    112–17, 122, 128–9, 137–8
dehumanizing, dehumanization 1, 13,
    21, 24–5, 47, 78, 83, 95, 99, 107,
    108–10, 116, 118–19, 121, 129,
    135, 138, 144–6, 150, 161, 163,
    165, 167–8, 170, 174, 178–80
    see also human
demonizing, demonization, 1, 14, 26, 30,
    53, 63–4, 67, 69, 88, 103–4, 138,
    144–5, 155, 168, 179
dialogue, dialogical, 2, 6, 10, 12–13, 18,
    21, 25–6, 44–6, 57, 64, 67, 86,
    88, 93, 98–9, 102–3, 106, 109,
    113, 116, 119–25, 127–30, 133–7,
    139–45, 150–7, 161, 165, 167–76,
    181
dichotomy, 18–21, 29, 41–4, 44, 52–3, 56,
    63, 68–9, 95, 101–2, 145, 147, 150,
    167
difference, different, 1, 2, 5–10, 12–14,
    16–22, 24–7, 29, 31, 33–4, 36–7,
    43, 45–7, 50, 55–6, 60–1, 63–5,
    71, 73, 77–8, 80–4, 87, 89, 92–3,
    95, 98–9, 101–2, 105–6, 108, 111,
    114–15, 117, 119–24, 128, 130–6,
    138–44, 146, 150, 152–9, 161–3,
    167, 169–73, 175, 177–8, 180–1
discourse
    dual, 61, 63, 96, 100–102, 150
    first-order, 19, 29, 38–40, 44, 46, 50,
        63, 120, 149, 174
    second-order, 19, 29, 32, 40, 44, 46,
        63, 120, 149, 173

distortion, 18–19, 21, 35, 43, 62–3, 67, 68, 76, 96, 100, 107, 117, 126, 145–7, 160, 164, 168, 170
  distorted relations, 1, 11–13, 19, 84, 108, 145–7, 163–5, 168, 178, 181
diverse, diversity, vii, 9, 18, 21, 26, 29, 36–41, 45, 52, 59, 64–5, 73, 75–7, 92, 95, 103–6, 108, 111–12, 114–17, 119, 129, 132–3, 136, 138, 143, 153, 168, 171, 175, 181
dominance, dominant, 7–8, 13, 16–17, 21, 25, 29, 37, 44, 50, 52, 54, 61, 70, 77, 86, 89, 92, 101, 103–5, 110, 123, 156, 158–9
domination 16, 22, 24, 26, 47, 70, 78, 81, 85–6, 88–9, 92, 99–100, 103–4, 109–10, 116–18, 122, 138, 145, 147, 149, 157, 160, 164–5, 170, 177–80
  see also powers
  Domination System, 21, 26, 48, 78–81, 83, 88, 91, 99, 103, 112, 120–1, 144–6, 153, 164–5, 168, 170, 172, 178–81
Dupuis, Jacques, 112–17, 128

ecclesiology, ecclesiological, 7, 16–17, 22, 82, 113, 167–8, 170–5, 179–80
ecumenical, ecumenism, 6–8, 47, 50, 57, 61, 64, 105, 117, 151,155, 168–9, 172–5, 181
embody, embodiment, 2, 5, 11, 21–2, 25, 59–60, 70–71, 76, 79, 81, 83–4, 86–92, 100, 103–4, 106–7, 110, 114, 118, 122, 131, 139–42, 144–6, 148, 153, 161, 164, 174, 177–81
empire, Empire, 5, 11, 24, 116, 145, 151, 156, 169
engage, engagement, 1–3, 6, 8, 10–13, 19–21, 24, 27, 42, 48, 52, 54–5, 57, 59, 61–5, 67, 69–71, 73, 75–7, 80–83, 86–92, 96, 98–9, 103–7, 109–110, 118–19, 121, 123–4, 127, 129, 131, 138–9, 142–5, 147, 150, 153, 161, 163, 165, 167–71, 173–5, 177–9, 181
Enlightenment, post-Enlightenment 8, 18–19, 40, 50–51, 53, 67–9, 86,

100, 105–6, 114, 133, 148, 155, 157, 174
  see also culture
epistemology, 29, 41, 43, 59, 61, 69, 96, 100–102, 104–7, 117, 119, 132
eschatology, 33, 51, 71, 74, 126, 134, 168
ethic, ethical, 5, 11, 18–20, 27, 29, 34–42, 46–9, 73, 80, 82–6, 99, 102, 105, 107, 120, 131–2, 134–9, 143, 148, 150–51, 157, 160
evangelical, 27, 49, 53, 61, 63–4, 73, 105–6, 110
experience, experiential, vii, 2, 5–10, 12, 14, 18, 24–5, 27–30, 32–43, 45–6, 49, 51, 53–6, 59–63, 68, 73–6, 81, 89–90, 96–8, 101–6, 109, 112, 117, 130, 134, 140, 145, 149–50, 152, 156, 160, 162, 165, 168, 172, 177, 180–81
  experiential-expressive, 43,

finality, finalities, 13, 22, 49, 53–4, 57, 62, 64, 66, 70–71, 77–8, 86–7, 90, 95, 100–105, 110, 117, 119–20, 126, 130–31, 148, 150, 165, 168, 171, 174
Fiorenza, Elisabeth Schüssler, 5, 11, 20, 78, 80, 85–6, 98, 103–104, 108, 143, 164, 177
flourishing, 116, 162

gang, or herd, 24, 26, 71, 91, 117, 145, 171
globalization, 8, 68
Griffin, David Ray, 120, 131–5, 137, 139–41, 159, 162–3, 176

Hegel, GWF, 24, 123, 170–71
Heim, S. Mark, 58, 132–5, 138–9
Hick, John, vii, 2, 7–10, 18–19, 23–52, 56, 59–60, 63–4, 71, 73–80, 86–7, 92, 96–7, 99–106, 108–110, 112, 115, 117, 119–22, 125, 131–6, 139–43, 147–52, 154–6, 158–9, 165, 167, 172–4, 179
  agapé, Agapéing, homoagapé, 31, 129
  Copernican revolution, 28, 38, 103
  critical realism, 28, 30
  deification, deify, 32, 35, 73–5, 97

experiencing-as, seeing-as, 30, 34
inhistorization, 31
noumenal, noumenon, 29, 33, 40–41,
    45, 63, 71, 101–2, 140, 158
phenomenal, phenomenon, 29, 32–3,
    40–41, 45–6, 63, 101–2, 105, 134,
    156, 158
Real, transcendent reality, 27–30, 33–6,
    38–43, 45–7, 62, 99, 101, 103, 105,
    109, 120, 122, 131, 134, 136, 140,
    147–51, 155, 159, 161, 174
saintliness, 36, 105–6, 147–9, 173
historicity, 55, 61–2, 87, 96, 98, 176
history, historical, 1–2, 13–15, 19–20, 25,
    31–3, 41–2, 46, 49–51, 53–62,
    64, 66–8, 70–71, 77, 79–80, 87,
    95–100, 103–5, 108–110, 112–18,
    123–4, 128, 133, 136, 141–2, 145,
    147–8, 159–62, 165, 172, 175–6,
    178, 181
    historical Jesus 1–2, 10, 20, 70, 77, 92,
        96–100, 103–4, 133, 136–7, 142,
        165, 174–6, 178–9
        see also tradition of Jesus
    historicization, 2, 75, 77, 92, 98, 100,
        175
    mythicization of history, 2, 77, 92, 98,
        100, 175
Hodgson, Peter C., 2, 7, 17–19, 21–2, 24,
    41–2, 69, 80, 87, 101, 116, 120–24,
    128, 132–3, 142, 159, 161, 170–71,
    181
honesty – see truth-as-Honesty
Horrell, David, 82–5
hospitality, 97, 143–4
human, humanity vii, 1–2, 5, 7, 9, 11–14,
    16–21, 24–6, 28, 31–2, 34–5, 37,
    39, 41–2, 44, 47–8, 52–5, 57,
    59–63, 65–6, 71, 77–92, 95–6,
    99–101, 103–4, 107–112, 114–16,
    121, 123–4, 130, 132–7, 140–54,
    156–7, 159–65, 167–8, 170–1,
    173–81
    see also dehumanize
    Human Being, 2, 73, 78–81, 83–4,
        86–92, 100, 103–4, 130, 142,
        144–5, 148, 153, 167, 177–8

humanization, mutual, 3, 16, 21, 36,
    79, 86, 107, 118, 130, 148, 164–5,
    168, 171, 175, 180
humanity of God, 26, 78–80, 82, 91–2,
    100, 104, 114, 153, 167, 177, 181
humanity of Jesus, 1–2, 8–9, 20, 24–6,
    31–2, 36–7, 55, 63, 74, 78–92, 98,
    110–15, 136, 141–2, 150, 160, 167,
    177–81
humility, 22, 53, 57, 59, 61, 66, 70, 108,
    111, 163, 177, 181
    see also critical humility

idealize, idealization, 1, 8–10, 12–14, 19,
    21, 25, 30, 35, 37, 42, 63, 69, 77,
    79–80, 84, 87–9, 92, 95, 98–9, 104,
    108, 110, 120–21, 145–7, 149–50,
    152–3, 160, 164, 167, 178–9
identity, 1, 5, 8, 10, 17, 22–4, 26–7, 65, 80,
    84, 87–8, 92, 95, 104, 106–8, 122,
    130, 133–4, 139, 147, 158, 167,
    169–70
    Christian identity, 6–7, 9, 12–13,
        16–17, 21, 25–6, 39–45, 60–64,
        95–100, 103–4, 106–9, 115–16,
        122, 134–5, 139, 170
    Jesus' identity 17, 20, 31, 35, 76, 87–8,
        98, 103–4, 110, 165, 169
        see also christology; humanity of
        Jesus; incarnation; Jesus; tradition
    personal/others' identity, 1, 6–7, 22–3,
        65, 80, 84, 87, 133, 167, 175
ideology, ideological, 1, 14, 16, 19–24, 37,
    44–7, 97, 103, 109, 120–27, 130,
    145–8, 152, 154–60, 164, 168–72,
    175–7, 181
immanence, immanent, 36, 38, 41, 43,
    65–6, 74, 110–11
imperialism, 2, 14, 54, 70, 86, 95,
    105–106, 108, 112–13, 117, 122,
    125, 132, 137, 147–60, 163, 173,
    176, 181
impotence, 8, 10, 35, 47, 70, 73, 167
incarnation 31–2, 34–9, 45–6, 48, 53,
    55, 74, 77–8, 92, 97–8, 101, 108,
    110–11, 114–16, 133–7, 142, 151,

155, 160, 176
    see also christology; Jesus
indifference, 8, 10, 24, 37, 108, 120, 163,
    167, 178
individual, 1, 6, 7, 17–22, 24–5, 27, 39, 42,
    63, 71, 78, 80–81, 86–7, 92, 96–8,
    103, 106, 123, 130, 140, 143, 145,
    147–9, 155, 164, 167, 171, 173
individualism, 18, 49, 62, 68, 127, 147–8,
    164
insularity, 8–10, 35, 86, 167
integral worldview, 11, 13, 63, 65, 79, 132,
    146
interpretation, reinterpretation, 2, 19,
    29–32, 38–46, 53, 57–8, 62–4, 71,
    73, 76–81, 85–93, 95, 97, 103, 108,
    110, 123, 126, 133–4, 140, 152,
    161, 172–6
interrelatedness 12–13, 21, 26, 63, 71, 76,
    124, 127, 133, 142, 174
    see also relation
    interpenetration, 11, 12, 17, 63, 65,
        71, 79, 103, 132–3, 135, 142, 146,
        160, 175
    intersubjectivity, 20–21, 25, 31, 54, 63,
        65, 69, 71, 77, 95, 98, 109
Islam – see tradition
Israel/Palestine, 6

Jesus, or Christ *see also* christology;
    human; incarnation; relation;
    tradition
    the Shaken One, 2–3, 5, 10–12, 14, 16,
        18, 25, 62, 73, 84, 87–93, 95–8,
        100, 103–4, 108–110, 114, 118–20,
        124–5, 129–31, 138–9, 142, 144–5,
        147, 150, 153, 160, 162–5, 167–72,
        174–81
Jew, Jewish, 20, 66, 73, 75, 84–5, 89–92,
    95, 104, 108, 118, 121, 128, 137,
    143, 151, 157, 164–5, 167–8,
    172–3, 176–7
Judaism – see tradition
justice, injustice vii, 22, 47–8, 69–71, 73,
    85–7, 107, 112, 122, 129, 136–8,
    142–65, 168–72, 177–80
    see also liberation; oppression

Kant, Immanuel, Kantian, 19, 27–9, 33,
    39–42, 45–6, 48–9, 63, 86, 96–7,
    101–3, 105, 109, 119, 134–5, 147,
    155, 173
kingdom of God – see *basileia*
Knitter, Paul F., 112–15, 126–40, 143, 156,
    176
kyriarchy, kyriarchal, 11, 22, 78, 107, 109,
    146, 148, 163, 168, 177

language, 17, 27, 30–36, 38–46, 56, 63, 65,
    74–5, 87, 101–3, 108–111, 123–4,
    127–30, 134–5, 140–41, 151–3,
    159, 161–2, 168, 175
    language-system/s, 34–6, 38, 46, 63,
        161
least, last, belittled vii, 10–11, 24, 36–7,
    48, 67, 69, 71, 83, 104, 107, 120,
    146, 152, 162–3, 169, 175, 180
    see also oppressed; other, invisible;
    outsider; victim
liberal, liberalism, 7, 9–10, 39, 45, 49, 59,
    102–103, 106, 108, 115, 117, 119,
    130, 149–50, 152, 154–60, 173,
    176, 181
    postliberal, 30, 117, 129–30
liberation, liberative, 2, 7, 11, 13, 18, 21–2,
    47–8, 69–70, 80–82, 86–7, 91–3,
    99, 108–110, 116, 120–21, 128–9,
    144–54, 156, 158, 160–65, 168–72,
    178–80
liberation theology – see theology
Lochhead, David, 120, 124–5, 127, 176

marginalizing, marginalized 1, 8, 19,
    21, 47, 69, 73, 86, 89, 100, 173
    see also least; oppressed; other,
    invisible; outsider; victim
McFarland, Ian, 15, 17, 21, 62, 107, 146
mediation, 18, 21, 28, 38, 44, 59, 62–3, 71,
    96–100, 102, 110, 160, 169–72,
    175, 177, 180
meta-narrative, grand narrative 14–19,
    66–9, 95–6, 103, 120, 154, 164
    see also universality
metaphor, metaphorical, 31–6, 39, 41–5,
    65, 74, 87, 89, 98, 103, 105, 109,
    111, 123, 140, 175

Milbank, John, 65, 106, 122, 147, 151–2,
    154–60
Min, Anselm, 5–6, 8, 18–19, 65, 70, 100,
    147, 161–2, 168
modern, modernity, 7, 9, 18–21, 34, 52, 61,
    63, 67–9, 73, 86, 96, 98, 103, 106,
    117, 119–20, 126, 132–3, 148–50,
    157, 167, 174
    modernism, modernist 18–19, 29–31,
        33, 41–6, 49, 56, 63, 67–9, 96,
        100–101, 110, 117, 119–20, 148,
        159
    see also Enlightenment
    counter-modern, 19, 63, 69, 86, 110,
        120
    see also postmodern
monologue, monological, 6, 127, 155, 158,
    173
mutual, mutuality 2, 3, 7, 11, 16, 21–2, 36,
    57, 62, 65–6, 73, 76, 78–80, 82,
    85–6, 91–3, 104–5, 107, 110–111,
    114–18, 120–21, 127–8, 130, 133,
    136, 138, 142–4, 146–8, 150, 153–
    4, 157, 160–65, 168–75, 180–81
    see also humanization
myth, mythological 2, 27, 32, 34–6, 39, 41,
    43–5, 47, 68, 73–5, 77–84, 86–92,
    96–100, 103–4, 122, 132, 134,
    144–5, 148, 153, 155, 158–9, 167,
    175–9
    see also history

Newbigin, Lesslie, 2, 7–10, 18–19,
        23–6, 29, 37, 49–71, 73, 76–80,
        86, 88, 92, 96–7, 99–106, 108–114,
        116–17, 119–20, 125–7, 129, 132,
        137–9, 143, 147–54, 157, 160, 165,
        167, 172–4, 179
    discontinuity, discontinuous, 31, 50,
        53–5, 105, 153, 174
    election, 49, 57–8, 60, 66, 96, 100, 132
    plausibility structure, 50–51, 53, 58,
        60, 68, 132
norm, normative, normativeness, 42, 46–7,
        49, 82–4, 90, 99, 105, 109, 112–13,
        121–2, 124, 137–8, 147, 150,
        152–6, 162–3, 167–8, 174, 177

objectify, objectification, 1–2, 5, 8, 11–13,
        17–22, 25, 31, 34, 37, 51, 54, 63,
        67, 77–8, 82, 88, 91, 95, 99, 102–3,
        106–7, 109–110, 112, 122, 124–5,
        127, 140, 145–6, 150, 164, 167–9,
        170–71, 173, 181
objective, objectivity, 22, 25, 28–9, 34,
        49–52, 59–63, 98, 104, 109, 122,
        126, 137
Ogden, Schubert M., 121–2, 131, 133
Oman, John, 28, 50, 53, 59
ontological, ontology, 35, 44, 65, 77, 92,
        98, 101, 108–111, 131–4, 137, 162,
        176, 178
orthodoxy, 19, 25, 29–31, 37, 52–3, 61, 77,
        82, 97, 106, 112, 134, 158, 177
open-mindedness, 14
oppression, oppressed 2, 8, 13, 18–19, 24,
        37–8, 47, 69–71, 81, 85, 104, 113,
        137, 146, 152, 156, 162, 164, 168,
        171, 177, 181
    see also least; marginalized; other,
        invisible; outsider; victim
other *see also* tradition:
    othering, 5, 11, 47, 104, 152
    other-regard, 73, 82–5, 87, 92, 95, 102,
        107, 109, 118
    concrete other (Benhabib), 7, 11–13,
        24, 45, 52, 64, 175
    generalized other (Benhabib),
    invisible other 2, 3, 8, 24, 26–7, 47–8,
        60, 69–71, 73, 87, 90–92, 110,
        145–6, 151, 159, 163–5, 168–9,
        175, 178
    see also least; marginalized;
        oppressed; outsider; victim
    imaginary other (Žižek), 12,–13, 35,
        75, 146
    impossible Thing (Žižek), 12–13, 30,
        35, 40, 55, 146
    symbolic Other (Žižek), 13, 30, 35,
        75, 146
outside, outsider 9, 15, 17–18, 21, 24, 36,
        44, 58, 61–2, 71, 79, 84, 88–91,
        101, 104, 108, 125, 128–9, 137,
        142–3, 146, 151–2, 172, 175, 179
    see also least; marginalized;
        oppressed; other, invisible; victim

Panikkar, Raimundo, 115–16, 135–6, 139, 143, 156–7
partial, partiality, 1–3, 5, 11, 19, 23, 25, 27, 37–8, 40, 43, 45–6, 48, 57, 60–63, 70–71, 73, 76, 78, 80, 92, 95, 101, 105, 109–110, 126, 149, 168, 172
particularity, particular, the, 1–2, 5–6, 8–9, 12–14, 17, 20–26, 30, 37–42, 44–6, 49, 57, 59–60, 62–6, 68, 79–80, 86–8, 92, 95–6, 100–102, 104, 106, 108–9, 112–19, 122–9, 131–45, 148–51, 154–6, 159, 161–5, 168–72, 177, 181
Pattison, Stephen, 8, 23, 98, 150, 153
Penrhys, 6
perichoresis, 65, 136
Pieris, Aloysius, 136–7, 139, 164
plural, plurality, 2, 7–8, 13, 16, 20–22, 24–9, 32, 34, 38, 40, 42, 44–6, 57–60, 62, 64, 68–9, 73, 78, 86–7, 90, 96–7, 101–3, 105–6, 108–117, 119–44, 149–63, 168, 170–71, 173–4, 176–8
    deep pluralism, 2, 5, 16, 26, 86–7, 117, 120–21, 128, 131, 133–4, 138–43, 168–9, 171, 176
    general pluralism, 131–3, 137
    superficial pluralism, 120, 131, 133–8, 150, 173
    scandal of plurality, 20, 119, 129, 139, 142
pneumatology 64, 116–17
    see also Spirit, Holy
politics, political, vii, 5, 7, 16, 18, 21, 47–9, 75–83, 85–6, 89–93, 99–100, 103–8, 128, 145–65, 168–72, 175–80
    sociopolitical, 1, 8, 19, 22, 25, 27, 47, 69, 71, 90–92, 129, 136, 142, 145, 148, 169, 179
postmodern, postmodernism 17–20, 25, 31, 33, 61, 68–9, 86, 103, 120–21, 123, 143, 161, 165, 167, 170
    see also modern
powers of domination, 2, 11–13, 16, 18, 21–2, 24, 26, 47, 56, 63, 70, 75–6, 81–3, 85, 88–92, 99, 107–110,

127, 138, 145, 147, 151, 159–62, 169–70, 177–9
privatization, privatize, 9, 17, 52, 145, 149
problematize, 5, 18–22, 67, 73, 77, 85, 92, 95, 97, 110, 124, 133, 145, 173, 176, 179
process – see theology

Real, transcendent reality – see Hick
relation, relationality *see also* distortion; interrelatedness; other; powers; solidarity; tradition:
    Jesus' relationality, 1, 5, 17, 20–21, 24–6, 42, 48, 63, 109–110, 142, 176
    social relations, vii, 1, 5, 8, 17–19, 22–7, 42–3, 47–8, 57–9, 63, 69–71, 82, 89–92, 95, 100, 104, 109–110, 116, 129–32, 136–8, 142–65, 167–70, 174–6, 178–81
relativize, relativity, 19, 47, 54–5, 100–102, 112, 120, 122–3, 128, 140–41, 149–51, 155, 158, 163
    relativism, relativist, 9, 12, 30, 35, 47, 61, 68, 106, 111, 116–17, 120–21, 134, 136–7, 149, 152–3, 157, 160–63, 169, 171, 173, 178
revelation, revelatory, 6, 15, 26, 32–4, 39–42, 47, 49, 51, 53–6, 59–63, 73–7, 89, 96–101, 110–12, 123, 126–7, 131, 149, 151, 160, 171
    anthropic revelation 25, 98 *see also* Human Being
    revelational positivism, 59–61, 96, 160
    self-revelation, 32, 34, 47, 49, 51, 53, 55–6, 59–62, 73, 127, 149
revision, revisionist, 19, 68–9, 101, 117, 170
Ricoeur, Paul, 33, 43–4, 108, 123
Ruether, Rosemary Radford, 37, 147, 151, 156

sanctity, 22, 26, 95, 105, 122, 161, 168, 175
Schleiermacher, Friedrich, 28–9, 33, 53, 143
scripture – see Bible

secular, 9, 52, 54, 59, 68, 96, 117, 129, 134, 154, 156, 173–4
shadow side, 8, 13, 23, 26, 42, 61, 89, 95, 98–9, 135, 144, 146, 150, 153, 160, 168, 174–5
shaken, shakenness 2–3, 5, 8, 11–12, 14–16, 19, 21–7, 39, 45–8, 59–62, 64, 67, 69, 71, 73, 80, 84, 87–92, 95–7, 104, 107, 118–21, 125, 127, 130–32, 135, 138, 142–4, 147, 153, 160, 163–5, 168–81
    see also Jesus; solidarity
Shanks, Andrew, vii, 2, 5, 14–18, 22–4, 30, 37, 43–6, 63, 87, 95–7, 101–3, 105, 117, 145, 161, 168–71
Sobrino, Jon, 37–8, 70–71, 147
solidarity, solidarities, 1–2, 5–8, 10, 12–18, 21–7, 29, 39, 45, 47–8, 50, 59, 64–5, 73, 80–84, 86–7, 89, 91–3, 107, 118, 121–2, 124, 128, 130, 137, 142, 145–7, 150, 154, 161–5, 167–71, 175, 177–80
    of others, 5, 7, 10–11, 13, 17–19, 21, 23–4, 26, 39, 45, 47–8, 64–5, 69, 71, 87, 91–2, 100, 104, 107, 109, 112, 118, 120, 131, 143–4, 146, 148, 150, 153, 160, 163–5, 168, 170–72, 177–8, 181
    of the shaken, 14–16, 22–3, 64, 130, 168, 170, 173
Sölle, Dorothee, 24, 162, 180–81
Soskice, Janet Martin, 44
Spirit, Holy 23, 56, 58, 60, 63–5, 83, 95, 107, 109–110, 112–18, 123, 127–8, 133–4, 137, 170, 176
    see also pneumatology
Stassen, Glen, 73, 85–6, 165
stranger, 144
subjective, subjectivity, 25, 31, 33, 52, 60–62, 98, 127, 149–50, 157
substance (*ousia*), 31–2, 35, 136
Suchocki, Marjorie Hewitt, 132–3, 147, 152–4, 156
suppression, 1, 8–9, 14, 17, 21, 26, 42–3, 45, 49, 62, 91, 97–8, 145, 172
system, System 21, 24, 26, 48, 51, 71, 75, 78–83, 85, 88–9, 91, 99, 104, 112, 120–22, 144–5, 151, 153, 164–5,

168, 170, 172–5, 178–81
    see also Domination
systematic, 8, 25, 61, 87–8, 123, 158

Theissen, Gerd, 20, 75–7, 79, 92, 98, 103, 175
theology
    contextual, 6–7
    dialogical, 64, 120–22, 130, 143, 145, 169
        see also dialogical
    ecumenical 169 *see also* ecumenical
    liberation 7, 18, 21, 152, 156, 161, 164
        see also liberation
    political 18, 24, 169
    process, or Whiteheadian, 139–40, 162
    public, 70
thoughtfulness 14, 22
    see also attentiveness
tradition, a, or traditions, 1–3, 5–6, 8, 11–13, 20–21, 23, 27–30, 33, 36, 39–40, 42, 44, 46, 50, 64, 69, 75, 86–8, 105–8, 112, 117, 119, 146, 148–59, 162–3, 173–6
    Christian or Judaeo-Christian, vii, 1–3, 5, 9, 12–13, 15–24, 26, 29–30, 32, 37, 39–48, 56–7, 60–64, 68, 73–7, 82–93, 95–118, 119–44, 145–65, 167–81
    Hinduism, 27, 29, 50, 54–6, 59, 134, 143, 149, 159
    Islam, 20, 29, 33, 143
    Judaism, 73–6, 85–92, 157, 173, 176–7
    of Jesus, 1, 13–14, 24, 26, 42, 76, 81, 85–93, 95, 103–4, 108, 110, 118, 121, 131, 145, 157, 163–5, 167–9, 172, 176–81
    other traditions, 1–2, 6, 8, 11, 18, 22, 26, 28–9, 36–8, 40, 45–8, 54, 57, 61, 64–7, 73, 77, 87, 89–90, 93, 96, 99–102, 105–6, 108, 112–18, 119–44, 145, 148, 152–64, 168, 173, 175–7, 181
transcendence, transcendent, 5, 14–15, 27, 33–43, 45–6, 55, 63, 82, 101, 109–112, 130, 133–4, 136, 140, 147, 174

transform, transformation 1, 10–11, 13,
    17–18, 26, 36, 38–9, 41, 46–9, 52,
    69–71, 73, 76, 78–82, 86–92, 99,
    104–5, 118, 120–22, 131, 134, 136,
    142–6, 148, 156, 160–65, 168–72,
    175, 177–81
    see also humanization; mutuality
transgression, 22, 26, 64, 90, 119, 122,
    161, 168
Trinity, trinitarian, 2, 23, 38, 41, 45, 53, 56,
    60, 64–6, 95, 102, 109–118, 136–9,
    157, 175
truth-as-correctness, 14, 23, 37, 46, 97,
    103, 108, 120, 145, 164, 167–8
truth-as-Honesty, 14, 22–3, 37, 46, 96–7,
    103, 108, 120, 130, 145, 164, 168,
    176

universality, 14, 20–21, 39, 41, 44, 54, 62,
    79, 86, 119, 133, 135, 139, 143,
    145, 156, 158, 171
universalizing, 25, 42, 62, 79, 86, 105, 155,
    177
universal ethical religion, 19, 39–40, 42,
    46, 48–9, 80, 102

universal pretender, 21, 25, 40, 46, 62, 71,
    112, 116, 147, 149, 159–60
Ustorf, Werner, 8, 13, 23, 67–8, 99, 130,
    147, 150, 160–61

victim 22, 81, 88, 92, 137, 147, 152, 173,
    178–80
    see also least; marginalized;
    oppressed; other, invisible; outsider
victor, 178–9
    victory, 53, 68, 71, 75, 178–9

West, the – see culture
Wink, Walter, 2, 11–13, 17, 19–22, 63, 73,
    77–92, 98–100, 103–4, 106–7, 116,
    142, 145, 150, 153, 167, 170, 172,
    174–9
Wisdom, 74, 86, 104, 141–2, 164

Žižek, Slavoj 2, 5, 11–13, 24, 30, 35, 75,
    87, 146, 171–2, 178, 180
    see also other
    hard kernel, 12–13, 171
    traumatic encounter, 5, 12, 180